# GAZETTEER OF BRITISH GHOSTS

An illustrated guide to 236 haunted sites

Peter Underwood

**Underwood Publishing**

*To my wife*
*JOYCE ELIZABETH*
*for everything*

# CONTENTS

# A GEOGRAPHICAL DICTIONARY OF
# BRITISH GHOSTS - EDITORIAL NOTE

'**B**ritish' refers to the antiquated sense of the term: 'United Kingdom of Great Britain and Ireland' (1801-1922), before the formation of the Irish Free State (in 1922). Since so many accounts concern the reemergence of the past 'within' the present - the present haunted by the traumatic events of the distant past, its use may be understood as a structural necessity.

Entries marked with an asterisk [*] are those about which Underwood had personal knowledge, either having interviewed the witnesses, carried out an investigation of the case, or visiting the place in question himself.

Known changes to the status of a property specified within an entry are mentioned in square brackets. As are explanations of the meaning of specific terms.

At the end of each entry Underwood indicates a nearby hotel which may be of assistance to those who plan a visit or itinerary to some of these haunted places. Over time, many of these hotels have closed, or been demolished.

Each entry can be found on a corresponding *Gazetteer of British Ghosts* Google Map; each one is also being revisited online in the Ghostly Gazetteer (via Wordpress).

Find out more about Underwood's life and work at peterunderwood.org.

# ILLUSTRATIONS

*With the exception of five, marked by an asterisk, the photographs listed below were taken by Christopher Underwood - including the cover image of Bisham Abbey.*

1. 'Woodfield', Aspley Guise, Bedfordshire
2. *Haunted Berry Pomeroy Castle, near Totnes, Devon
3. *The 15c. 'Crown' inn at Bildeston, Suffolk
4. Bisham Abbey [detail of cover image]
5. *Borley Rectory, Essex
6. The village of Bramber, Sussex
7. The ruins of Bramber Castle, Sussex
8. The Friary, East Bergholt, Essex
9. The courtyard of the Hop Bag Inn, Farnham, Surrey
10. Farnham Parish Church, Surrey
11. Flansham Manor, Sussex
12. The Tulip staircase at The Queen's House, National Maritime Museum, Greenwich
13. Ham House near Petersham, Surrey
14. Fountain Court, Hampton Court Palace
15. Lonely Warbleton Priory near Heathfield, Sussex
16. The Black House, Higher Brixham, Devon
17. Hinton Ampner Manor House, near Alresford, Hampshire
18. The Ferry Boat Inn, Holywell, St Ives, Huntingdonshire
19. Ladye Place, Hurley, Berkshire
20. Bosworth Hall at Husbands Bosworth, Leicestershire
21. *Langenhoe Church, Essex
22. Walpole House, Chiswick Mall
23. The 'Old Burlington', Church Street, Chiswick
24. *Ludlow Castle, Shropshire
25. Markyate Cell, Hertfordshire
26. Penkaet Castle, Pencaitland, Scotland
27. St John's Priory, Poling, Sussex

28. Sherrington Manor, Selmeston, Sussex

29. Upton Court, Slough, Buckinghamshire

30. The house near Gravesend, Kent, once known as Southfleet Rectory

31. Sixteenth-century Thorington Hall, Stoke-by-Nayland, Suffolk

32. The parish church of West Drayton, Middlesex

33. Spinney Abbey, Wicken, Cambridgeshire

**M**y earliest memories of my dad involve him writing. Forever making notes and formulating ideas. He wrote pieces for the Ghost Club, contributed to Books and Bookmen, and wrote letters. He initiated correspondence but also took care to reply to any letters received. In later years he would have them sent to his club so that he could call there and deal with them in his own time. In more recent times he would be scornful of the various social media, mindful that a 'like' was never as good as a two page handwritten reply.

By the time success was within reach and *Gazetteer of British Ghosts* approached publication in 1971, I had been married five years and had a young child, spending my time as a young father, a bank clerk and a 'weekend hippy'. Although dad had always entertained the whole family with his well-told tales of ghostly goings on - and it always made for great dinner table chatter - I had never been directly involved with his work. But here was a studious book on the subject of ghosts and where they might be found and things were getting serious.

I attended several Ghost Club meetings over the years and remember a talk by Colin Wilson being particularly impressive. I also remember being at some of the annual dinners, although the one I remember best was when afterwards, the two of us sped to what was then the National Film Theatre (now the BFI Southbank), where he was to introduce an all-nighter of Boris Karloff films.

I did much proof reading for the *Gazetteer* and had a good time seeking out the various haunted houses to photograph -

sometimes alone but several times together. Peter would drive us hither and thither. I would be leaping out to take a picture. And then we were off again. Up gravel drives, shady lanes and behind garden walls. Sometimes with permission. Sometimes not. It was fun, even if for me, it wasn't all-consuming.

When the book came out to such acclaim I was astonished and found the whirlwind of interviews and favourable reviews bewildering. There was so much coverage that I began to think this was the norm. Although many more of dad's books would be successful, none ever caught the public imagination quite like this one. Looking back as I peruse the volume some 50 years later, it becomes clear that the simple yet appealing format (with the review style entries complete with nearby hotel information), would indeed set the heart racing for anyone the least bit interested.

As the years passed and dad continued with more and more books, this one still remained like a beacon for others to try and emulate or even copy. The only thing it lacked we always agreed was a map! And now, thanks to a grandson and that despised 'modern technology', is a new imprint - this time complete with a Google Map.

**Chris Underwood**

April 2017, London

## INTRODUCTION BY PETER UNDERWOOD

There are more ghosts seen, reported and accepted in the British Isles than anywhere else on earth. I am often asked why this is so and can only suggest that a unique ancestry with Mediterranean, Scandinavian, Celtic and other strains, an intrinsic island detachment, an enquiring nature, and perhaps our readiness to accept a supernormal explanation for curious happenings may all have played their part in bringing about this state of affairs.

Another question I am repeatedly asked is whether I believe in ghosts and my answer is that belief does not come into it as far as my work in this field is concerned. I try to investigate and study reportes of these phenomena dispassionately but I am impressed by the wealth of evidence for ghosts and hauntings: strikingly similar reports from all over the world since the beginning of recorded history. I am quite certain that I have spoken to many people who are genuinely convinced that they have seen apparitions, phantoms, spectres, ghosts - call them what you will.

My interest in ghosts and haunted houses probably stems from the fact that my maternal grandparents lived in a reputedly haunted house and as a child I heard all about ghosts and soon found that other people believed that they too, lived with them. As a boy I was intrigued that adults should take the subject seriously and I began to collect notes of hauntings and then press-cuttings and reports.

A collection that has today grown into an enormous collection of data on the subject, and from this material, the result of over thirty years study of the subject, I have selected most of the famous cases of haunting and many hitherto unpublished accounts of ghostly phenomena to offer a representative account of apparently paranormal activity throughout the British Isles.

The entries marked with an asterisk [*] are those about which I have personal knowledge, either having interviewed the witnesses, carried out an investigation of the case, or visited the place in question myself; and I hope that in reading between the lines, it would be possible to glimpse my opinion on some of these fascinating mysteries.

It is interesting to note, for example, that there are often children up to and around the age of adolescence in the affected houses who may be conscious or unconscious participants in the disturbances and I have also often noticed in such houses a dominating mother or a woman who is unhappy or frustrated.

The entries are arranged in alphabetical order of the place where the ghost has been sighted or where the curious happenings have occurred, something that has never been attempted before on this scale.

I hope the work will be of value as a reference book and as a guide to ghost-hunting, although I must emphasize that the inclusion of a haunted house in this volume does *not* necessarily mean that the house is open to the public.

At the end of each entry I have indicated a nearby hotel which may be of assistance to those who plan a visit or itinerary to some of these haunted places [*many hotels have since closed or been demolished*].

I did consider referring readers to various volumes containing fuller details of some of the cases included, but decided against this, because many well-known hauntings are dealt with - with varying reliability - in many books. The select bibliography at the end of this work includes most of the best books of true ghostly experiences published to date.

I would like to acknowledge the help I have received from many correspondents and people I have talked to, for their cooperation extending over many years. To my wife for inexhaustible patience and understanding. To my daughter for reading the first draft and for many helpful suggestions. And particularly to my son Chris who has provided most of the excellent photographs.

I am always interested to receive first-hand or reliable accounts of ghosts and haunted houses: a subject that has interested me for almost as long as I can remember and will probably continue to interest me until, perhaps, I become a ghost myself!

**Peter Underwood**
The Savage Club,
London S.W.1

## *ABBOTS LANGLEY, HERTFORDSHIRE

Here the apparition of a former housekeeper has been seen from two different angles at the same time.

From enquiries on the spot, it appears that the housekeeper - Anne Treble, was treated badly by the wife of a former rector soon after the First World War. Anne lies buried in the churchyard but her ghost is said to have been seen in three places; walking between the church and nearby vicarage, appearing at Mass on All Soul's Day inside the church, as well as in her old bedroom at the vicarage, where the daughter of a former rector used to wake up and see the back of the ghostly Anne - seemingly looking out of the window towards the church.

An interesting and unusual aspect of the case is that the face of Anne used to be seen and recognized at the same time in cottages facing the rectory, just over the road!

I traced a former rector who found the ghost very active when he first moved into the vicarage and told me that while deciding on alterations to the rambling Queen Anne house, the local builder pointed to the fireplace which stood out from the wall in what, the rector was to learn, was the haunted room, and said gloomily: 'Not much use repairing that; it will be out again within six months.' Asked to elaborate, he continued: 'Annie it was; died a horrible death in this room and the place will never be free of her.'

Nevertheless the fireplace was repaired - and within six months it fell out again! Now the rector began to make searching enquiries. He consulted a surveyor and asked whether subsidence could have caused this to happen, not once but on at least three previous occasions? The surveyor blamed bad workmanship. Again the fireplace was repaired and within a few months it was out again. Since then it has remained unrepaired.

Soon after moving into the vicarage, the rector met a parish priest who had been assistant curate at Abbots Langley, who told him that on All Soul's Day, ten years previously, he had seen the manifestation of an unknown woman at Mass in the church - a woman who disappeared when the priest had turned to give the Invitation and who had not been seen at all by the priest's wife.

The curate's description was found to correspond exactly with that of a former vicar's housekeeper - and when the curate and his wife went to the vicarage with the rector after the service, the haunted fireplace was found to be newly cracked!

A year later an Irish vicar saw the same woman in his congregation and reported the facts of the matter to his bishop with the result that Bishop Michael Furse, in full canonicals [*the complete costume of an officiating clergyman or ecclesiastic*], exorcized the house in accordance with the mediaeval Service of Exorcism [*consisting of prayers banishing evil spirits*].

Thereafter, apart from a mysteriously broken grate [*a metal frame for holding fuel in a fireplace or furnace*], the church and vicarage had peace for some years, although the succeeding incumbent's wife kept the door of what was now the 'guest room'(!) locked because of unaccountable noises.

Another assistant curate heard footsteps approaching him from the west end of the church when he was there alone late one night. He felt some clothes brush past his face as he knelt in prayer. He heard the footsteps continue towards the east end of the church, then they ceased. He has reminded me that this occurred on the evening of All Hallow's Day.

On several occasions one rector made a point of spending the night of All Hallows Day in the 'guest room' at the vicarage and keeping particularly vigilant at the Eucharist [*the Christian service, ceremony, or sacrament commemorating the Last Supper, in which bread and wine are consecrated and consumed*] in the church on that day, but he saw no materialization. Nor has the young daughter of the present rector who told me, very proudly, that she sleeps in the haunted room!

*Langley Hotel, Kings Langley, Herts.*

## *ABERDOVEY, MERIONETHSHIRE, WALES

Here the ghostly bells of Aberdovey are still said to be heard occasionally, their ringing approaching from the sea on still summer evenings.

Much of the coastline of Wales has altered beyond recognition since the days of the Romans. Today it is difficult to imagine someone standing on the hills above Aberdovey, looking seawards and seeing 'a rich and fertile plain and prosperous cities with marble wharves and churches whose towers resounded with beautiful peals and chimes of bells stretching for miles towards the west'.

The encroaching sea now covers these cities but at low tide the sunken tree trunks of the submerged forests may still be seen sometimes between Aberdovey and Towyn.

The story of the sea's triumph is told in the legend of Seithenyn the Drunkard, one-time Lord High Commissioner to Gwyddno Garanhir, lord of Ceredigion, whose rich dominions were protected from the insatiable sea by strong seawalls and dykes.

The care and preservation of these walls were entrusted to Seithenyn who, however, spent days and nights feasting at his palace by the sea, heedless of the stormy waves and the weakening walls. One night the raging seas rolled in and the wall was washed away.

The cities and their inhabitants were lost forever, only a handful of men escaped, but among them was Taliesin the king's bard and his songs tell the story of the fair cities under the sea and of how bells of Mantua, the greatest city swallowed up by the sea, may now and then be heard - distant-sounding chimes, sweet and low, like a call to prayer or the rejoicing for some forgotten victory.

*Penhelig Arms Hotel, Aberdovey, Merionethshire, North Wales*

## ABBOTSFORD, ROXBURGHSHIRE, SCOTLAND

The home of Sir Walter Scott, the novelist, for the last twenty years of his life. Scott died in 1832. He had built the villa, which he called Abbotsford, and between 1817 and 1825 added farm buildings to make a picturesque estate which today contains many Scott relics.

It was in 1818, during some of the alterations, that Sir Walter complained of a 'violent noise, like drawing heavy boards along the new part of the house'. The next night, at the same hour, two a.m., the noises were heard again.

On this occasion, Scott investigated 'with Beardie's broadsword' under his arm, but could discover no reason or cause for the sounds. At the time of the disturbances, George Bullock, Scott's agent who was responsible for the alterations at Abbotsford, died suddenly.

*The George and Abbotsford Hotel, Melrose, Roxburghshire, Scotland*

## *AIRLIE, KIRRIEMUIR, SCOTLAND

Music, like the wail of bagpipes and the beating of a drum, faint but definite, is said to herald the approach of the death of the head of the Airlie family and the ghostly Airlie drummer has been heard, it is claimed, for generations.

A former minister of Airlie published a history of the famous old Scottish family and gave fully documented and corroborated proof of this 'drum of death'.

In 1881, the drum was heard by Lady Dalkeith and Lady Skelmersdale, and they remarked at the time that what they heard sounded like the traditional Airlie Drummer. The death of Lord Airlie in America took place the same night and it was discovered that the sound of the Drummer was heard approximately an hour before his death.

After the death of the last Lord Airlie in 1968, Lady Airlie (whose second son, Mr Angus Ogilvy, married Princess Alexandra in 1963) informed me that as far as she knew the drum of death had not been heard.

*Royal George Hotel, Perth, Scotland*

## ALWINTON, NORTHUMBERLAND

A lonely spot here is said to be haunted by a cowled monk-like figure which appears to have no face, hands or feet and seems to hover above the ground. The haunting was investigated by the Newcastle Institute of Psychic Research in 1967.

*The White Swan Hotel, Alnwick, Northumberlandshire*

## *AMERSHAM COMMON, BUCKINGHAMSHIRE

When actor Dirk Bogarde lived at Bendrose House, an old farmhouse where Cromwell is reputed to have stayed, he told me that the oldest bedroom - a gloomy, timbered chamber - was definitely haunted.

While he was there, seven people slept in the room at different times and, without previously being aware of the others' experiences, all discovered themselves waking suddenly between three and four in the morning with the feeling that an electric shock was passing through their bodies.

The experience seemed to last about four minutes. In addition, unexplained footsteps were heard from one particular corridor.

*Crown Hotel, Amersham, Bucks.*

## *ARUNDEL, SUSSEX

Arundel Castle, the ancestral home of the Dukes of Norfolk, has twelfth-century and perhaps earlier foundations, although the present building is mainly nineteenth century in mediaeval style, and there are four ghosts: a girl, a boy, a dandy and a white bird.

The castle is first mentioned in the will of King Alfred the Great. The third Duke of Norfolk was an uncle of Catherine Howard, fifth wife of King Henry VIII, and the castle has been owned by the Norfolk family since 1580.

A story of unrequited love led to the occasional appearance of a young girl, dressed in pure white, who has been seen on still, moonlit nights in the vicinity of the tower on the brow of the hill, called Hiorne's Tower, from the top of which the lovelorn girl threw herself in desperation.

The great kitchen of the castle is said to be haunted by the ghost of a former kitchen boy who was ill-treated by the head cellarer [*the person in a monastery who is responsible for provisioning and catering*] two hundred years ago. He died young and his ghost has been heard, and more rarely seen, cleaning the pots and pans as if his very life depended upon it, long after the kitchen staff have retired to bed.

The ghost of a dandy dates from the days of King Charles II. This figure, also known as the 'Blue Man', has been seen at night poring over old books in the library. He is dressed in blue silk and there he sits… nobody knows what he is looking for or why he cannot find it.

The 'White Bird' of ill portent flutters against the windows of the castle when the death of one of the Howard family is imminent and there are those who claim to have seen the bird just before the death of the last Duke of Norfolk.

For good measure the sounds of Cromwell's cannon have been heard from time to time here, battering the ramparts of the castle as they did under the command of Sir William Waller over three hundred years ago.

*Norfolk Arms Hotel, Arundel, Sussex*

## ASCOT, BERKSHIRE

Where a phantom horseman was long reputed to ride at night near a spot where a new road roundabout was laid in January, 1967.

*Berystede Hotel, Ascot, Berks.*

# *ASPATRIA, CUMBERLANDSHIRE
## (NOW PART OF CUMBRIA)

[*Gill House is now a Private Residence*]

When Gill House was used as a hostel for members of the Women's Land Army during the Second World War, there were many reported incidents which were never satisfactorily explained. These included:

- Strange noises and 'horrible smells' which were only experienced during the hours of darkness.

- A phantom shape which was seen walking through closed doors.

- And one girl awoke with the feeling that she was being strangled.

Two W.L.A chiefs decided to spend night in the 'haunted dormitory' but left before the morning. The local vicar heard raps travelling around the room and at one time the disturbances became so bad that the affected room was closed. The late W.J. Phythian-Adams, Canon of Carlisle, investigated this case at the time and showed me the papers and reports about the haunting.

We discussed some of the unusual phenomena experienced at the house when it was occupied by girls. We decided that it was difficult to decide how many of the reported incidents were subjective. After the W.L.A girls left Gill House, I heard nothing more of the haunting.

*Skinburness Hotel, Skinburness, Silloth, Cumb.*

## *ASPLEY GUISE, BEDFORDSHIRE.

'Woodfield', Woodcock Lane, was said to be haunted a few years ago when the sounds of galloping hooves were heard. A phantom man on horseback was seen entering the grounds and a pair of lovers were said to haunt the hundred-year-old house.

I was invited by the Borough Council to take part in a series of investigations at 'Woodfield' in an attempt to establish whether there was any substance to the owner's claim that the house was haunted and that the rates should be reduced accordingly.

There is evidence to suggest that an inn once occupied the site of the house and there is a persistent legend, long accepted by many of the local people, to account for the curious happenings. This concerns thwarted lovers. It is said that some two hundred years ago a house on the site was occupied by a girl and her father. The girl had a secret lover who used to come to the house whenever his sweetheart's father was away.

One night he returned unexpectedly, and in a panic the pair just had time to hide themselves in one of the large cupboards in the pantry before he entered the house. Unknown to them, however, the girl's father had seen the guilty pair through the window, watched them enter their hiding-place and now, in his anger, he trapped them by pushing a heavy table and other furniture against the door of the cupboard, leaving them there to die.

Some time later, it is said, the notorious highwayman, Dick Turpin, broke into 'Woodfield' and accidentally discovered the bodies of the two young people. Realizing that he had stumbled upon some ghastly secret, he woke up the old man and, on hearing the full story, agreed to remain silent on condition that he could use the house as a hideout whenever he wished to do so. The bodies were removed from the cupboard and buried under the floor of the cellar.

Mr B. Key, the owner of 'Woodfield' at the time of the investigation, told me that there was some evidence to suggest that Dick Turpin had in fact visited the house on more than once occasion, and the ghostly hoofbeats that had been heard galloping down the hill were thought to be those of Turpin's famous horse, 'Black Bess'. At various times, the ghosts of the murdered lovers - and especially the girl - were reported in the house and garden of 'Woodfield'.

I spoke to one witness who maintained that he had seen a ghostly man on horseback dismount and hurriedly enter the grounds, seemingly through a thick hedge. I established that in fact that particular spot, many years before, was an entrance to the property.

During the course of a number of seances held at the house

over a period of several weeks, apparent communicators included a girl who said she had been shot. She gave her name as 'Bessie' and her story roughly agreed with the accepted legend.

At length the medium succeeded in persuading the entity that she was, indeed, dead and 'Bessie' agreed not to haunted 'Woodfield' any more. The seances were quite inconclusive, and I have no knowledge of anything further being done in an attempt to establish the reality of the haunting.

Mr Key's rates appeal, he informed me, took place at the Shire Hall, Bedford, but did not end conclusively for after the Chairman of Bedfordshire Quarter Sessions Appeals Committee and Counsels had discussed the matter privately, the appeal was withdraw. A year later Mr Key tried again to get the rates assessment reduced.

He told the Bedfordshire Quarter Sessions Appeals Committee on this occasion that no one would rent the place and claimed that people still heard the sound of galloping hooves in Weathercock Lane and saw a horseman disappear through the hedge.

He added that a phantom white lady had also been seen at the top of an embankment there, and produced other reasons, but this appeal was dismissed by the Chairman, who said that Mr Key's reasons were 'devoid of merit and without point or substance'. The loss of this appeal was included in the British Broadcasting Corporation's news broadcast, and provided one of the very few occasions when a reputedly haunted house was mentioned in a news bulletin.

*Bedford Arms, Woburn, Beds.*

## AYLSHAM, NORFOLK

Nearby Blickling Hall, that lovely symmetrical seventeenth-century house of mellowed red brick, probably stands on the site of the birthplace of Anne Boleyn, and there seems no doubt that Anne enjoyed many months of happy childhood hereabouts.

She died by the executioner's axe on Tower Green on May 19th, 1536, and every anniversary (notwithstanding the alterations in the calendar over the years), a phantom coach drawn by headless horses and driven by a headless coachman, is said to convey her ghost - carrying her head on her knees - towards the Hall where coach and horses and Anne vanish into thin air.

When news reached old Blickling Hall of the execution of Anne and her brother George (Lord Rochfort), apparitions of four headless horses were said to have been seen racing over the countryside, dragging a headless man behind them.

The man's head was safely tucked beneath one arm, his hair was tangled and spattered with blood, and the grisly vision was completed by the accompaniment of a pack of 'shrieking demons!' Travelling in a straight line, the visitation was said to have to cross twelve bridges before morning brought release.

Another version of the story states that Sir Thomas Boleyn (Anne's father) is doomed each year to drive over forty bridges in the country, followed by a pack of yelling demons.

*Bell Hotel, Norwich, Norfolk*

## BALLECHIN HOUSE, STRATHTAY, NEAR DUNKELD, PERTHSHIRE, SCOTLAND

[*The original* Ballechin House *was uninhabited by 1932, and most of the house was demolished in 1963, after a fire, leaving only the former servants quarters and outbuildings. The current owners built a beautiful extension in 2009 within the remains of the original outer walls of* Ballechin House's *lower floor, and the house was renamed* Old Ballechin]

A haunted house that was the source of controversy as long ago as 1897, when such public figures as Lord Onslow, Andrew Lang and F.W.H. Myers had letters on the case published in *The Times.* There is still considerable discussion on the curious 'Haunting of B___ House', as it is called, today.

In 1892 Lord Bute was told of the haunting by a Jesuit priest, Father Hayden, S.J., who said that he had heard loud and unexplained noises there while sleeping in one of the rooms. He changed his room, but the loud noises seemed to follow him, and he heard something which he described resembling 'a large animal throwing itself violently against the bottom of the bedroom door'. He also heard raps and shrieks.

The following year, Father Hayden met by chance a young woman who had been a governess at Ballechin House some twelve years previously, and she told him that she had left because so many people complained of queer noises in the house. She volunteered this before Father Hayden told her he had been to Ballechin, but it was subsequently established that the noises had occurred in the two rooms which he had occupied there.

In 1896, the house was let to a family for twelve months. They left after eleven weeks, forfeiting more than nine months rent, having heard rattling, knocking, tremendous thumping on doors, heavy footsteps and other noises they could not explain:

- Bedclothes were pulled off beds.

- A silky rustling noise was heard when no lady was present.

- Groans, frequently accompanied by heavy knocking, sometimes aroused the whole household.

- A fanning sensation was reported, as thought a bird were flying around.

- The sound of heavy breathing was heard - and felt.

- And an icy coldness usually preceded the manifestations.

Lord Bute rented the mansion and arranged for two psychic investigators, Colonel Lemesurier Taylor and Miss A. Goodrich-Freer (Mrs Hans Spoer) to carry out research. They reported on the first morning after their arrival 'a loud clanging sound' which was heard throughout the house. This noise was repeated at frequent intervals for two hours.

The sound of voices was heard, and footsteps in locked and empty rooms: the noise of something being dragged along the floor. Pattering sounds, explosive bangs, thumps, knockings and other noises were reported by these experienced observers.

Messages were received during experiments with an Ouija board and one communicator, giving her name as 'Ishbel', asked the investigators to go at dusk to a nearby glen. This they did, and Miss Freer reported seeing, against the white snow background, a slim black figure, a woman dressed like a nun, moving slowly up the glen. She disappeared under a tree. Miss Freer subsequently reported seeing the same figure many times. Sometimes weeping. Sometimes talking 'in a high note, with a quality of youth in her voice'.

The case is a puzzling one, and a recent assessment of Miss Goodrich-Freer is of little help in elucidating the mystery.

*Queen's Hotel, Blairgowrie, Perthshire, Scotland*

## BARBRECK, ARGYLLSHIRE, SCOTLAND

A mysterious 'hooded maiden' has been seen repeatedly on this estate on Loch Craignish, in the valley of the River Barbreck, between Ardfern and Ford. The figure of a girl with long hair and a pale face has been seen sitting on a rock, wearing a skirt of a dark but unidentified tartan. She seems to be wearing a hood which hides her features.

She always disappears when shepherds or fishermen approach her.

*Caledonian Hotel, Oban, Argyll, Scotland*

# BARNACK, NORTHAMPTONSHIRE

*[The Rectory is now a Private Residence]*

The old fourteenth-century rectory had a 'Haunted Room' troubled by a ghost called 'Button Cap'. Novelist and historian Charles Kingsley spent much of his childhood at Barnack, where he wrote sermons and poems at the age of four.

He knew all about 'Button Cap', and used to say that he had heard the ghost walk across the room in flopping slippers many times. Often it would turn over the leaves of the book young Charles was reading.

The ghost was believed to be a former rector of Barnack, who wore a flowered dressing gown and a cap with a button on it. During his lifetime, he was said to have defrauded a widow and orphan, and his restless ghost was thought to be searching for the incriminating deed.

There seems to be no account of anyone seeing the figure, but anyone who spent any time in the 'Haunted Room' always heard him - sometimes making a noise like barrels rolling about. In later years, Kingsley put the noise down to rats!

*George Hotel, Main Road, Stamford, Lincs.*

# *BASINGSTOKE, HAMPSHIRE

Both Kingsclere Road, particularly in the vicinity of a plot of land known for hundreds of years at Catern's Grave and a nearby hilltop, have long been regarded as haunted. There are many reports of muttering dark figures being heard and seen in the shadows of a clump of fir trees - reports that go back over fifty years.

A visitor on the road beside Catern's Grave approached what he thought was a man lighting a cigarette in his cupped hands, but when he reached the figure, he found it be a monk - hands held before him in prayer. 'He had fixed, staring eyes,' this witness told me, 'his face was grey and lined and as I looked at him I found myself being drawn towards him.'

'Although I tried to pull back, I was at first unable to do so; but at length I turned and started to run. Then it seemed that his spirit - or being - pushed mine out of me, and possessed my body. Halfway along a path, we had a terrific struggle; I felt myself shaken until my whole body ached and quite suddenly, I found that I had shaken off whatever had possessed me. It was a very unpleasant experience, and I will never go that way alone again at night-time.'

A Basingstoke man once overtook a procession of muttering men along the Kingsclere Road. He hurried past them and then noticed a glow in the darkness. Suddenly, he felt and then noticed a glow in the darkness. Suddenly he felt blows raining down on his back, as though the muttering men were trying to drive him away from Catern's Grave. He ran desperately and succeeded in escaping.

*Red Lion Hotel, London Street, Basingstoke, Hants.*

## BASINGSTOKE, HAMPSHIRE

Bramshill House, near Basingstoke, was built in 1327 and has long had the reputation of being haunted. An ancient chest in the panelled gallery is said to have been the 'deathbed' of a young bride who died on the eve of her wedding.

A former queen of Romania, while staying at Bramshill House, was among those who claimed to have seen the young bride's ghost walk at night through the Long Gallery, wearing a white, ankle-length gown.

There is also an apparition of a 'Green Man' seen near the lake in the grounds where, according to legend, the Black Prince was drowned, and the house has always been associated with an early Prince of Wales who died in mysterious circumstances at Bramshill with more than a suspicion of murder by poison.

In recent years the property has been occupied by a police training college.

*Red Lion Hotel, London Street, Basingstoke, Hants.*

## *BATTLE, SUSSEX.

The great Abbey was founded by King William I (William the Conqueror), to commemorate his victory over King Harold in 1066, and was built on the actual spot where the battle was fought. By founding the Abbey, he sought to atone for the awful slaughter - and show his gratitude for victory.

On the spot where Harold fell and the gorgeous gem-studded standard was captured, a High Altar was built within the Abbey Church, but all that now remains to mark the site is a fine fir tree. It is here that the famous 'bloody fountain' is said to have sprung up after a shower - a sign of the immense efflux of Christian blood that was shed here.

The 'fountain of blood' is still reported to be seen occasionally by visitors, and the figure of Harold himself, complete with arrow through his eye, and dripping with blood, has been reported on occasions, sorrowfully surveying the dismal scene.

*George Hotel, Battle, Sussex*

## BEDFORD, BEDFORDSHIRE

*[Willington Manor Farmhouse is now a Private Residence]*

The Right Honourable Joseph Bradshaw Godber, a former Secretary of State for Foreign Affairs, lives with his wife and sons at nearby Willington Manor, a gracious seven-bedroomed Elizabethan house that has been in the possession of the Godber family for many years. At one time it belonged to Sir John Gostwick, Master of Hounds to King Henry VIII, but having twice been burnt down over the centuries, it is now largely Georgian in aspect.

Mr Godber has not seen or heard the ghost, but Mrs Godber has heard it many times. 'Often the dogs have woken me by their barking at three a.m. on the dot and I have heard footsteps and a tinkling bell. My husband used to say that it was the grandfather clock, but when that broke down, the sounds were still heard.'

There is no story or legend to account for the noises, although they may possibly be connected with a skeleton found bricked up in a wall during some rebuilding in the early part of the century.

*Lion Hotel, Bedford, Beds.*

## *BERRY POMEROY CASTLE, NEAR TOTNES, DEVON

You approach the ruins of Berry Pomeroy Castle along a winding glen banked high with shrubs and trees, when suddenly, you find the ruins before you, perched on a spur of the hillside. A strange, deserted place - it is said to harbour at least two ghosts.

Here, from the Norman Conquest until 1548, lived the family of de la Pomerai. In that year the castle was sold to the Lord Protector Somerset and his son, 'Lord' Edward Seymour, built most of the Seymour mansion which stands, gaunt and gutted, within the precincts of the old castle.

Elliott O'Donnell told me that he had traced back reports of the haunting of Berry Pomeroy Castle many hundreds of years, but that it became widely known when an eminent physician, Sir Walter Farquhar, referred to it in his memoirs.

He recounts how he was called one day to attend the wife of the Steward of the Castle, who was seriously ill. While waiting to see the patient, he was shown into a lofty, oak-panelled room, which had a flight of stairs in one corner leading to a room above. As he was looking round the room, the door opened and a beautifully-dressed lady entered, wringing her hands and obviously in great distress.

Taking no notice of the occupant, she walked across the room, mounted the stairs, and then paused and looked directly at the physician who saw, before she disappeared from sight, that she was very young and of a remarkable beauty.

At length the doctor saw his patient who was so ill that he returned to the castle the following morning, and was pleased to find her much better. Afterwards, he discussed the marked improvement with his patient's husband and, during the course of conversation, remarked on the beautiful lady he had seen on his previous visit, expressing his curiosity as to her identity and cause of her mental anxiety, whereupon he was surprised to find the Steward very upset.

He was told that the figure he had seen was a ghost and that her appearance always preceded the death of someone closely associated with the castle. The apparition had been seen shortly before his son was drowned, and nothing would convince him that his wife would not die.

Sir Walter did his best to reassure the distracted man, pointing out again that his wife's condition had improved vastly. But within a few hours, the lady was indeed, dead.

On making enquiries, Sir Walter learned that the ghost was that of the daughter of a former owner of Berry Pomeroy Castle, who was as wicked and cruel as she was lovely and who, because of her many crimes and licentious living, was doomed after her death to haunt forever the home of her forebears -

and the scene of some of her evil deeds. Sir Walter also traced accounts of the haunting during which the beautiful but evil lady lured those who saw her to some unsafe spot in or near the castle, where they were liable to have a serious accident.

Perhaps the best-known story of haunted Berry Pomeroy concerns another lady owner of the castle, one of two sisters, Margaret and Eleanor de Pomeroy, who both loved the same man. Lady Eleanor was mistress of the castle at the time, and she was so jealous of her beautiful sister, that she caused her to be imprisoned in the castle dungeons, where she was starved to death. Now, on certain nights, it is said that she rises from her dungeon, leaves St Margaret's Tower in flowing white robes, and walks along the ramparts, beckoning those who see her.

Another apparition at Berry Pomeroy is an unidentified woman in a long, blue, hooded cape. She is thought to have smothered her baby and cannot find rest: according to some sources, she is a young daughter of one of the Pomeroys, and the murder took place in one of the upper chambers.

Many visitors have remarked on the indefinable sense of deadness and evil, of loneliness and desolation, at Berry Pomeroy, and a number of photographs taken have included shadowy figures which cannot be explained.

In 1968 a visitor took her two children of seven and nine there for a picnic, expecting them to romp and explore and enjoy themselves. Instead, they kept sedately by their mother's side for most of the time, and when they did venture into the ruins, they soon ran back to say that it was horrid and that they wanted to go home.

When one remembers the young knights who plunged to death with their horses into the valley of the north side, rather than be taken as slaves by their enemies; of the unhappy Lady Margaret, starved to death in the dungeons; of the other

Pomeroy who killed her offspring, and of the tragic and violent happenings here over the years, perhaps it is not surprising that something remains which can be picked up occasionally by some people, especially the young.

*Palace Hotel, Paignton, Devon*

BETTISCOMBE HOUSE, SEE MARSHWOOD
VALE, BETWEEN BROADWINDSOR
AND LYME REGIS, DORSETSHIRE

## *BILDESTON, SUFFOLK

The fifteenth-century Crown Inn has long had the reputation of being haunted. Twenty years ago I went there, following reports of mysterious footsteps being heard in the rambling old inn.

Once they were heard by a policeman whose investigations were as completely unsuccessful as those of everyone else who has tried to discover the origin of them over the years. There are many reports too of 'touchings' and loud hammering noises. At one time the landlord thought that the latter could be accounted for by youths hammering at the front door of the inn.

But when next the knocks came, the landlord, ready for them this time, slipped quickly upstairs and looked out of a window which gave him an uninterrupted view of the front step. There was no one there but the hammering noise continued.

A British Legion secretary told me that once when he was in the bar, he pointed to a man wearing an overcoat and old-fashioned hat who was standing in the private part of the house, and asked the landlord who the stranger was. The landlord turned round but the figure had vanished, and it seems that there had in fact been no human being there.

*Great White Horse Hotel, Ipswich, Suffolk*

## *BISHAM ABBEY, BERKSHIRE, NEAR MARLOW, BUCKINGHAMSHIRE

A Tudor house, now belonging to the Central Council of Physical Recreation, it was long reputed to be haunted. A Preceptory of the Knights Templars, that became a stately Abbey, formerly occupied this site. The mansion that remains is essentially the same building that King Henry VIII gave to his discarded Queen, Anne of Cleves.

Richard Neville, Earl of Warwick, known as the king-maker, knew Bisham. His bones are buried hereabouts.

The property passed into the hands of the Hoby family, one of whom, Sir Thomas Hoby, had custody of the Princess Elizabeth during the reign of Queen Mary. He must have been a gentle gaoler [*jailer, a person in charge of a jail or of the prisoners in it*], for after her accession, Elizabeth appointed him Ambassador to France, and it is the ghost of his wife, the Lady Elizabeth Hoby, that has for so long been alleged to haunt this beautiful old house.

Lady Hoby was a scholar. She wrote Greek and Latin verse, and composed religious treatises. The haunting of Bisham Abbey, handed down from generation to generation, is in accord with her character, for such a highly accomplished and intellectual person might well have had little patience with a dull child, slow at learning, such as her son William is said to have been. His work was slovenly and untidy and his copy-books were usually full of ink blots.

His mother seems to have been in the habit of severely chastising the boy, and one day, perhaps when his copy-books were really disgraceful, she thrashed him so unmercifully that he died.

Soon afterwards, Lady Hoby herself died, and not long after her death her ghost was reported to be seen gliding from a bedroom, in the act of washing bloodstains from her hands, in a basin of water which floated before her 'without visible means of support'.

This is the ghost which has been repeatedly seen over the centuries, recognized by comparing it with old family portraits, still hanging in the hall. Lady Hoby is represented with a very white face and hands and dressed in the coif, weeds and wimple of a knight's widow. Those who have seen her always say she appears in the negative (speaking in the photographic sense), with black face and hands and white dress.

The same figure has been reported in the grounds and two boys, returning late one evening from fishing, saw an unexplained figure as they walked along the river bank by Bisham: an old woman dressed in black and sitting in a boat. Both she and the boat disappeared as the watchers approached.

There have been reports in the past, too, of visitors being woken up in the night by the sound of footsteps shuffling along corridors no longer there, and sometimes there is the sound of hysterical weepings.

When Admiral Vansittart lived at Bisham, he ridiculed the idea of ghosts, until one night when he played a late game of chess with his brother in the panelled room where Lady Hoby's portrait hangs. 'We had finished playing,' he said, 'and my brother had gone up to bed. I stood for some time with my back to the wall, turning the day over in my mind. Minutes passed. I looked round. It was Dame Hoby. The frame on the wall was empty! Terrified, I fled the room.'

During alterations in 1840, workmen are said to have found some antique copy-books pushed into the wall between the joints and the skirting, beneath a sixteenth-century window-shutter and several of these books, on which young William Hoby's name was written, were covered with blots. Unhappily, this evidence is the only known reference to the existence of William Hoby.

The copy-books were later lost. Lady Hoby had four children by her first husband: Edward, Elizabeth, Anne and Thomas, and by her second husband one son - Francis, who is recorded as having died in his infancy. Edward and Thomas grew to manhood and were knighted. The two girls died within a few days of each other in 1570.

*George and Dragon Hotel, The Causeway, Marlow, Bucks.*

## BLACKBURN, LANCASHIRE

A few miles north of Blackburn, on the way to Preston, stands mediaeval Samlesbury Old Hall, with its two 'ghost' lovers. One is a lady in white, who is said to have been the daughter of a previous owner of Samlesbury Hall, and the other - a knight who loved her.

The girl's brother slew the knight, so goes the story, and the ghosts of the lovers are said to be seen occasionally in the vicinity of the murder, hovering above the present level of the ground.

*Barton Grange Hotel, Present, Lancs.*

## BLANDFORD, DORSET

Long-vanished Eastbury Park was built by George Dodington in the middle of the eighteenth century, and allowed to fall into ruin by a late owner, Earl Temple, who found himself unable to afford such a huge place. At one time, he even offered £200 a year and free residence to anyone who would take the mansion and keep it in repair.

Earl Temple, it seems, had a fraudulent steward named Doggett, and it is his ghost which haunts or haunted the road and long drive from the park gates to the house. He, according to tradition, robbed his employer, oppressed the tenants, and eventually shot himself.

On the stroke of midnight, on certain unspecified nights of the year, a coach with headless coachmen and headless horses was said to drive out of the park, pick up Doggett and return to the house where he would alight from the coach, enter the house, and proceed to the panelled room where he had shot himself. The sound of the pistol shot would again be heard, ending the ghostly episode.

Doggett was recognized by his knee-breeches, which were always tied with a yellow silk ribbon, and when workmen exhumed his body, during the demolition of the neighbouring church where he was buried, his legs were found to have been tied together with yellow silk ribbon - and the material was as bright and fresh as the day it had been tied - nor was the body decayed. Little wonder that the local people averred that he was a vampire.

*Crown Hotel, West Street, Blandford Forum, Dorset*

BLICKLING HALL, SEE AYLSHAM, NORFOLK

## *BORLEY, ON THE BORDERS OF ESSEX AND SUFFOLK, NEAR LONG MELFORD

[*For more on Borley Rectory, see The Ghosts of Borley (1973)*]

Here is the site of 'the most haunted house in England', Borley Rectory, built in 1863 and destroyed by fire in 1939.

Everyone who lived in the house and literally hundreds of visitors asserted that they heard, saw or felt things they could not explain. The famous Borley 'nun' has been seen by dozens of reputable witnesses, including three former rectors of the parish, visiting clergymen, doctors, and two of the present occupants of the cottage near the site.

The full story was published by famous psychical researcher Harry Price in his books: '*The Most Haunted House in England*' (1940), and *The End of Borley Rectory* (1946). His findings and handling of the case was attacked by three members of the Society for Psychical Research in 1956 (after

Price's death), but an Examination by another member of the same Society published in the 'Proceedings' of the S.P.R in 1969 rehabilitated Price, and the haunting remains as baffling and as fascinating as any in the annals of psychical research.

Certainly there exists more evidence for this haunting than for any other alleged haunted house anywhere in the world.

In the 1900s Borley Rectory, as a haunted house, had everything: it was a gaunt, ugly, isolated monstrosity approached by a winding, lonely, overshadowed country lane. The red-brick house had a window bricked up here, a wing added there, and the whole impression was grotesque and ominous - and yet the place held a strange fascination for its successive inhabitants.

Firstly the Rev. H. D. E. Bull, who built the house and added to it as his family increased, and who died there in the haunted Blue Room in 1892. Then his son, the Rev. Harry Bull from 1892 until he too died there in the Blue Room in 1927. The Rev. Guy Eric Smith, an Anglo-Indian, from 1928 to 1930. The Rev. Lionel Foyster, from 1930 to 1935, and - although he never really lived in the house - the Rev. Alfred C. Henning, from 1936 to his death in 1955.

Subsequently many curious happenings have been reported from the site of the vanished rectory, the vicinity of the cottage, and the church just across the road.

The rambling rectory acquired a 'haunted house' reputation almost as soon as it was occupied, and the Rev. and Mrs H. D. E. Bull knew all about the legend that a monastery formerly occupied the site and that a monk, attempting to elope with a nun from a nearby nunnery, had been hanged and the hun bricked up alive. The ghostly nun was supposed to walk each July 28th.

I talked with several of the children of the Rev. H. D. E. Bull, and in particular with Ethel Bull, the last to survive, and she told me of the remarkable experience she had with three of her sisters on the afternoon of July 28th, 1900. She and Freda Mabel were returning from a  garden party in the late afternoon, and as they reached the rectory gate, they all saw a nun-like figure gliding slowly along a path that had long been known as the 'Nun's Walk'.

The face of the figure was not visible, and they heard no sound, but the 'nun' appeared to be solid and Ethel thought she might be telling her beads. Ethel and Mabel stood by the gate watching the figure while Freda ran into the house and fetched a fourth sister, Elsie, who also saw the figure and, thinking there was nothing strange about it, went forward to ask what she wanted, whereupon the figure vanished.

Mr P. Shaw Jeffrey, M.A., a former headmaster of Colchester Grammar School told me that he visited the rectory in either 1885 or 1886 and saw the 'nun' several times.

Mr Shaw added that Harry Bull told him that he too had seen the ghost nun, both before and after he took over the living of Borley. I talked too with a resident of nearby Cavendish, who used to go to the rectory for instruction in Latin when Harry Bull was rector.

Once, when he was spending the night there the Rev. Harry Bull came to his bedroom door after everyone in the rectory had been awakened by a loud peal of bells. Mr Bull was much perturbed by the ringing for which there seemed to be no normal explanation. He was concerned lest it foretold misfortune for himself or his family.

On another occasion Harry Bull, 'a puckish, lovable man', said that if he was dissatisfied with his successor, he would try to make his presence felt from beyond the grave in some singular and unusual way - 'such as throwing moth balls about: that's it, mothballs; then you'll know it's me'.

GAZETTEER OF BRITISH GHOSTS

After Harry Bull's death, moth balls did in fact fly about the deserted rectory. A doctor who knew Harry Bull described him to me as 'one of the most normal men you could meet'. Harry Bull told many people that he had seen the ghost nun. That he had seen and heard phantom coach-and-horses, and had witnessed a wealth of varied psychic phenomena which left him in no doubt but that the rectory was haunted.

Eric Smith and his English wife were the third occupants of the haunted rectory, and it was not long before the Smiths were puzzled and alarmed to find curious quite inexplicable things happening in and around the house. Mrs Smith saw what she took to be a horse-drawn coach with lights on in the drive. Rooms in the rectory lit up mysteriously. Bells rang. Footsteps were heard. And she would frequently complain of the curious occurrences to neighbours and friends.

Mr Smith, too, heard and saw things for which he could find no explanation. Once he heard words like *'Don't, Carlos, don't!'* when he was near the archway on the first floor leading to the chapel. Soon he appealed to a daily paper for assistance, and they sent down Harry Price, who lost no time in obtaining evidence pertaining to the haunting from all the principal witnesses, little thinking that twenty years later he would still be occupied with this enigmatic case.

The Smiths welcomed Price and his investigators. They supplied him with details of their experiences. Entertained him and gave him facilities for his researches. And repeatedly asked him to produce a printed report on the case. His initial book on the haunting was received by them enthusiastically and which no criticism whatever.

But within nine months they left the rectory (giving as their reason 'lack of amenities'), residing at Long Melford for another nine months when they moved to Norfolk, and later to Kent. Mr Smith died in 1940. Mrs Smith now lives in East

Anglia, her memories of Borley Rectory, of Harry Price, and of her husband - confused and muddled.

In October, 1930, the Rev. L. A. Foyster (a relative of the Bulls) and his much younger wife, Marianne, moved into the rectory and from then until they left almost exactly five years later, the unusual happenings at Borley reached their zenith. Messages were discovered on walls and pieces of paper - appealing for *'Light'*, *'Mass'* and *'Prayers'* - bottles materialized and flew about and de-materialized. Articles appeared and disappeared. Noises of practically every description were reported. Phantom figures were seen.

Things were so bad and regular that the Rev. L. A. Foyster kept a diary of events and circulated among his family details of the curious happenings. Among the contemporary evidence in my possession for this period is the testimony of Dom Richard Whitehouse, a nephew of Lady Whitehouse of Arthur Hall, Sudbury. Dom Richard approached me in 1956 with a view to our meeting and we discussing Borley in detail. The result was a lengthy discussion in London followed, at my request, by a written and signed account of his evidence and views.

This letter or statement of facts puts fairly and squarely on record an independent account of the psychic phenomena occurring at Borley at this period, for Dom Richard witnessed movements of objects without human contact. Pencilled wall-writing. An unexplained outbreak of fire. Door-locking and unlocking. Bell-ringing and other inexplicable noises. And the materialization and dematerialization of bottles.

His evidence alone, it has been suggested to me, establishes the haunting of Borley Rectory for all time. (I reproduced this evidence in the *'Examination of the Borley Report'* published by the Society for Psychical Research in their Proceedings in March, 1969).

Other contemporary evidence for paranormal activity at the

rectory at this period includes that of Captain V. M. Deane. He told me at a meeting of The Ghost Club in 1948 that there is not the slightest shadow of a doubt: in good light showers of bottles and stones fell amongst observers who saw the phenomena with their own eyes, heard them with their own ears, and handled the objects, thus using three of the five senses.

Mr Guy L'Estrange, J.P. has told me about the bottles he saw thrown and broken. How one missed his ear by about an inch, and of the tremendous din caused by the violent ringing, 'by no human hands', of the thirty bells in the hall.

The Rev. L. A. Foyster died in 1945. Marianne, who has lived a strange and unhappy life, now resides in Canada where, under pressure, she has told conflicting stories of her life at Borley Rectory, the people she met there and her subsequent life.

After the departure of the Foysters, the haunted rectory was empty. Harry Price had the foresight and ingenuity to rent the property for a year for the purpose of scientific investigation. He arranged a rota of investigation of high integrity who spent varying periods at Borley.

Their detailed reports provide further evidence of unexplained happenings. The principal investigator was Sidney H. Glanville, a retired consulting engineer, with whom I spent many hours both in London and at his home at Fittleworth. Glanville became deeply interested in the Borley haunt as a scientific problem, and he compiled a typed manuscript with pasted-in photographs, cuttings, booklets, posters, tracings and plans that became known as '*The Locked Book of Private Information*' after Price acquired it, had it bound in morocco and fitted it with a Bramah lock.

Glanville became convinced of the genuineness of the Borley haunting based on his own experiences, and the evidence he had obtained first-hand from witnesses. All of which he collated and presented in his scrapbook of Borley. With his permission, I took a verbatim copy of the 'Locked Book' to add to my Borley Dossier.

Other people, apart from the occupants and investigators, experienced curious happenings at Borley. The inhabitants of the rectory cottage had their own stories to tell over the years: the Coopers, who lived there from 1916 to 1920, told me of the 'padding' noise they heard night after night, of the 'black shape' in their bedroom with its distinctive smell, and of the ghostly coach-and-horses and the hooded figure Mr Cooper saw in the courtyard.

The Arbons, who were at the cottage in the 1930s, have curious experiences to relate: the Turners, there from 1947 to 1950, reported many strange things at the time. The Bacons and the Williams who are there now have also testified to many unexplained occurrences.

In 1926, a journeyman-carpenter saw the sad-faced figure of a nun, waiting at the gate of the rectory on four successive mornings as he walked up the lane on his way to work. On the last occasion it occurred to him that she might want help, so immediately he had passed he, he turned, but she had vanished, and he never saw her again.

Years later, a local doctor had an almost identical experience. Clive Luget, Rector of Middleton, told me many interesting details about the haunting, for he was actively associated with several successive rectors of Borley, and he entertained no doubts as to the authenticity of the numerous manifestations he and others had witnessed there.

The property was sold to Captain Gregson in December, 1938 and in February, 1939 (seemingly fulfilling a planchette prediction made eleven months earlier) the place was gutted by fire. Later that year, Dr A. J. B. Robertson organized and controlled a Cambridge Commission which conducted investigations and experiments as what was left of the rectory.

These inquiries continued until 1944, and the detailed report issued later shows that peculiar temperature variations were scientifically recorded. A luminous patch was seen. Footsteps were heard. Knocks and other noises were heard - on one occasion eighteen knocks in a row - stones were thrown. Strange smells were noticed. Unexplained lights were seen.

All this evidence was presented soberly and factually by Mr Robertson, M.A., a Fellow of St John's College, Cambridge, holder of an honours degree in Chemistry, a Doctor of Philosophy, and a member of the Society for Psychical Research.

Over the Christmas holiday of 1939, the Rev. Canon W. J. Phythian-Adams, D.D., Canon of Carlisle, read '*The Most Haunted House in England*', and produced a brilliant theory involving a young French Roman Catholic, brought to this country in the seventeenth or eighteenth century, betrayed and murdered and her remains buried on the site.

The Canon suggested digging, and Price dug in the cellars and found human remains which medical experts believed to be those of a young woman. In particular, a jaw bone showed evidence of a deep-seated abscess, which must have caused considerable pain to the owner.

It is interesting that many witnesses of the ghost nun have described her as 'miserable', or with 'face drawn' or with a 'pale face' or 'sad' and never as looking happy or laughing. The remains were buried in Liston churchyard and thereafter the Canon and Price kept up a lively correspondence until that day in 1948 when Price had a sudden heart attack and died.

When he left Carlisle, Canon Phythian-Adams, with whom I discussed Borley and its mysteries both in London and at my home, presented me with all his correspondence pertaining to the Borley haunting, and this too is in my Borley Dossier [later published as *The Ghosts of Borley*].

Since the death of Harry Price, I have collected a wealth of first-hand contemporary evidence for unexplained happenings at Borley, both in the vicinity of the rectory site, and in the nearby church and churchyard.

There are many reports of unexplained footsteps in and around the church: they come from such diverse witnesses as an archaeologist, a nursing sister, a Sunday school teacher, a visiting rector and his wife, a student, a headmistress, a poet and literary consultant. They include a member of The Ghost Club who, one September evening of the full moon, heard heavy footsteps hurriedly approach the church, yet when he stood up in the church porch ready to greet whoever was coming along the path, the sounds ceased instantly.

There are reliable reports of unexplained organ music being heard from the locked and empty church. Among witnesses for this phenomenon are Mrs Norah Walrond (Norah Burke, the novelist), the Rev. A. C. Henning, a visitor to Borley, Mrs A. G. Wilson and her thirteen-year-old sister-in-law, Vivienne Wilson, who both heard the sounds at the same moment. Early in 1970 the sounds were heard yet again during the course of investigations by a party of scientists.

The nun-like figure has been seen many times since the destruction of the rectory, both on the rectory site, and in the churchyard. The present occupants of the cottage are Mr and Mrs R. Bacon, their children, Terrence and Jose, and Mrs Bacon's father, Mr Williams. All have experienced curious happenings which they cannot explain in rational terms. Terrence claims to have seen the 'nun' three times, and Mr Williams to have seen her once.

In 1952, I interviewed a Mr Cole of Great Cornard, who once saw in Borley churchyard, in 1951, a nun who looked rather sad, and seemed to be sheltering under a tree. She looked quite normal and wore a black hood, a white collar, a golden-coloured bodice, and a black skirt which stood open about eight inches down the front, disclosing a blue under-dress. When Mr Cole approached the figure, she suddenly disappeared.

In 1949, the Rev. Stanley C. Kipling of Barnoldswick, Lancashire, visited Borley to read the lesson at the funeral of a friend. As he stood at the west door, he saw the figure of a veiled girl in the churchyard.

As he watched, she passed behind a shrub to another close by, and then vanished. He told me that she appeared to be a 'frail' girl, aged about eighteen to twenty-three, and he distinctly saw the shape of a nun's hood on her head, from which the thick veiling hung.

A couple of months later, two 'ghost-hunters' reported seeing a figure in black walk silently towards the priest's door at Borley church. No sound broke the silence of the night, although the figure appeared to be walking on the pathway. No door opened. The figure simply disappeared.

Curious odours were experienced when the rectory still stood, and this phenomenon too has survived the fire. Unexplained smells of incense, of violets completely out of season, of corpse-like smells and distinctive, heavy smells, often localized and stationary, even if a wind was blowing. All have been reported at Borley. Among the unusual noises reported since the rectory fire are:

- Numerous raps (once experienced by BBC producers).

- The noise of a panting dog which seemed to follow the late Mrs Williams along the Nun's Walk.

- Noises of heavy furniture being moved and of crashing crockery, when nothing has been moved or broken.

- And voices, happy and laughing, that Mr Turner heard night after night for a fortnight when he was clearing the old Bull orchard.

In 1970, distinct thuds were heard on the rectory site which seemed to have no normal explanation.Careful examination of the evidence for the haunting of Borley Rectory suggests that this was a unique case, perhaps caused by successive occupants of a similar psychic awareness or sensitivity living in a house built on the site of an earlier building with a tragic history. But whatever the reason, this is a truly remarkable case of haunting which will be dealt with in detail in the *Borley Omnibus*, now in active preparation [later published as *The Ghosts of Borley*].

*Bull Hotel, Long Melford, Suffolk*

## *BOSCOMBE, HAMPSHIRE

Twenty-eight-year-old secretary Margaret Best was repeatedly tucked into bed by a 'ghost' for over nine months in 1964.

She told me that she would wake up in the middle of the night conscious that 'something' was in the room. Although she never saw anything. Then she would feel the bedclothes being tucked in all round her divan bed. She would lay still, not daring to let the presence know that she was awake, and soon the 'influence' in the room would go away.

Occasionally, objects in the room were moved, too. A curious feature of the case was the fact that the 'ghost' seemed to visit the flatlet [*a very small flat*] yat more or less regular intervals.

Sometimes Margaret Best had the impression of being strangled, and she discovered marks on her throat consistent with this actually happening. The disturbance ceased as mysteriously as it began.

*Fircroft Hotel, Owls Road, Boscombe, Bournemouth, Hants.*

## *BRAMBER, NEAR STEYNING, SUSSEX

A village that is reputed to have ghostly children that run after passers-by, begging for food.

Eight hundred years ago, when Bramber Castle was owned, together with forty manors, by William de Braose, King John suspected the loyalty of the powerful lord and demanded his children as hostages. Although the family fled to Ireland, they were captured and taken to Windsor Castle, where they were starved to death. The story of the ghosts of these starved children used to be well-known in the vicinity of Bramber.

Usually about Christmas time, the emaciated figures of a little boy and a little girl would be seen gazing wistfully at the ruins of their former home, and sometimes they would be seen in the village, at night time, begging for food.

Starved and in rags, the pathetic ghosts would pursue anyone who say them, holding out their hands in mute appeal. Should anyone attempt to speak to them, they simply vanished.

*Three Tuns Inn, High Street, Steyning, Sussex*

# *BREDE PLACE, NEAR RYE, SUSSEX

*[Brede Place is now a Private Residence]*

Once described by the architect Sir Edwin Lutyens, who designed the Cenotaph in Whitehall and the British Embassy at Washington, as the most interesting haunted house in Sussex.

In 1350, one of King Edward III's knights - helped by monks - erected this mediaeval manor house. In 1570, the Oxenbridge family added two wings, and the following owners - the Frewens (one of whom was related to Sir Winston Churchill, who planted a golden yew tree here on one of his visits), restored the house and improved the garden, adding much period furniture, tapestries and pictures.

The present owner is Mr Roger Moreton Frewen, who told me of the history and hauntings associated with this beautiful home.

In the eighteenth century, the house was a favourite haunt of smugglers, and it is thought that a horror story about a former owner, Sir Goddard Oxenbridge, was invented to keep prying eyes away from it. He was presented as a giant ogre who devoured babies.

Eventually, the story goes, the children of East and West Sussex succeeded in capturing the giant and sawed him in half with a wooden saw at a spot marked on the map as Groaning Bridge. The story was spread around that various portions of the luckless giant would appear in different parts of the house forever!

The chapel and its adjoining rooms are particularly haunted and perhaps this fact has some connection with the bones of a priest that were found buried underneath the original altar during restoration in 1830, wearing a gilt cross round his neck.

One owner used to say that she could draw a line through the house to divide the part that was evil and that which was not. 'The rooms adjoining the chapel,' she stated, 'which used to have a room over it but which was so haunted that it had to be taken down - and the dungeons beneath the house are certainly haunted.'

In 1936 sculptress Clair Sheridan, née Frewen and her son Dick, made the house their home. After Dick's death, his mother became much drawn to the occult and saw several ghosts at Brede: Marthe, a Tudor maidservant who is said to have hanged from an oak tree in the grounds and haunted the dell where she died, Father John, a priest who lived at Brede hundreds of years before, and other ghostly visitants.

During the 1939-45 War, members of the British Army were at Brede Place and there were several reports of ghostly monks being seen by various officers. Some Canadian officers also had a number of ghostly encounters. Chairs and tables moved without anyone being near them. Boots and other articles of clothing were shifted and found hidden in odd parts of the house. On one occasion, the ghost of Father John is said to have walked through a file of men in one of the corridors.

*George Hotel, Rye, Sussex*

## *BRISTOL

In the early 1990s a fine house in the best residential part of Bristol was reputed to be haunted by a 'horrible, pale-faced' servant girl. She was said to have been the natural daughter of a wealthy man who owned the house some fifty years earlier. A half-witted, hunch-backed creature, she always wore a cheap pink dress and lived a miserable life - half-starved and often beaten, until in the end she drowned herself in a pool in the garden.

A widowed colonel's wife and her three daughters took a long lease of the house in the early part of this century and settled comfortably into the house, but were unable to obtain a housemaid for several weeks. Yet, soon after they moved in, one of the daughters passed on the stairs a young girl, in a pink dress, busily sweeping with brush and pan as if her very life depended upon it.

Thinking that her mother must have obtained a temporary maid, the daughter gave the girl no more than a glance. But the impression that she obtained was distinctly unfavourable.

The girl had appeared to be untidy and sluttish - her cap soiled and askew, she was practically hump-backed and had such a white, unhealthy face.

The ghost girl was next seen by another daughter of the colonel's widow. This time, she seemed to be aware of the daughter's presence, and slithered down the stairs, grinning hideously over her shoulder as she closed a door behind her.

Montague Summers, that remarkable student of ghosts, witchcraft and vampires, told me that when he visited the house, he also saw a most repulsive-looking and dishevelled little maid in a dirty pink frock, near the front door. The creature grinned and then slipped away through a red baize door at the back of the hall.

A week later, one of the colonel's daughters, alone in the house at the time, went down to the basement to fetch some hot water and was astonished, when she pushed the kitchen door open, to see the girl in the pink dress, apparently busy at the kitchen range, with her back towards the door.

'What on earth are you doing here?' the daughter of the house asked. The figure swung round, an impudent leer on her white face and, without a word of explanation, scuttled off into an adjoining room, from which there was no other exit.

At last, the widow's daughter thought, I'll catch you face to face. But the scullery was empty and there was no sign of the mysterious girl in the pink dress. Suddenly frightened, she turned and ran upstairs, pausing to recover breath on the landing when, to her horror, she saw, grinning at her through the landing window, thirty feet from the ground, the white face of the ghostly housemaid she had left a moment before in the kitchen!

'How I got out of the house I don't know,' she told Montague Summers. But she was found in the porch in ad dead faint, and was so ill afterwards, that she went to Brighton to recover, which took several months. By then, her mother and sisters had left the house and found another, without a ghost.

Montague Summers told me that the family who moved in after the colonel's widow stayed less than a month. The next tenants left abruptly within an even shorter time.

As stories of the ghost spread, and the house stood empty, and as Summers was fond of saying, he was sure it would always be empty - except for the ghost-maid.

*Dunraven Hotel, Upper Belgrave Road, Bristol*

## BURFORD, OXFORDSHIRE

The ancient Priory, hard by the River Windrush that ran red with blood twelve hundred years ago, after a battle between the kingdoms of Mercia and Wessex, is said to be haunted by a little brown monk. And by the sound of a bell that rings at two o'clock in the morning. Little is known of the origin of either haunting.

Richard, Earl of Warwick (1428-71), was one of the Lords of Burford. King Charles II came here with Nell - for there is still a room called 'Nell Gwynne's Room. King William II stayed here. A Lord Abercorn was tried for murder of a man whose body was found in the grounds, while in the nineteenth century, the place became neglected, and was avoided by the local people because it was said to be haunted.

Sir Archibald Southby bought it some sixty years ago, restored and repaired the property, but never had any luck there. Lady Southby always said it was 'very haunted' - that it would never be peaceful until it went back to the church - for Augustinian monks were here a long time ago.

In 1947, the Priory passed into the hands of the Anglo-Catholic Church, and some twenty sisters of the Benedictine order now reside in the Priory itself, while the old Rectory houses the convent's chaplain, and the gardener and his wife. Both houses are haunted.

At the old Rectory, there are stories of articles being thrown about. Of screams being heard from an empty room. Of things disappearing in front of one's eyes. And of an overwhelming atmosphere of sadness.

The figure of a man dressed like an old-fashioned game-keeper has been seen by the sisters, carrying an out-of-date gun under his arm and walking right through anything that is in his path.

The sound of singing has been heard in the garden, not far from the old monks' burial ground. The little brown monk has been seen by many people in the entrance hall of The Priory.

Lady Southby used to say that visitors frequently saw the strange figure in the hall, and a relative of one of the sisters saw the same figure on two occasions.

Another visitor saw a monk in brown habit on the path leading to the chapel itself, and in one of the corridors outside the nuns' cells.

In this strange, silent place, footsteps have been repeatedly heard that have no normal explanation. Doors have opened and closed. Distinct knocks have been heard on doors and walls. The mysterious bell has been heard to ring on many, many occasions. It always rings at two o'clock in the morning. The time that the mediaeval monks of Burford were called to worship.

*The Cotswold Gateway Hotel, Burford, Oxon.*

## *BURY ST EDMUNDS, SUFFOLK

The remains of the mighty abbey which once housed the shrine of St Edmund, King of the East Angles, who was martyred by the Danes, include the Gateway where occasionally ghostly, monk-like figures have been reported.

When I was there in 1942, I met several local people who told me of their personal experiences in and around the Abbey Gateway, a place which has been described as 'one of the most spiritually-powerful spots in England'.

Some years ago, a former Rector of Risby, the Rev. A. F. Webling, told me that he had received messages from his two dead sons, and that several of the former Abbey monks 'influenced' him when he was writing a book on the last years of St Edmund's life.

One dead Abbot had told him that St Edmund's body had been taken out of the sarcophagus and placed in another part of the church, where it was buried deep - as a protection against defilement.

There was some talk years ago of excavation on the site of the transept [*in a cross-shaped church, either of the two parts forming the arms of the cross shape, projecting at right angles from the nave*] facing the high altar, in the hope of discovering the saint's remains, but as far as I know this was never undertaken.

*Suffolk Hotel, Bury St. Edmunds, Suffolk*

## *CAISTER, LINCOLNSHIRE

The local church has long been reputed to be haunted by a monk who plays the organ. In January 1967 the vicar, Canon Ernest Pitman, decided to end the story once and for all by placing a tape-recorder in the old church one night and locking the door.

Next morning, when he ran the tape, there were footsteps echoing through the empty church, and loud and clear notes from the church organ - with banging noises that were not part of the traditional ghost story!

*Yarborough Hotel, Old Market Place, Grimsby, Lincs.*

## CALDMORE GREEN, WALSALL, STAFFORDSHIRE

*[What was once the The White Hart Inn is now a Private Residence]*

The old White Hart Inn has a haunted attic where a mummified baby's arm was once found. There is a story too, of an elderly maid who committed suicide here in the early 1990s.

A few years ago, the licensee heard curious noises and cries which appeared to come from the attic, and when he investigated, he found the imprint of a tiny hand on a dust-covered table in the attic.

He had heard the noises before, and thought that there must be a logical explanation. But after his visit to the attic, and the evidence of a former licensee's wife, who woke up on night to find a white form standing by her bed, he had second thoughts about the place not being haunted.

*George Hotel, The Bridge, Walsall, Staffs.*

## CAMBRIDGE, CHRIST'S COLLEGE

A haunting known as 'the college mystery' concerns a mulberry tree in the Fellows' Garden, planted by Milton, where, on certain nights of the full moon, a tall, elderly, stooping figure is seen at midnight.

It is thought to be the ghost of Christopher Round, who murdered another Fellow and lived in repentance for forty years.

The figure walks in the solitude of the garden with his hands behind his back. Occasionally, a heavy and ponderous step, for which no explanation has ever been discovered, is heard mounting the staircase of the college to the first floor.

*Blue Boar Hotel, Cambridge, Cambs.*

# *CANTERBURY, CITY WALL, SUDBURY TOWER

[*The Tower being named after Simon Theobald of Sudbury,
Archbishop of Canterbury 1375 to 1881*]

Eighty-year-old Charles Denne told me that he had dwelled here with a ghost for twenty years.

It all began when he retired one evening to his bedroom at the top of the tower - where he lived all alone.

After a busy day repairing shoes, he was having a rest before getting his evening meal when he heard someone knocking at his bedroom door. There were three distinct knocks. And then the door opened. Although he knew that he was alone on the premises, Mr Denne told me that he did not feel afraid, as he saw that his late visitor - apparently as solid and substantial as himself (although wearing very out-of-date clothes and what looked like a grey robe), walk slowly toward his bed.

Mr Denne said that he felt a strong feeling of friendliness emanating from the stranger, and as he rose from his bed to offer the visitor his hand in welcome, the strange figure - with its grey square-cut beard, bowed three times - and disappeared.

He never saw the figure again. But he often felt the presence in his bedroom. And on occasions he was aware of a pair of hands 'tucking him in' at night-time.

Also, he often heard strange tapping noises, which sometimes came before he had the feeling that his 'visitor' was in the room with him.

*Chaucer Hotel, Canterbury, Kent*

## *CHATHAM, KENT

Two neighbouring houses in Magpie Hall Road are reported to have been haunted at night for over twenty years by unexplained noises, rapping and footsteps - noises which always stopped when a light was switched on.

Time after time, the occupants told me, footsteps followed by rapping - as though someone wanted to come in - were heard from the vicinity of the stairs and bedrooms. Sometimes the rapping sounded louder and more violent than at others, but always it stopped when a light was switched on. It usually began about midnight, and sometimes went on till about five o'clock.

Years ago, a man committed suicide in one of the houses by cutting his throat. And in the same house, a previous occupant complained that she had seen a 'form' she could not account for.

*King's Head Hotel, Rochester, Kent*

## CHEAM, SURREY

The Century Cinema was the scene of curious and unexplained happenings a few years ago, when sounds of shuffling feet were heard by some cinema staff, including the manager, apparently coming from the empty stage.

When some of them, with three local reporters, held a midnight watch in the silent cinema, the all heard the mysterious shuffling noise on three occasions from the right-hand side of the stage.

The noises, which could not be traced to mice or any other rodent, may have had some connection with the disappearance of a workman, who helped to build the cinema some forty years ago.

His lunch-bag and hat were found hanging on a nail near the part of the building which is now the stage and his wages were never collected.

He seems to have disappeared without trace, and some people have wondered whether something happened to him, and whether the ghostly shuffling footsteps that are heard from time to time are his.

*Drift Bridge Hotel, Reigate Road, Epsom, Surrey*

# *CHELTENHAM, GLOUCESTERSHIRE

*[The former school is now a Private Residence]*

There is a large house here, formerly a school, and now divided into flats, where the ghost of a nun used to appear each New Year's Eve at six-fifteen p.m.

Miss Margot Vincent Smith, formerly of Randolph Crescent, Edinburgh, was a nurse at the house when the building was used as a girl's school, and she first saw the apparition in 1939.

She was shown the figure, some fifty yards from the house at the far end of the open playground, by the headmaster, from an upstairs window.

As they watched, the figure moved backwards into a sitting posture, although no seat was visible. It appeared to be wearing a white habit, complete with hood. The headmaster asked Miss Smith to remain watching while he descended to see whether the figure was also visible from a lower floor window, but a moment later - it vanished.

Miss Smith, who was interviewed at Wandsworth Training College in 1951, stated that she also saw the apparition the following New Year's Eve. But on that occasion the figure appeared at seven-fifteen p.m. - one hour later (because British Summer Time was in force).

The 'nun' was seen at the precise spot as the previous year. On this occasion, Miss Smith and the headmaster went to the edge of the playground. The figure seemed to be solid and looked as clear-cut and distinct as when viewed from a distance. There was bright moonlight. When the headmaster directed a torch on to the figure, the light immediately went out and the torch could not be made to work.

They had intended to attempt to speak to the figure on this occasion, but the headmaster, after his experience with the torch, made no attempt to do so.

Miss Smith, with no obstruction between her and the ghostly form, began to feel somewhat uneasy, and the watchers retired to the school-house. Soon after 1940, Miss Smith left the school.

I had been in touch with Professor H. H. Price, a past-President of the Society for Psychical Research - and at that time Wykeham Professor of Logic at Oxford, concerning the case. We decided to visit Cheltenham together and try to find out whether the 'nun' had put in any appearances in recent years. We found the house and located the owner, who told us that she had no knowledge of the haunting. She would not permit an investigation under any circumstances. So we had to give up what had promised to be an interesting exploration of a recurring manifestation.

*Queen's Hotel, Cheltenham, Glos.*

## *CHENIES, BUCKINGHAMSHIRE

Chenies Manor House was visited by King Henry VIII with Anne Boleyn and, seven years later, with Catherine Howard. King Charles I came here as a prisoner of the Parliamentarians in 1648. It is now owned and occupied by Lt. Col. Alastair MacLeod Matthews and his charming wife, Elizabeth.

They moved into the house in 1956, and realized immediately that they had a ghost - for they were disturbed in the small hours of the morning by heavy and distinct footsteps and the creaking of floorboards. They investigated and traced the sounds to an anteroom of the apartment which Queen Elizabeth I had occupied nearly four hundred years before.

Once, Lt. Col. Matthews heard limping footsteps outside his bedroom and noticed that the time was about two o'clock as he got out of bed and followed the sounds. He traced them to the vicinity of the ancient gallery where two hundred of Cromwell's men were reputed to have slept.

More recently, the Matthews had house-guests, and it was arranged that they should occupy the Pink Room - until Mrs Matthews pointed out that there was no wardrobe in that room, nor a convenient place where one could be installed.

Her husband then consulted the plans of the house, and discovered that there used to be a small prayer room in the corner of the room above, although there was no corresponding space in the Pink Room.

He took measurements, which showed that there certainly should be a room of some kind in the corner of the Pink Room. It was decided to have the wall broken down. After they had broken down two-and-a-half-thicknesses of brickwork, they found themselves in a space which was in fact a priest's hiding

The wall of the little room bore a year in the 1660s and, quite distinctly, the date of September 9th. A door was duly hung to the room.

One night when Matthews' children were being rather troublesome, Lt. Col. Matthews decided to sleep in the Pink Room. It was a very window night, he told me, and he read himself to sleep with a candle - for electric light had not then been installed in that part of the house.

The door to the little room had a 'Suffolk latch', and since the night was so boisterous, Matthews made sure that he gave the door a really good pull-to before settling down for the night.

He was quite certain that the door was absolutely secure, and all the windows tightly closed. Suddenly, a puff of wind blew out his candle, so he decided to settle down for the night. He awoke early in the morning to find the windows and the door to the little room wide open - and when he eventually arose he discovered that the date was September 9th!

*The Bedford Arms Hotel, Chenies, Bucks.*

## CHILTON CANTELO, SOMERSET

For over two hundred years, the skull of Theophilus Brome has been kept at Higher Chilton Farm.

Tradition asserts that he requested that his head should be preserved at the farmhouse near the church where he died - in August 1670. Repeated attempts to inter the head have resulted in 'horrid noises', heard throughout the farmhouse.

In the late 1860s, a sexton [*a person who looks after a church and churchyard, typically acting as bell-ringer and gravedigger*] began to dig a hole to bury the head, but when his spade broke into two pieces, he declared that he would never again attempt 'an act so evidently repugnant to the quiet of Brome's head'.

Brome was probably actively engaged in the Civil War, and may have given the directions about the preservation of his head on account of the practice at the time of the Restoration for the bodies of those who had been against the monarchy to be taken from their burial-places and for the heads to be cut off and exhibited.

During restoration of the church, Brome's tomb was opened and the skeleton found inside - minus the head. It seems likely, therefore, that the head, or rather the skull, preserved in a special cabinet over a door in the hall at the farmhouse is indeed that of Theophilus Brome.

*Portman Arms Hotel, East Chinnock, Yeovil, Somerset*

CLAYDON HOUSE, SEE MIDDLE CLAYDON,
NEAR AYLESBURY, BUCKINGHAMSHIRE

## *COGGESHALL, ESSEX

There are many reports of local ghostly visitations. Vague accounts of inexplicable happenings at the Abbey. And at the Gatehouse, at Cradle House, Guild house and at some of the cottages.

At number 47 Church Street, in 1966, the occupants, Mr and Mrs Michael Grand and their two daughters, Isabel and Rebecca and son, Simon, were convinced that paranormal occurrences took place ever since they had moved into the house four years previously.

The rambling old house used to be an inn, and later the residence of a baker. Still later - about 1959 - it was reconstructed by a local builder, but it still has a distinctly weird atmosphere. No reports of curious happenings seem to have been recorded before the reconstruction. But during the re-building, a hidden room was discovered on the ground floor, and it is in the vicinity of this room that most of the unexplained phenomena have occurred.

There is now a modern door leading from the previously hidden room into the present morning room. This door will suddenly open and shut by itself for no apparent reason, when there is no breath of wind.

The door of the kitchen too, has opened by itself - just like the doors in the hall.

Curious smells. The unexplained appearance of objects. A sudden sensation of coldness. Footsteps. The feeling that a 'presence' is in the house. All have been reported by the Grants.

Mr Grant said that sometimes 'there seems to be a eerie mist flitting past the bottom of the stairs', at other times the same thing has been seen at the top of the stairway. Pictures have fallen off walls in various rooms, quite inexplicably, but the Grants were not worried by the happenings - merely curious.

Cradle House, near Markshall Old Rectory, is said to be visited from time to time by ghostly white monks who dance in the garden, coming in through the gate near the little brook. The property now forms two cottages, but it used to be known for its hidden stairway and recesses where the monks from Coggeshall Abbey held secret meetings.

The Guild house, Market End, has a small room under the eaves of the roof, and here a mysterious light has been seen. After experiencing an overwhelming impression that someone was in the room, occupants have sensed - or seen - an unidentified 'little man' who stood at the foot of the bed.

*Red Lion Hotel, Colchester, Essex*

## CONNEMARA, IRELAND

At Renvyle House, many seances took place - with such literary luminaries as W. B. Yeats, James Joyce, and Oliver St John Gogarty taking part. Yeats always maintained that he personally raised the ghost of a remote member of the Blake family, who used to own the property - a man who had strangled himself with his own hands.

It is said that the ghost still haunts the house.

*Renvyle House Hotel, Killary Harbour, Connemara, W. Ireland*

## COOKSTOWN, COUNTY TYRONE, NORTHERN IRELAND

A model council house was reported by the occupants Mr and Mrs Mullan, and by visitors to be haunted by an indistinct figure resembling a man. He was claimed to have been seen by a number of people in the vicinity of the house.

Inside the property, unexplained footsteps were heard many times - pacing the floor of one of the bedrooms.

*Conway Hotel, Belfast, N. Ireland*

## *CRANFORD PARK, MIDDLESEX

Hardly anything remains now of the dark and ominous mansion, for so long the seat of the Fitzhardinge Berkeleys. It was a member of that illustrious family, the Hon. Grantley Berkeley, who first told of the ghost in the kitchen of the old house.

He, together with his brother, returned home late one night, went down into the kitchen in search of food, and there both distinctly saw the tall figure of an elderly woman. As they entered, she walked from one side of the room to the other.

Thinking she must be one of the maids, they called out to her, but by then the figure had reached the other side - where she vanished. Puzzled, they searched diligently, but could find no trace of the woman, or of how she could have vanished.

Grantley Berkeley's father used to describe a man he once saw in the stable-yard who, on being challenged, vanished as completely and inexplicably as the woman in the kitchen.

*Grenada Hotel, Lampton Road, Hounslow, Middlesex*

# *CRESLOW, NEAR AYLESBURY, BUCKINGHAMSHIRE

Creslow, the smallest parish in the county, has - or had - the largest field: the 'great pasture' containing three-hundred-and-twenty-seven acres and a romantically-situated old house, now vastly altered, that once had a famous 'haunted room'.

The surrounding 'Creslow pastures', long celebrated for their exceptional fertility, were once Crown property. Cattle and produce from these fields supplied the tables of the monarchs from Queen Elizabeth I to King Charles II.

Creslow Manor House was originally built by the Knights Templars, who acquired the land in 1120, and added to by the Knights Hospitallers of St John of Jerusalem. In succeeding years, much has been destroyed, and much added - notably the gabled Elizabethan octagonal turret and groined crypt or dungeon.

The confiscation of monastic property during the reign of Henry VIII made Creslow pass to the Crown, with more alterations. Some seventy years ago, the chapel - once attached to the manor house - was a stable, and the farmyard formerly part of the graveyard.

There is still Tudor panelling and plaster decorations in parts of the house which must have been even more picturesque, romantic and isolated among high trees a hundred years ago when its haunted room gained and held its reputation.

It was about 1850, it seems, that a former High Sheriff of Buckinghamshire visited Creslow to attend a dinner party. His house was some miles distant, and as the weather turned stormy, he was pressed to stay the night - provided that he had no objection to sleeping in the haunted room.

He said he was interested in the possibility of meeting a ghost, for he did not believe in the supernormal. Being a strong and fit man, he was convinced that any practical joker would more than meet his match - should anyone think to 'play the ghost' that night.

The room was prepared accordingly. He desired no fire or night-light, but took with him a box of matches - so that he might light a candle if he wished to do so. He armed himself with a cutlass and a pair of pistols - amid much joking between himself and his hosts.

Morning came, clear and bright, after the stormy night. The other guests gathered round their host and hostess in the breakfast. Someone remarked that the visitor who had slept in the haunted room was not present. A servant was dispatched to summon him, but soon returned saying that his repeated knocking had brought no answer - and that a jug of hot water left outside the room an hour ago, was still there.

Two or three of the gentlemen went up to the chamber, and after also knocking loudly several times, entered - to find the room empty! No servant had seen anything of the guest. But, since he was a county magistrate, it was thought he had left early to attend a meeting.

Then it was found that his horse was still in the stable. And so, at last, perplexed and a little worried, the guests sat down with their hosts to ear, and were in the middle of their breakfast, when in walked the missing guest!

He had, he said, locked and bolted his room on entering it the night before, then proceeded to examine carefully the whole place. Only when quite satisfied that no living creature but himself was in the room, and that every entry was sealed, did he go to bed, expecting to have a good night's rest.

But shortly after dropping off to sleep, he was awakened by the sound of light footsteps, accompanied by a rustling noise - like that of a silk gown. He got up quietly, lit a candle, and searched the room, but could find nothing to account for the noise which had ceased as soon as his feet had touched the floor.

He looked under the bed. In the fireplace. Up the chimney. At both doors - fastened and locked as he had left them. Glancing at his watch, he found the time was a few minutes after midnight. Since all seemed quiet again, he returned to bed and was soon asleep.

Then he was awakened again, by the same noises - but this time they were much louder. He heard the violent rustling of a stiff silk dress and distinct footsteps which told him, he thought, exactly where the figure was in the room.

This time he sprang out of bed, darted to the spot where he felt the figure must be, and tried to grasp the intruder in his arms. But his arms met and there was nothing there. The noise moved to another part of the room, and he followed it, groping near the floor to prevent anything passing under his arms - but still he found nothing.

Eventually, the sounds died away at the doorway to the crypt, and the visitor returned to bed, leaving a lighted candle burning. But more than a little perplexed at being totally unable to detect the origin of the noise, or account for its cessation, when he lighted the candle.

Mr D. G. Hares told me in 1967 that the inside of the house had been extensively altered and no room remained as it once did. He had no personal knowledge of any ghost at Creslow.

*Bell Hotel, Aylesbury, Bucks.*

## CROWBOROUGH, SUSSEX

Windlesham Manor was the home of Sir Arthur Conan Doyle for the last twenty years of his life, and he and his wife were buried in the family vault in 1955. The house was first reputed to be haunted in 1968, when the manageress of the property (now a home for retired gentlefolk) said that she had seen no ghost, but had sensed an extraordinary atmosphere.

Certainly, the local people regarded the house as haunted. Sir Arthur died at the Manor in 1930, at the age of seventy-once, a dedicated spiritualist.

*Country House Hotel, Croft Road, Crowborough, Sussex*

# CUMNOR, NEAR ABINGDON, BERKSHIRE

*[Cumnor Hall no longer exists - parts of it were incorporated into Lytham Church; 'Cumnor' was in Berkshire until 1974 - which is why Underwood listed it as a Berkshire haunting]*

Here, before it was destroyed, stood Cumnor Hall, the scene of Amy Robsart's mysterious death after her 'fall' down a staircase - a death probably engineered by Queen Elizabeth I and Amy's husband, Robert Dudley, Earl of Leicester - one of the Queen's favourites.

When the hall was demolished in 1810, the ghost of Amy Robsart was said to have haunted the place of her death for two-hundred-and-fifty years.

Her figure was most often seen in the vicinity of the fatal staircase. But her ghost is also said to have made a nuisance of itself by frequenting Cumnor Park - so much so that nine parsons were called from Oxford to 'lay the ghost'. They duly 'laid' her in a pond, known afterwards as 'Lady Dudley's Pond', and it was said that thereafter the water would never freeze in it.

However, her apparition seems to have survived the exorcism, and her ghost was still said to revisit at intervals the scenes of her past life.

Amy Robsart's ghost is also reported to have appeared to her husband to warn him of his approaching death.

*Crown & Thistle Hotel, Abingdon, Berks.*

## CWM, NEAR RHYL, WALES

The 'Blue Lion Inn' is reputed to be haunted by a farm labourer, John Henry, who was murdered here in 1646. The present landlord, Mr S. Hughes, who owns a private menagerie, will tell you that he has found different cages opened mysteriously during the night - and his pets missing.

Once, Mr Hughes caught a glimpse of the ghost, and he and many other people have heard footsteps at the old inn which cannot be explained.

*Hotel Marina, Rhyl, Flint, Wales*

## *DARTMOOR, DEVON

Two miles north of Widecombe-in-the-Moor, there is a lonely stretch of countryside with a roadside grave where fresh flowers have appeared mysteriously for years.

Jay's Grave is said to be the final resting place of a young girl, Mary Jay, who hanged herself in a barn which used to stand on the site of the grave. According to the custom of over a hundred years ago, she was buried in unconsecrated ground on the spot where she committed suicide.

Ever since, it is said, fresh flowers have appeared on Mary's grave and no one has ever discovered where they came from.

From time to time, there are stories too of unexplained figures being seen in the vicinity of the grave. In August 1967, a seventeen-year-old girl and her fiance saw someone, or something, crouching over the grave as they passed the spot in a car

Rosemary Long described how the crouched figure straightened itself and stood up as they passed, looking like a huddled man at the head of a grave. He appeared to have a dark blanket over his head and body, and around the bottom of the blanket there was a white line. The blanket stopped about a foot above the ground - yet there were no legs to the figure, and no face was visible. Other local people and visitors have had similar experiences there.

*Wooder Manor Hotel, Widecombe-in-the-Moor, Devon*

## *DARTMOOR, DEVON

According to legend, the ghost of Sir Francis Drake (1545-96) has been seen on the moor, riding with a pack of spectral hounds whose cries are so terrible that any dog hearing them dies on the spot! (My wife and I once spent a night on Dartmoor and our dog whined and was restless the whole night.)

It is also said that Drake's ghost sets out for Plymouth from Tavistock in a black coach or hearse, drawn by four headless horses - and, some say, preceded by a dozen goblins whose eyes flash fire and whose nostrils emit smoke!

White Hart Hotel, Moretonhampstead, Devon.

## DEDDINGTON, OXFORDSHIRE

*[The 'Vicarage' has since been demolished]*

In 1962, after the death of the vicar - the Rev. Maurice Frost, who had lived there for nearly forty years - the vicarage was thought to be haunted by his ghost. Servants fled when Mr H. Campbell Jarrett, who came from Italy to settle his cousin's estate, claimed that a mysterious hand stopped him leaving the drawing room.

Between eight-thirty and nine o'clock in the morning, the beds were pressed down with nobody touching them. There were noises in the study and coughs in the drawing room, when no human being was in the rooms. Mr Jarrett believed his cousin's ghost had returned to the vicarage to wind his antique clocks and look after his favourite books.

Mrs Betty Spencer, one of the maids at the vicarage, said she thought she heard Mr Jarrett cough in the drawing room, and decided to clean his bedroom - but found him upstairs, sitting on the bed, tying his shoelaces - so, presumably, she heard a ghost cough.

*Hotel Russell, Deddington, Oxon.*

## DISLEY, CHESHIRE

Lyme Park, enlarged in 1726 and 1817, is said to have been given to Sir Thomas Danvers as a reward for his bravery at Caen and Crecy, by the Black Prince. The house and park both have ghosts. At the house, unearthly peals of bells have been repeatedly heard. And the long gallery is known as 'The Ghost Room' because of a 'lady in white' that has been reported to walk here on many occasions.

She is thought to be Blanche, who died of grief when her betrothed, Sir Piers Legh, was brought back dead from Agincourt. His phantom funeral procession has been seen winding its way through the park, followed by the same faithful and inconsolable spirit figure seen in the house.

Years ago, a skeleton was found here in a tiny secret chamber under 'The Ghost Room', but whether they were the bones of a forgotten priest, a hidden offspring, a runaway or a secret enemy of the family, no one knows.

*Alma Lodge Hotel, Buxton Road, Stockport, Cheshire*

## *DORCHESTER, DORSET

Nine miles east of Dorchester, one and a half miles east of Waddock crossroads, stands the cottage where T. E. Lawrence lived, after he left the Royal Air Force in 1935. Here the ghostly form of Lawrence of Arabia has been seen, and the roar of a powerful motorcycle has been heard at dead of night.

Soon after his death, stories began to circulate that a figure in Arab costume had been seen entering Clouds Hill at night, and since then there have been persistent reports that his ghost has been there.

I know one person who is quite convinced that she had seen Lawrence, long after he was killed, on the Brough Superior motorcycle which he so loved to ride at night in the lanes and roads in this quiet area.

Farm workers have heard the noise of a motorcycle roaring towards them in the early hours, but always the noise stops abruptly just when the hearers expect to see it. Perhaps that last tragic journey that Lawrence took has somehow become impressed forever upon the atmosphere.

I have talked with men who served with Lawrence, and I like to think that the moving spirit of the Arab revolt does in fact visit again the little cottage he called Clouds Hill, where he found some peace at the end of a troubled life.

*Antelope Hotel, South Street, Dorchester, Dorset*

## DRIFFIELD, YORKSHIRE

Burton Agnes Hall, a fine Tudor mansion, and one of the stately homes of England, designed by Inigo Jones, and decorated by Rubens, still contains the skull of Anne Griffith in the Great Hall, in accordance with her dying wish three hundred years ago.

In the reign of the first Queen Elizabeth, the property was owned by the three daughters of Sir Henry Griffith, who spared no expense in improving their property. None was keener on this work that Anne, the youngest of the three sisters. She became obsessed with, and seemed to live only for - the beautiful house.

One day, while visiting friends, she was attacked and robbed by footpads, and left for dead. She was found barely alive, and lingered only a few days at her beloved Burton Agnes Hall, but before she died she beseeched her sisters to preserve her head within the walls of the house forever.

She added that if this wish was not granted, she would endeavour to return from the grave and make the house uninhabitable for any human beings. Her sisters duly promised, but after she died, they decided that her gruesome wish had been the wandering of a dying mind, and her body was duly interred in the family vault.

Not many days had passed however, before the sisters were reminded of their promise: loud crashing noises were heard, for which no cause could be discovered. A few nights later, the reverberating slamming of doors awakened the entire household. Again, no cause could be found for the noises.

Inexplicable groans echoed through the corridors night after night, and at length the sisters consulted their vicar, who advised them to keep the promise they had made to their dead sister.

When the corpse of Anne was disinterred, her body was found in perfect condition but headless - where the head should have been, they found a grinning skull. After the skull had been installed in the Hall, no further mysterious noises were heard until, many years later, a mischievous servant-girl threw the skull onto a passing farm cart, whereupon the horse stopped dead in its tracks and would not move.

The driver whipped the animal unmercifully, but - sweating with terror - the horse stood its ground. At length the servant admitted what she had done. The grisly relic was taken indoors again, and the cart went on its way.

Later owners of the mansion refused to regard the story seriously, and they buried the skull in the garden. However, they had so much bad luck, that they decided to bring the skull back into the house, and only then did things improve for them.

In the 1860s, a visitor to the Hall scoffed at the story of the skull, and did not believe in the haunting, until he heard noises like hobnailed boots in his bedroom, and doors banging all over the house. By morning, he had changed his mind, and never spent another night at Burton Agnes.

Today, the skull is built in behind a great carved screen, where it cannot easily be removed, and on the staircase of the Hall, there hangs a large oil-painting of Anne, strikingly depicted in black, together with her two sisters, looking down into the house she loved.

*The Bell Hotel, Driffield, E. Yorks.*

## EALING, MIDDLESEX

A haunted photographer's studio, built around 1900, attracted the attention of Dr George Owen in 1967, and resulted in an unusual film, which told the story of the disturbances - including interviews with witnesses, depictions of scenes of the haunting, and dramatic recreations of some of the haunting.

When he rented the derelict hall, the photographer did not know that in the house next door, a woman and a child had been murdered, and that an airman had been hanged for the crime - in 1943.

But he and his staff soon experienced incidents which convinced them that supernormal agencies were at work. Lamps hanging from the ceiling swung in unison. Footsteps sounded on the unfrequented flor. People were touched. Voices were heard.

Convinced that the place was indeed haunted, the photographer and his staff held seances at which a dead airman purported to communicate - speaking of an aircraft which at the relevant date was on the secret list, and insisted that he had not been guilty of the crime for which he had been hanged.

Various marks, consistent with the story related, appeared mysteriously on his neck and arm. It seemed certain that as the photographer was a young boy at the time, he could have had no direct knowledge of either the murder, which was described in some detail, or the secret aircraft.

*Carnarvon Hotel, London W5*

The local Friary used to have the reputation of being haunted. At night there is a distinctly eerie atmosphere in this area, which includes the church just across the road, where the bells are hung in a bell-cage behind the church - after, it is said, numerous unsuccessful attempts to hang the bells in the church belfry, during which at least one man was killed.

During the Second World War, soldiers were stationed at the Friary, and at that time, one particular door, which led into the sergeants' mess, would unlatch itself every night at ten minutes to eleven, and open to a distance of about eighteen inches.

A distinct drop in air temperature would precede this apparent phenomenon, and soldiers playing cards in the room would purposely stop at this time, to wait for the door to open. Each night, it would regularly 'oblige'.

On five different (but not consecutive) nights, arrangements were made for men to be situated on either side of the door, armed with clubs, to see whether anyone was playing tricks. But invariably, the temperature would drop and the door would open. No explanation was ever found for the curious happening.

One night, a young soldier of about eighteen was lying on his bed alone in another room when he saw the door - which connected with the next room, open by itself. He claimed he saw a vague, indistinguishable shape enter the room.

Next, he felt a pair of icy cold hands being placed on his face. Terrified, he screamed for help, whereupon whatever it was in the room with him immediately disappeared. Next morning, his hair had turned from jet black to white. Thereafter, all the soldiers refused to sleep in that particular room, and it was eventually sealed off.

On account of the reputation that it had acquired with officers and men, no one used a certain door at the Friary at this period - a door which led into a passage and was the quickest and most direct way into the building.

Without exception, they would all go a long way round to the front entrance, and then walk back through the building along the narrow winding passages - with recesses in the walls, marked with the names of those buried in them. The Friary was formerly St Mary's Abbey - a Benedictine nunnery.

*Red Lion Hotel, Colchester, Essex*

## *EDGEHILL, WARWICKSHIRE

Within a year of the first battle of the Civil War, fought on this hilly ridge in 1642, a pamphlet was published, describing the ghostly reappearance of the troops who fought and perished here. Witnesses quoted included clergymen, a Justice of the Peace, and several Army officers who had recognized some of the combatants.

The story goes that on the Christmas Eve following the battle, local people heard the sound of far-off drums, accompanied by groans and shouts and all the noise of battle. Then suddenly, there appeared in the air battalions of soldiers, with flags flying, drums beating, and with the infantry discharging small arms and cannon.

The phantom battle is said to have continued for two or three hours until the Royalists took flight, and soon afterwards the aerial apparitions vanished.

Witnesses hurried to Keinton and signed declarations of what they had seen, with the result that many people from the surrounding countryside went to Edgehill the following evening - and there witnessed themselves the same dreadful vision.

A week later, the spectral struggle seems to have been repeated yet again, lasting an hour longer this time; and it was seen once more on the ensuing night.

Stories of the strange spectacle reached the ears of King Charles I at Oxford, and he immediately dispatched Colonel Lewis Krike, Captain Dudley, Captain Wainman, and other offers, to inquire into the matter.

This the worthy gentlemen did, and in fact they themselves witnessed the phantom battle and recognized some of the combatants. All this they testified on oath before the King.

Periodically there are reports of the noise of battle still being heard at Edgehill, on the anniversary of the struggle (October 23rd).

The Rev. John C. Dening (with whom I have spent many hours discussing ghosts) visited the vicinity a few years ago, and succeeded in locating a number of people who had heard what they thought were sounds of the battle fought over three hundred years earlier.

*White Lion Hotel, High Street, Banbury, Oxon*

## *ELM, NEAR WISBECH, CAMBRIDGESHIRE

[*'Elm Vicarage' is now a Private Residence*]

Rambling, two-hundred-year-old Elm Vicarage is said to be haunted by a monk who died over seven-hundred-and-fifty years ago - and by a bell that tolls a death-knell.

Some years ago I was in touch with the rector and his wife, and learned that Mrs Bradshaw was the only one who heard the tolling bell. But her husband, the Rev. A. R. Bradshaw, would invariably hear of a death in the parish next day. This happened, I was told, thirty-one times in two-and-a-half years!

In common with so many cases, this haunting began with accounts of unexplained footsteps. These were heard, night after night, soon after the Bradshaws went to live at Elm Vicarage. At first, the rector would get up and go in search of an intruder.

But after some extremely cold nights, wandering about the house, unable to find any normal cause for the nocturnal footsteps, or even locating exactly where they came from, Mr Bradshaw gave up trying to discover their origin. The mysterious footsteps continued - until a ghostly monk, Ignatius, appeared.

Mrs Bradshaw told me that when she brushed against the ghostly monk one evening in an upstairs corridor, 'he' said: 'Do be careful.' Mrs Bradshaw, with commendable pluck, asked the visitor who he was and received the reply: 'Ignatius, the bell-ringer.'

The form appeared to be wearing a brown monk's habit and sandals. After that first occasion, Mrs Bradshaw met the monk many times, and gradually learned his history. It seems that he died over seven hundred years ago in a monastery that used to occupy the site of the present rectory.

Ignatius said that one of his responsibilities had been to watch the flood waters rising in the nearby Fens, and to warn his brothers if there was any danger. One night, he was asleep, and did not ring the warning bell, when the waters rose to a dangerous level. The water rushed in, some monks were drowned, and Ignatius was in disgrace.

I asked Mrs Bradshaw to describe exactly how Ignatius usually became visible, and whether he always appeared at the same spot. She told me that she had seen him in various parts of the house, sometimes in the upstairs corridor, where he had first appeared, sometimes in the parlour - occasionally elsewhere.

He appeared first as a fine outline, then gradually emerged into the figure of a man aged about thirty-three, with 'dark curly hair and thin ascetic features'. It was usually dusk when she saw him and he always dressed in a brown monk's habit that looked old and worn.

One September night, Mrs Bradshaw was going to sleep, as she occasionally did, in a bedroom usually reserved for visitors. Afterwards, this room was used as a box room, and the door kept securely locked. The family dog invariably slept on Mrs Bradshaw's bed, but this night he whimpered and cried and repeatedly ran out of the room. He had to be brought back three times, and at length he was persuaded to stay.

Mrs Bradshaw put out the light and went to sleep. She awakened with the feeling that something was being tied around her neck. She reached for her torch, and discovered that a tendril of wisteria from the wall outside the bedroom window had made its way through the open window and law across her throat.

She tore it away, and then felt the bedclothes being pulled from her. Terrified, she felt herself being violently picked up and thrown sideways across the bed. Speechless with fright, she became aware of a vague black shape looming over her, and through what appeared to be a haze, a pair of gnarled hands materialized and clutched at her throat.

She tried hard to scream, but no sound would come. The hands tightened their hold now, and she had to use every ounce of her willpower to fight the increasing pressure, for she found that she was powerless to defend herself physically.

Suddenly, she saw Ignatius. He came towards her, reached for the twisted hands clutching at her throat, and pulled them away. As the pressure on her throat relaxed, Mrs Bradshaw dropped back exhausted on to the bed. She hardly had time to catch her breath before she became aware of the horrible vague creature bending over her again.

It had a huge head and a red face. The dog was on the bed, snarling and fighting something invisible. Summoning all her remaining strength, Mrs Bradshaw tore herself free and rushed into her husband's room.

The marks on her throat remained for almost a week. The first her husband knew of the episode was when he was awakened by his wife. But he confirmed to me that her throat was badly bruised, and that the marks remained visible for days.

When she next saw Ignatius, Mrs Bradshaw asked him who had attacked her, and she was told that he was a man who had been murdered in that room. Later, Ignatius told Mrs Bradshaw that he would not be seeing her so often in the future; his having saved her life had gone some way towards completing his penance, and he was hopeful of complete forgiveness and rest.

At all events, Mrs Bradshaw is quite convinced that a ghost saved her life that night.

*Duke's Head Hotel, King's Lynn, Norfolk*

## EMNETH, NORFOLK

A lonely hundred-year-old cottage was occupied for several years by a fitter and his former beauty-queen wife. As long as they lived here, mysterious things happened: windows opened inexplicably, the radio, television set, cooker and alarm clock were all switched on, on different occasions, when no living person was in the room.

Door latches rattled. Locks were undone. Ornaments were smashed. Furniture broken. In 1967, Mr Thorpe said 'There is a strange atmosphere here, as though someone were in the spare room.'

*Duke's Head Hotel, King's Lynn, Norfolk*

## EPWORTH, ISLE OF AXHOLME, LINCOLNSHIRE

One of the best documented cases of the poltergeist infestation concerned the parsonage of the Rev. Samuel Wesley (1662-1735), which - with alteration - is still standing. The disturbances took place during December 1716 and January 1717, and the evidence is contained in letters received by the rector's eldest son Samuel (1690-1739), from his mother, and other members of the family.

In addition, the Rev. Samuel Wesley himself wrote an account of the haunting. It was at the same parsonage that John Wesley (1703-91) was born - one of the nineteen children of the Rev. Samuel Wesley. At the time of the curious happenings, he was thirteen-and-a-half years old.

The first recorded incidents were 'several dismal groans', followed by a 'strange knocking' - usually three or four at a time. This continued for a fortnight, and was heard in various parts of the house. But most frequently in the nursery.

Everyone in the house heard the knockings, which grew in intensity and number. Often, nine loud knocks would be heard very near the Rev. Samuel Wesley's bedstead. He never found anything to account for the noise, or saw anything to explain them.

One night, noises came from the bedroom above that which was occupied by the Rev. Samuel Wesley and his wife, sounding as though people were walking about. This was followed by the noise of running footsteps up and down the stairs.

When they reached the bottom of the stairs, the noise of rattling money was heard at their feet, and then the noise of dozens of bottles being smashed.

The following night, Samuel Wesley asked a friend - the rector of a nearby parish - to spend a night at the house. As the three sat up waiting, the knockings were heard in the very early morning. Sometimes, a rasping noise would be heard, as if a clock were being wound up. Sometimes, the sound of a piece of wood being planed.

But more frequently, the knocks - three at a time: silence: then three more - would continue for many hours.

Once while looking in at the nursery to ensure the children were asleep (the younger children usually slept through the disturbances), the rector heard several loud and deep groans, and then more knocking.

Soon the noises increased in volume, and the Wesleys were disturbed day and night. They became utterly convinced that 'it was beyond the power of any human creature to make such strange and various noises.'

A maid was so frightened by hearing a 'most terrible and astonishing noise as of someone expiring' at the door of the dining room, that she dared not move from one room to another by herself. One of the daughters - Hetty - while sitting on the stairs waiting for her father, saw 'something like a man' come down the stairs behind her, with a loose nightshirt trailing behind him - which caused her to flee to her room!

Another apparition was seen by Mrs Wesley, under one of the girl's beds. Something 'like a badger', but apparently without any head. It seemed to run directly under Emily's petticoats. The same form was seen one evening in the dining room when a servant entered: it ran past him and through the hall under the stairs. He followed with a candle, but could find no trace of it.

Later, he saw it again in the kitchen, and this time he likened it to a white rabbit. The stairway seemed to particularly attract this ghost, and the sounds of footsteps were heard going up and down them, at all hours of the day and night, dozens of times. Vast rumblings were heard, and a gobbling noise - like a turkey cock.

Sometimes, the latch of the Wesley's bedroom door would be lifted when everyone was in bed, and one night, when there was a great noise in the kitchen, and the latch of the yard door was also lifted, another of the daughters - Emilia - went and held it tight on the inside. But still it lifted up, and the door itself was pushed hard against her, although nothing was visible outside.

The Rev. Samuel Wesley was frequently interrupted while at prayer by loud noises, and he was pushed by an unseen force three times. He followed the noises into practically every room in the house, and would sometimes sit alone and ask to be told what it wanted. But he never heard any articulate voice. Only once or twice two or three feeble squeaks. The ghost, or poltergeist, came to be called 'Old Jeffrey', after a former occupant who had died in the house.

It was noticed that soon after the noises began, the wind usually rose and whistled loud around the house. Often, the sounds seemed to be in the air in the middle of the room. A mastiff which had barked violently the first time 'it' came, never did so afterwards, but seemed to be conscious of it before the family, and would run, whining or silent, to shelter.

Independent accounts of the disturbances were recorded by members of the family, visitors, and in 1720 the Rev. John Wesley enquired into the whole matter, speaking to each of the people concerned. He compiled an account which was published in three issues of *The Arminian Magazine*, and reprinted sixty-four years later in the same periodical.

This certainly suggests that he was as convinced of the authenticity of the disturbances when he was over eighty as he had been when he was twenty.

Harry Price has pointed out that the poltergeist seemed to centre on Hetty Wesley - then aged around nineteen. There are reports of her 'trembling strongly in her sleep', and of her confused breathing and flushed face prior to and during 'visits' from 'Old Jeffrey', who seemed to follow her about the house, and to have a particular predilection for the bed on which she was lying.

After about two months, the disturbances ceased as mysteriously as they began.

*Mount Pleasant Hotel, Rossington, near Doncaster, Yorks.*

## FARINGDON, BERKSHIRE

The lonely hundred-year-old Oriel Cottage, Wicklesham Road, was the scene of 'ghostly rumblings, bangings, cold draughts and strange shadows' in 1963 and 1964. Police stayed a night and reported that there was 'no doubt there are strange noises… [but] there is nothing the police can do about it.'

A mysterious shape was seen by twenty-one people who stayed a night at the cottage, and they all felt a cold draught around their feet, for which they could find no rational explanation.

'We are sick with fear,' the family said in December, 1963 - 'it's all so uncanny.' The family then consisted of Mr and Mrs Norman Wheeler and their children Colin (nineteen), Betty (fifteen), Joy (ten), and Rosalie (five).

At the height of the disturbances, the girls were afraid to go upstairs for a fortnight, and slept huddled round the living-room fireplace. Yet the Wheelers had lived at the cottage, undisturbed, for eighteen years.

The mysterious knockings and bangings brought Mrs Wheeler to the edge of a nervous breakdown. Mr Wheeler ripped up floorboards to try to find the source of the noises, and architects checked the walls for flaws, but could find no material cause for the noises.

A medium identified the entity as a troublesome lodger who had lived at the cottage prior to the Wheelers moving in, and who had committed suicide. After a thirty-minute exorcism service by Canon Christopher Harman, a member of the Churches' Fellowship for Psychical and Spiritual Studies, the Wheelers reported that the disturbances had ceased.

*Crown and Thistle Hotel, Abingdon, Berks.*

# *FARNHAM, SURREY

['*Clarendon House*' is the former site of the '*Hop Bag Inn*']

The 'Hop Bag Inn', Downing Street, was once on the main coach route, when coaches were drawn by horses. In those days the inn was called the 'Adam and Eve'. In recent times, the sounds of horses and heavy wheels have been heard in the courtyard.

A visitor staying at the inn was awakened by the sounds one night, and when she looked out of her window into the yard - where the sounds seemed to originate - it was quite deserted. It was a bright moonlit night, but nothing could be seen that might have accounted for the loud and distinct noises. There is a story associated with the inn that goes back to the old coaching days - when a coach came over Long Bridge and pulled into the yard here for the driver to break the news to a waiting girl that the lover she was waiting for would not be coming for her.

He had been shot dead by highwaymen.

If the mysterious sounds heard here have their origin in this coach of bygone days, it is only one of several phantom coaches that are said to haunt the vicinity of Farnham.

*Bush Hotel, The Borough, Farnham, Surrey*

## *FARNHAM PARISH CHURCH, SURREY

There are a number of apparently well-authenticated ghost stories associated with this pleasant church. During the last war, a firewatcher reported hearing men's voices, chanting what sounded like Latin from within the dark and empty church.

He investigated, and noticed a number of tiny pinpoints of light at the far end of the nave. He saw them moving, and realized that the moving lights were candles being carried in procession round the interior. Far from being frightened, he only felt a deep sense of peace.

Only afterwards, when he thought about what he had seen, did he begin to have a feeling of apprehension. Of all the nights he spent in the vicinity of the church, this was the only time he saw or heard anything of a ghostly nature. But he could never be shaken on this particular experience.

A visitor, kneeling at the back of the church, raised her eyes and saw a pre-Reformation High Mass being celebrated at the altar. She watched, spellbound - the gold-clad celebrant and his brightly-dressed assistants wreathed in the rising incense smoke.

She said afterwards that the church seemed half-full of people. Some motionless. Others moving up and down the north aisle. But unlike the celebrants, they were colourless and shadowy. She strained her ears for the sound of ghostly music. But the arrival of the rector and a church warden shattered the strange atmosphere, and she found the church suddenly empty - as it had been when she arrived.

A former curate used to say that he saw on occasions a semi-transparent veil descend during the preaching of the sermon, cutting of the chancel [*the part of a church near the altar*] and altar, as well as figures and lights moving dimly behind the veil.

Other visitors to the church have experienced the same 'vision'. This curate, in the company of another parson, saw a little old lady enter the church while the church bell was ringing for evensong. But when they followed her, they found she had disappeared, and that the church was deserted. This happened not once, but several times, and it seems certain that the little old lady was no physical being.

*Bush Hotel, The Borough, Farnham, Surrey*

## FELBRIGGE, NEAR NORWICH, NORFOLK

Noble Felbrigge Hall, built on the site of an older Felbrigge residence, was long the home of the Windhams, a family that included the patriotic statesman, William Windham, and the notorious 'mad Windham' - who died in 1866.

Later, the house passed to the Kitton family, and one of the Miss Kittons told the traveller and author Augustus Hare (1834-1903) that 'Mr Windham comes every night to look after his favourite books in the library. He goes straight to the shelves where they are. We hear him moving the tables and chairs about. We never disturb him thought. For we intend to be ghosts ourselves some day, and to come about the place just as he does.'

*Bell Hotel, Norwich, Norfolk*

## FERNHURST, NEAR HASLEMERE, SUSSEX

On the eastern side of Fernhurst, near Blackdown Hill, there are a few remains of Verdley Castle. According to legend, this was the place where the last bear was killed in Sussex - and perhaps in England.

It was slain on Christmas Day, in the Great Hall of old Verdley, where it has sought refuge from the locals who had discovered the poor beast in the snow, nosing for food. It is said that at this time of the year, the growls of the cornered beast - and the shouts of the yokels - have been heard in the vicinity.

*Georgian Hotel, Haslemere, Surrey*

# *FLANSHAM MANOR, FLANSHAM,
# NEAR FELPHAM, SUSSEX

In the 1930s, the manor was a guest house. Many visitors seemed to have 'bumped' into a phantom called Cuthbert. The deep lounge hall has a small gallery running overhead, which goes through a doorway at one end, and connects with the bedrooms.

One night, all the residents and guests were out, except for the owner and a friend. Suddenly, they both heard footsteps coming from the passage upstairs at the other end of the gallery. They knew there was no one else in the house, but decided to investigate. When they walked across the hall, and looked up at the gallery, they saw the door slowly closing. And yet no living person was in fact in the house, except themselves.

Years before, a child sleeping in a bathroom had awakened night after night by strange sounds, thuds, bumps - actually seemingly coming from within the room - almost as though someone or something was being dragged out of the cupboard, along the floor, and through the haunted doorway.

*Clarehaven Hotel, Wessex Avenue, Bognor Regis, Sussex*

## *FORRABURY, CORNWALL

Forrabury has long had a tradition of ghostly bells sounding from beneath the waves. They are supposed to have originated with the conveyance by sea of new bells for the local church. All went well, until the captain of the boat used profane language - whereupon a violent storm broke, and the ship sank with all hands.

There are local people, too, who claim to have seen phantom boats with phantom crews rowing silently to the spot where the ship sank.

*Tolcarne Private Hotel, Doctor's Corner, Boscastle, Cornwall*

## *FULMER, BUCKINGHAMSHIRE

Near this delightful village, there is a ford which runs across the road. Many people have reported hearing curious and apparently ghostly noises hereabouts. One man, a technician at nearby Pinewood Film Studios, heard the sound of a horse and trap which sounded quite distinct - yet there was no sign of any such vehicle.

The noise did not seem to be advancing, but sounded as though the trap was in one spot - yet moving. Another witness said she heard the sounds of hooves at one side of a field near the same spot, not once but many times. The same noise had been heard by a friend of hers.

*Royal Hotel, Slough, Bucks.*

## FYVIE, ABERDEENSHIRE, SCOTLAND

Fyvie Castle is famous for its ghost room, a murder room and a secret chamber. In 1920, the famous 'green lady ghost' is said to have been seen wandering forlornly and silently along the corridors and disappearing through the panels of a dark, wainscotted apartment.

A few years before a monster fungus had grown up in the gun-room, and when masons and carpenters had removed the plant and were repairing the carpenters had removed the plant, and were repairing the room, they discovered a complete skeleton.

This discovery seemed to signal the commencement of psychic disturbances, and Lord Leith gave instructions for the skeleton to be rebuilt into the wall - whereupon 'normality' was restored.

*Kintore Arms Hotel, Inverurie, Aberdeenshire, Scotland*

## GALASHIELS, SELKIRKSHIRE, SCOTLAND

Nearby Buckholm Tower (ruins) is reputed to be haunted by a former Laird of Buckholm. Weird stories are told of strange noises heard in the dungeon, and there is talk of an everlasting bloodstain on an old beam.

Two hundred years ago, a laird of Buckholm, a man called Pringer - whose family still owns the property - ill-treated his young wife and ten-year-old son so badly that she ran off with the boy. Left on his own, the laird's behaviour became wild and violent. His great delight, in those days of the Covenanters [*a Scottish Presbyterian movement that played an important part in the history of Scotland, and to a lesser extent that of England and Ireland, during the 17th century*], was to hound these upholders of the forms of worship no longer countenanced by law. He kept two ferocious dogs - the terror of the local inhabitants - expressly for this cruel purpose.

Known as a local supporter of the Government, the laird was called upon one day by a captain of the Dragoons, to assist in breaking up an unlawful assembly of Covenanters on nearby Ladhope Moor.

Delighted to assist, shrewdly guessed where the gathering would take place. But when he arrived on the sport, he found that the assembly had somehow received warning and had disbanded - all except on old man, Geordie Elliot, whose wife had once been in the Pringe Service. His son, too, had stayed by his father's side when the old man had been thrown from his horse and was badly hurt. Both were known as Covenanters.

The wicked laird of Buckholm was for disposing of both men on the spot, but the captain decided that they might be able to give information about their fellow Covenanters. It was arranged that Pringle should hold them prisoner for the night, and that the captain would send an escort for them the following day.

Back at the Tower, the prisoners were thrown into the dungeon, which exists to this day with its grisly row of iron hooks suspended from the ceiling.

When the captain and his troops had left, the laird dined and soaked himself with brandy, well-pleased with the day's work. The hours passed. Brandy followed brandy.

Hours later, the servants were awakened by loud cries from the direction of the dungeon where the prisoners had been left for hours. They heard the laird stagger and curse as he made his way downstairs. Fearful sounds reached their ears and several servants hovered at the dungeon door when at length the laird stumbled out, muttering something like 'swine should be treated as swine…'

He staggered towards the main door. When he opened it, there stood an old woman. Pringle stopped dead in his tracks. It was Isobel Elliot, looking for her menfolk. The laird muttered some drunken oath, and dragged her to the dungeon. A piercing scream broke from the woman's lips when she saw, suspended from the hooks like carcases of swine, the bodies of her husband - and her son.

Screaming and wild-eyed, the distraught woman ran out of the dungeon, fell headlong, and sobbed uncontrollably. The drunken laird stood looking down at her, perhaps for the first time realizing the enormity of his crime.

Slowly, old Isobel rose to her feet. In a quiet tone, she cursed Pringle for what he had done. She called down the vengeance of God upon him, so that the memory of his evil deeds - like hounds of hell - should haunt and pursue him, waking and sleeping, and he should find no place of refuge in this life, or in eternity.

GAZETTEER OF BRITISH GHOSTS

After that, Pringle firmly believed that he was haunted. He would imagine frequently that ghostly hounds were at his throat night and day. Before long, he died a painful death, full of horror at the last moments, which were accompanied by convulsions, as if his body was being worried and torn to death.

As the first anniversary of the laird's death approached, a ghostly figure was seen in the vicinity of the Tower, running for his life from baying hounds. On the eve of the anniversary, the baying of dogs and the sound of someone calling desperately for help were heard - there was also the noise of hammering on the great door.

A terrified old retainer called out to ask who was knocking. A voice answered, asking to be admitted 'for mercy's sake'. It sounded like the voice of the dead Laird of Buckholm! The faithful manservant at length plucked up enough courage to throw open the door. But as he did so, there was only silence, and nothing to see in the dark night.

The following night, on the actual anniversary of the death of the laird, the baying of hounds was heard for the third time, coming now from the dungeon. Again a voice the old servant recognized cried out for help. Everyone in the place was terrified and stood listening to the dreadful commotion in the dungeon: baying hounds, frenzied breathing, blood-curdling screams. And finally silence.

Every June, it is said, these same sounds are heard by those who are able to hear them, from the depths of the dark and mysterious dungeon of Buckholm Tower.

*Douglas Hotel, Galashiels, Selkirkshire, Scotland*

## GATESHEAD, CO. DURHAM

A council house in Bronte Street, occupied by the Coulthard family, was the scene of 'poltergeist' activity in 1963 and 1964. Exorcism was carried out by a local clergyman, but had no lasting effect. Ornaments were thrown, bottles smashed, slippers shot up from the floor, plates and crockery crashed down, and chairs and other objects were moved. The householder fled and appealed for alternative accommodation.

*Springfield Hotel, Gateshead, Co. Durham*

GILL HOUSE, ASPATRIA,
CUMBERLAND; SEE ASPATRIA

## *GLAMIS CASTLE, GLAMIS, ANGUS, SCOTLAND

The oldest inhabited and most impressive castle in Scotland. It is famous for the story of the Monster of Glamis - and the secret room...

It was in this splendid castle that Duncan was murdered by Macbeth, and a bloodstain remained forever where King Malcolm II is said to have been killed - so that the whole floor was boarded over.

The place is, as might be expected, haunted by several ghosts. Among them, the little Grey Lady - so I was told when I was there in 1968 - had been seen quite recently by the present Lord Strathmore.

The Dowager Countess Granville saw her one sunny afternoon, kneeling in one of the pews. The sun, coming through the windows, shone through the outline of the little figure. Lord Strathmore walked into the chapel one afternoon and saw the same figure in the identical place. Once he saw her walk into the chapel. Others have seen the same form - but who she, nobody knows.

High up in the uninhabited tower of Glamis, there is a room where, in the days of King James II of Scotland, one Alexander, fourth Earl of Crawford, known as 'Earl Beardie', quarrelled while gambling with a Lord Glamis and two chieftains. They were doomed to play dice forever in that room. The cook at the castle will tell you that she has heard the rattle of dice - and stamping and swearing - coming from that empty room at dead of night.

The legend of the Monster of Glamis relates that somewhere around 1800, a monster was born to be heir of Glamis. Misshapen to an awful degree, he had no neck, only minute arms and legs, and looked like a flabby egg. But he was immensely strong, and a special room was built in the castle where he was kept from the eyes of everyone.

His existence was known only to four men at the time: The Earl of Strathmore, his eldest son, the family lawyer, and the factor of the estate. Each eldest son was told the secret and shown the rightful Earl when he reached the age of twenty-one.

There are still records at Glamis, showing that a secret chamber was built there in 1684, and since the monster is said to have lived to an incredibly old age (some think he only died in 1921), the secret may account for so many Lord Strathmores being unhappy men. A Lady Strathmore is said to have asked one of the factors outright about the story - for no Countess of Strathmore was ever told of the monster - and the factor refused to satisfy her, saying 'It is fortunate you do not know the truth, for if you did, you would never be happy.'

The present Lord Strathmore knows nothing about the monsters - presumably because the creature was dead when he reached his majority. But he has always felt that there was a corpse or a coffin bricked up somewhere in the walls.

A former Lord Halifax was convinced, after spending a night there, that the Blue Room at Glamis was haunted. He thought he saw the ghost of 'Earl Beardie', and recounted how two visiting children often saw shadowy figures flitting about the castle in the vicinity of the Blue Room, where they would not sleep. Sir Shane Leslie told me that the ghost of 'Beardie' had been seen by one of his aunts when she stayed at Glamis.

The small dressing room off the Queen Mother's main bedroom used to be haunted. People who slept there often felt the bedclothes being pulled off, but there have been no disturbances since the room has been turned into a bathroom.

Among the other haunted places at Glamis, there is the room where the door opens by itself every night. Even when it is bolted or wedged by some heavy object.

- There is a tongueless woman who runs across the park, pointing in anguish to her wounded mouth.

- 'Jack the Runner', a strange thin figure who races up the long drive to the castle.

- A madman known as 'The Mad Earl's Walk'.

- A ghostly little black boy has been seen sitting by the door of the Queen Mother's sitting room, and is thought to have been a page boy who was badly treated.

- Noises of hammering and loud knocking are heard in a room in the oldest part of the castle.

- A female figure has been seen hovering above the clock tower, surrounded by a reddish glow. She is thought to be a Lady Glamis who was burned to death on Castle Hill, Edinburgh, charged with witchcraft, and with being concerned in an attempt to poison King James V.

- A tall figure once walked into a room occupied by a Provost of Perth, clad in a long, dark cloak, fastened at the throat with an unusual clasp.

- A woman with mournful eyes and a pale face peers out of an upper lattice window, hands clutching at the panes.

There are indeed ghosts aplenty at Glamis, and whether one visits this historic and ancient pile in brilliant sunshine, or on a stormy night, it is not difficult to believe that strange happenings have taken place here.

Once, a party of youngsters decided to try to discover the locality of the secret room. They visited every room in the castle - the total is over a hundred - and hung towels and sheets out of the windows to mark them. They were sure that they had visited every room, but when they gathered outside, they counted seven windows in the massive castle with nothing hanging from them. The mystery of Glamis was still unexplained.

*County Hotel, Forfar, Angus, Scotland*

## GLOUCESTER, GLOUCESTERSHIRE

Some ten years ago, there was an old house where a vicar used to live, in a little village on the outskirts of Gloucester - almost hidden from the road by high trees.

Beneath the house there was a rambling kitchen - unused in living memory - from which there were at times sounds that seemed to suggest that people were walking about.

One day, the vicar went to see whether he could discover the causes of the noises and, standing in the centre of the old kitchen, he saw the figure of a monk. The vicar asked whether he could help the monk. The monk, by way of reply, looked sadly at him, walked across the kitchen and - when he had almost reached the opposite wall - vanished.

After this, the vicar saw the monk on several occasions in the old kitchen. The figure always vanished a few seconds after being seen. It never spoke. It always had a sad look on its face. The vicar began to make enquiries, and discovered that there had been a monastery nearby, but now only a few ruins marked the site.

On another occasion, the vicar noticed that the floor of the old kitchen seemed to sag in the middle, and thought that he better go see about repairing it. And when workmen took up the floor, it was found that the flooring rested on two huge wooden beams, which were almost rotted through with damp and age. Beneath them was a large, deep tank of water - possibly the water supply of years gone by. After the flooring had been repaired and replaced, the ghostly monk was never seen again.

*New County Hotel, Southgate Street, Gloucester, Cambridgeshire*

# *GRANTCHESTER, CAMBRIDGESHIRE

*[The 'Old Vicarage' is now a Private Residence]*

Rupert Brooke (1887-1915), the famous First World War poet, lived here at the Old Vicarage, a lovely house with a garden which must still be largely unchanged since those days, when it was the subject of one of his most famous poems.

Ever since they went to live there in 1911 (the occupants told me a few years ago), they heard a noise like someone walking about the top floor, moving books. They thought nothing of the sounds, and were not in the least frightened.

My friend Christina Hall suggested that the unexplained footsteps, heard coming to the garden towards the sitting room, are those of the poet, re-visiting the house he loved.

In his well-known poem Brooke refers to 'the falling house that never falls'. This is an odd little semi-ruined house at the bottom of the garden. And - I am told - it can be a very eerie place after dark. Curious poltergeist manifestations used to occur there at night-time, small objects being spilled out of boxes and arranged in strange little patterns. The most stringent precautions were taken to detect whether any living person had been able to get into the building during the night. And once the disturbances occurred after snow had fallen - yet there was no trace in it of any footsteps.

*Blue Boar Hotel, Cambridge*

## GREAT BEALINGS, WOODBRIDGE, SUFFOLK

Bealings House was the scene of a classic story of paranormal bell-ringing in 1834. The occupant of the Georgian mansion at the time, Major Edward Moor (1771-1848, a fellow of the Royal Society, retired from the East India Company, and author of a book on Hindu mythology), described the occurrences in a letter to his local paper. He subsequently published a short volume on the case, which includes accounts of unexplained bell-ringing at other places throughout the country.

On Sunday, February 2nd 1834, Major Moor, on returning home from church, was told that the dining-room bell had rung three times between two and five o'clock. The following day, the same bell rang again three times more during the afternoon, and once more, just before five o'clock, it was heard by Major Moor.

The next day, he was out and, returning shortly before five o'clock, he learned that all the bells in the kitchen had been ringing violently - and as he was being told this, a peal of bells sounded from the kitchen.

They were (and still are) nine bells in a row in the kitchen, around a foot apart, ten feet from the floor, and on enquiry Major Moor learned from the cook that the five bells on the right were the ones affected. These were the ones situated in the dining, the drawing over the dining room, an adjacent bedroom, and two attics over the drawing room.

While he was looking at these bells, which he was told had rung frequently since about three o'clock, the same five rang violently and with such force that he thought they would be shaken from their fastenings.

Major Moor's son was with him at the time and also witnessed the ringing. He had previously seen the bells ringing and had also heard them once before. In addition, the cook and another servant were present in the kitchen. About ten minutes later, there was another peal, and a quarter of an hour later yet another.

At six o'clock, when Major Moor and his son were sitting down to dinner in the breakfast room, the bell of that room rang once more, as if it had been pulled, although no one was near it at the time. During the meal, the five bells previously affected rang every ten minutes or so, and continued to do so at longer intervals when the six servants were at dinner in the kitchen until a quarter-to-eight, when the ringing stopped.

Next day, Wednesday, February 5th, a peal of bells was heard at eleven o'clock in the morning when Major Moor, his son and grandson, were in the breakfast room and while several of the servants were in the kitchen. Major Moor went to the kitchen and five minutes later the same five bells rang again, very violently. And four minutes later, yet again. One so violently that it struck the ceiling.

From then on the bells rang scores of times, and in conditions that convinced Major Moor and his family that no human being was responsible. They rang when no one was in the passage or room concerned, or outside the house, unobserved. Major Moor saw the bells ring in the kitchen when all the servants were present, and he became utterly convinced that the ringing noted by him and his family and others could not possibly have been produced by a living person.

The bell ringing lasted from February 2nd to March 27th, 1834, when it ceased as abruptly as it began. The cause was never discovered. The original bells, now disconnected, still hang at Bealings House.

*Crown Hotel, Woodbridge, Suffolk*

St Anne's Castle Inn, which claims to be the oldest inn in England, has long been famous for its haunted room. There are stories of over a hundred people who attempted to spend a night there, at different times, and who had curious experiences to relate. Noises of various kinds have been reported:

- Thuds, shuffles, bangs, raps - from the direction of the stout oak door.

- The noise of furniture being moved around.

- A cold draught has been felt.

- Curtains have been torn down.

- Bedclothes have been ripped off beds, and clothing scattered.

One visitor to this former retreat of royalist, monk and highwaymen, heard loud cries as he attempted to sleep in the haunted room. As soon as he rose from the bed, the noises ceased. But they began again when he lay back down again. This continued time after time, and he had no rest until daybreak.

Not long afterwards, a girl occupied the room for one night, and spent most of the time huddled by the window, waiting for the dawn. Several people reported seeing a black shape in the room, especially on one side of bed.

There are various stories and legends that attempt to justify the manifestations. Perhaps the most persistent one concerns the murder of a child in the four-poster bed that used to stand there, in the presence of the child's mother, a very long time ago. Investigator Harry Price found the contents of the room in a condition comparable to having been 'shaken out of a pepperpot' when he was there in 1944.

*County Hotel, Rainsford Road, Chelmsford, Essex*

# *GREENWICH, NATIONAL MARITIME MUSEUM

Two visitors from Canada - a retired clergyman and his wife - visited the National Maritime Museum in 1966, and took a photograph during normal opening hours, of the tulip staircase in The Queen's House, beautiful building erected by Inigo Jones for Anne of Denmark, consort of King James I, and subsequently completed for Henrietta Maria, wife of King Charles I.

The staircase appeared to be deserted at the time. But when the photograph was developed - after the Hardy's had returned to Canada - there seemed to be a cowled figure climbing the staircase with 'his' left and ringed hand on the stair-rail, preceded by a less clear figure - also with a hand on the rail.

The original transparency was sent to The Ghost Club, who obtained expert opinion and assurance that there had been no technical interference. The only logical explanation was that there had been a person, or persons, on the stairs.

On a further visit to England in 1967, Mr and Mrs Hardy, who are not interested in psychic activity, were interviewed at length at Canada House by Richard M. Howard, then Honorary Secretary of The Ghost Club. He is of the opinion that they are incapable of conscious fraud.

There are no official records of any alleged Haunting at the museum, although an official told me that there have been stories of an unidentified figure being encountered in the tunnel beneath paved way immediately outside the Queen's House. A former employee of the museums stated that on several occasions he had noticed unexplained figures in the vicinity of the Tulip Staircase. And one of them Warders on duty at the Queen's house used to say that he heard footsteps there which he could not account for.

The Ghost Club organized an all-night vigil at the Queen's House and 'sealed off' certain rooms, placed 'controls' in strategic positions, noted atmospheric conditions, took thermometer readings every ten minutes, used sound recording apparatus, infrared and standard film in movie and still cameras, and attempted 'to tempt' the ghosts by resorting to periods of total darkness and silence, using also planchette, table-turning and automatic writing for communication.

Among the unexplained noises heard during the course of the investigation were:

- The single peal of a bell.

- The sounds of muttering, crying and footsteps.

The remarkably clear photograph remains an enigma and, if genuine, probably the best spontaneous ghost photograph in existence.

*Eltham Private Hotel, West Mill Road, Eltham, S.E.9*

## GRIMSBY, LINCOLNSHIRE

A council house was so badly haunted that Mr Ted Barningham, his wife and family, left the place in September 1967, after a 'ghost' appeared on closed circuit television at the house! It was thought to be the entity which had been terrifying the family for weeks beforehand. This time it appeared on the monitor screen as the head of 'an old man of hideous appearance'.

It was seen by a group of six people, including an electrical engineer, who had rigged up the apparatus. A television camera had been placed in the bedroom where most of the disturbances had taken place, and after a watch several hours, the face appeared on the monitor screen downstairs. When one of the parties rushed upstairs, the face disappeared. The engineer stated that he had tried every possible test with the apparatus, but could find no possible explanation for the occurrence.

*Ship Hotel, Flottergate, Grimsby, Lincs*

## HALTWHISTLE, NORTHUMBERLANDSHIRE

Near the Remains of the old Roman wall, an entire phantom hunt used to be seen galloping past, terrifying the dogs and cats of the neighborhood, who would run for miles to get away from the spectral hounds.

*Hadrian Hotel, Wall Village, Hexham, Northumb.*

## *HAM HOUSE, NEAR PETERSHAM, SURREY

Almost hidden by trees amid the Thames-side Meadows between Twickenham and Richmond, one is surprised to come upon stately Ham House - a silent reminder of a more leisurely past, its ancient iron gates unopened since the flight of King James II.

Ham House was built by Sir Thomas Vavasour in 1610, and intended, according to tradition, as a residence for the eldest son of King James I. But the young prince's sudden death in 1612 brought whispers of murder - although it is not Prince Henry who haunts Ham House, but the old Duchess of Lauderdale who is said to revisit the scene of her triumphs and infamies during the days of Cromwell and of King Charles II.

The scheming and powerful Duchess, formerly Countess of Dysart, reputed to have been Cromwell's mistress, was daughter of William Murray, First Earl of Dysart, who built the magnificent great staircase at Ham. Elizabeth, his only child, while still married to Sir Lionel Tollemache, chose for her lover John Maitland.

In 1672, with Sir Lionel dead, she married this member of Charles II's Cabal Ministry. He lived to become the unpopular Duke of Lauderdale, favourite of King Charles II. Ham House was enlarged, sumptuously decorated and furnished anew with lavish splendour: these were the compensating deeds of the villainous Lauderdale and his wicked wife who were know to send innocent people to the rack.

For years after her death, the Duchess's boudoir remained as she had known it: her silver-headed ebony walking-stick where she had left it. It is this stick which is thought to be the original source of the mysterious tapping noises heard about the history-laden rooms of Ham House. At dead of night, that noise would be heard - '...tap, tap, tap...' - just as the old Duchess used to hobble about.

The story that is supposed to account for the haunting concerns a butler at Ham whose little girl of six stayed at the house on a visit at the invitation of the Ladies Tollemache. Very early in the morning, the child awoke suddenly to see an old woman scratching and clawing at the wall close to the fireplace. At first more curious than frightened, the little girl sat up in bed to see better what was happening. But the sound of her movements made the old woman turn round.

She came to the foot of the child's bed, grasping the bed-rail with her bony hands, and stared long and fixedly at the now-terrified child, who screamed and buried herself beneath the bedclothes. Hearing the screams, servants and occupants of the house rushed to the child's room, and although they saw no old woman, they comforted the child, listened to her story, and then turned their attention to the wall by the fireplace.

There they found papers which proved that in that very room,

Elizabeth - Countess of Dysart - had murdered her husband - to marry the Duke of Lauderdale...

When I was there, in August 1970, I learned of a phantom King Charles Spaniel, which is reputed to run yapping along the terrace at the original front of the house (now the back), where colourful herbaceous borders face the long unopened gates of this splendid house.

*Richmond Hill Hotel, Richmond Hill, Richmond, Surrey*

# *HAMPTON, MIDDLESEX

*[Penn Place has since been demolished - but is marked by a black plaque]*

Penn Place, the former home of Mrs Sybil Penn, nurse to the infant Prince Edward - later King Edward VI - is now occupied by Eric Fraser, the artist, who will tell you that his daughter used to see a 'lady in grey' in her bedroom when she was a little girl.

As he showed me the room, Eric Fraser explained that his daughter was only two or three years old at the time, and could not have known that the house probably incorporates part of the original house occupied by Mrs Penn, whose ghost, the 'lady in grey', is said to walk at nearby Hampton Court.

One morning, the little girl said casually, 'I've seen a nice lady in a grey dress. She came to my room last night, and I didn't mind.' After that first time, she told her parents on several occasions: 'I saw the grey lady again last night.' After a while, the child no longer mentioned the apparition, but it may be that the ghost still walks at Penn Place, and can be seen by those who have the extra-sensory perception of some children.

*Mitre Hotel, Hampton Court, Middlesex*

## *HAMPTON COURT, MIDDLESEX

The Old Court House, where the great architect Sir Christopher Wren lived during the years he was supervising work at Hampton Court Palace, and where he died, has been the scene of a remarkable psychic occurrence.Norman Lamplugh lived here for many years, until the outbreak of the Second World War. On one of the occasions when he held a garden party at the beautiful old house, two of the guests (on of them Norman's brother, Ernest) noticed a little boy of about eight years old, threading his way through the groups of guests dotted about the lawn. The two friends were standing on the landing of the main staircase, and they were puzzled for two reasons:

1. They knew that no children had been invited to the social event

2. And they were struck by the appearance of the child, for his fair hair was abnormally long, and he was dressed in a black-and-white costume of a page-boy of the time of King Charles II!

His breeches and doublet appeared to be of black velvet; he wore shiny black shoes with big silver buckles and white hose.

While the two men were discussing the boy, they watched as he easily and quickly wended his way between the guests, and approached the stairway. Unhurriedly, but with the confidence of someone who knew where he was going and without wasting any time he mounted the stairs and passed the two friends, who were in fact obliged to step back to make room for him.

The child took no notice of them, but walked on up the stairs to the top of the house, and there entered a room which had no exit other than the doorway on to the stairs, and disappeared.

No explanation was ever found for the mystery, and as far as I know, the phantom child was never seen again, although mysterious and unexplained footsteps are reported in the vicinity of the stairs on the night of February 26th, the anniversary of the death of Sir Christopher Wren.

The spirit of King Henry VIII seems to brood heavily over the mellow Tudor palace itself. He was at Hampton with five of his six wives, and it was here on October 12th, 1537, that his third queen, Jane Seymour, bore him a son - and died, a week later.

Her ghost walks here, or rather glides - clad in white - perambulating Clock Court. Carrying a lighted taper [*slender candle*], she has been seen to emerge from a doorway in the Queen's old apartments, wander noiselessly about the stairway, and through the Silver Stick Gallery. Quite recently, some servants handed in their notice because they had seen 'a tall lady, with a long train and a shining face' walk through closed doors holding a taper - gliding down the stairs.

Another courtyard, Fountain Court, used to be haunted by two male figures, which were seen by Lady Hildyard, who had grace and favour apartments overlooking the Court. She wrote to the Lord Chamberlain about the figures, and also complained about unaccountable rappings and other strange noises at night-time. Her letter was passed to the Board of Works, who did nothing; but not long afterwards, workmen laying new drains in Fountain Court came across the perfectly preserved remains of two young cavaliers of the Civil War period, buried two feet below the pavement.

It is possible that they were the remains of Lord Francis Villiers and a brother Royalist Officer killed in a skirmish between the King's forces and those of Parliament. But at all events, after the bones had received a decent burial, Lady Hildyard saw no more figures, and heard no more unexplained noises.

The famous White Lady of Hampton Court is reputed to haunt the area of the landing-stage, and a number of anglers reported seeing her one midsummer night a few years ago. There is also the ghost of Archbishop Laud (whose spirit is also said to appear in the library of St John's College, Oxford, rolling his head across the floor!), which has been allegedly seen by residents at the palace - strolling slowly without a sound (but complete with head!), in the vicinity of the rooms he once knew so well.

An example of the 'residential ghost' is also provided by the spectre of Mrs Sybil Penn, foster-mother of Edward VI. Records show that she was seen by a sentry here in 1881, and there are infrequent reports of her recurring appearances in succeeding years. As the nurse of Henry VIII's only legitimate son, Edward, she anxiously and conscientiously watched over the sickly child, and the sound of her voice and the whirr of her spinning-wheel must have been some of the first sounds heard by the young prince.

Edward never forgot his old nurse, nor did Mary Tudor - or Elizabeth - who granted her a pension and apartments at Hampton Court where both Elizabeth and Mrs Penn suffered an attack of smallpox in 1568. Queen Elizabeth survived, but remained marked for the rest of her life.

Mrs Penn was less fortunate, and died on November 6th. She was buried at nearby St Mary's Church, Hampton, which was struck by lightning in 1829, and although Mrs Penn's tomb and monument were removed to the new church, her grave was rifled, and her remained - scattered.

It was not long after this that a family named Ponsonby occupied the rooms in the palace, where once Mrs Penn had lived and worked. They soon began to complain of continually hearing the sound of a spinning wheel, and a woman's voice, which they could not account for.

The sounds seemed to originate through one of the walls in the south-west wing, and the noises became so persistent, that the Board of Works was called in. They discovered a sealed chamber which, when opened, was found to contain - amid other feminine relics - a much-used spinning-wheel, which may have been the one Mrs Penn used so often during her lifetime.

It was about this time that a sentry on duty one day outside these apartments, saw a female figure clad in a long grey robe and hood, emerging from the former rooms of Mrs Penn, and vanishing in front of his eyes. Another sentry deserted his post when he saw the phantom of an old woman in grey pass through a wall. Both asserted that the figures they saw resembled the stone effigy of Mrs Sybil Penn.

Oddly enough, the discovery of the spinning-wheel seems to have accentuated the curious happenings. For years afterwards, there were curious happenings in the vicinity of these apartments. Servants declared that they were awakened at night by:

- Cold hands on their faces.

- Stealthy footsteps perambulating the floor close to them.

- Mutterings in a sepulchral voice.

- Loud crashing noises.

They would also awake to find the whole apartment bathed in what they described as 'a ghastly lurid light'. Princess Frederica of Hanover, who knew nothing of Mrs Penn, came face to face with a 'tall, gaunt figure, dressed in a long grey robe, with a hood on her head, and her lanky hands outstretched before her'. She, too, declared that the figure resembled the faithful nurse's effigy. The well-authenticated ghost of Mrs Sybil Penn is known as the 'Lady in Grey'.

Perhaps the most famous ghost at Hampton Court is that of Lady Catherine Howard, who came here in 1540. A lovely girl of eighteen and bride of the fat, lame and ageing monarch. After little more than a year, ugly rumours began to circulate, and it was said that she behaved little better than a common harlot, both before and after her marriage.

The night she was arrested - her first step to the block - she broke free from her captors and sped along the gallery in a vain effort to plead for her life with her husband. But Henry, piously hearing vespers in the chapel, ignored her entreaties, and she was dragged away, still shrieking and sobbing for mercy.

As you go down the Queen's Great Staircase, you can see on the right-hand side the low-roofed and mysterious corridor containing the room from which Queen Catherine escaped, and to which she was dragged back, her screams mingling weirdly with the singing in the chapel. Her ghost re-enacts the grisly event on the night of the anniversary, running shrieking through what has come to be known as the 'Haunted Gallery'.

Those who have heard and seen her ghost include Mrs Cavendish Boyle and Lady Eastlake, together with many servants at the palace. All the witnesses say the figure has long, flowing hair. But it usually disappears so quickly that no one has time to observe it closely.

A hundred years ago, the 'Haunted Gallery' was locked and used as a storage room for pictures, but adjoining chambers were occupied as a grace and favour apartment by a titled lady who has recorded that once, in the dead of night, she was awakened by an appalling and ear-piercing shriek, which died away into a pulsating silence.

Not long afterwards, she had a friend staying with her, who was awakened by a similar dreadful cry, which seemed to come from the 'Haunted Gallery'. After the Gallery was opened to the public, an artist sketching some tapestry was startled to see a ringed hand repeatedly appear in front of it, but he hurriedly sketched the hand and ring. The jewel was later identified as one known to have been worn by Catherine Howard.

Towards the end of the last century, the ghost of Anne Boleyn was reported to have been seen here. Her ghost, dressed in blue, surprised a servant, who recognised the figure she had seen from a portrait in the palace. Anne is a perambulating ghost, and is reputed to haunt Blickling Hall, Hever Castle, Salle Church, Rochford Hall, Bollin Hall, Marwell Hall, the Tower of London, and the Undercroft of Lambeth Palace!

A police constable - with over twenty years experience in the force, once saw a group of ghosts in the palace grounds. Standing by the main gates, he noticed a party of people coming towards him along Ditton Walk. They consisted of some eight or nine ladies - and two men in evening dress.

The constable noticed that the only sound he heard was a rustling as of dresses. When the group drew near, he turned and opened the gate for them, whereupon they altered direction and headed north towards the Flower Post Gates. At the same time, the party formed itself into a procession - two deep - with men at the head. Then, to the policeman's amazement - and while he was actually watching them - the whole group vanished!

Among other accounts of ghosts at Hampton Court, there is the story of two devoted friends, one of whom - after the death of her first husband - married a German count, and went to live in Germany with her little girl Maud. The other was granted a residence at Hampton Court.

One night, when going to bed, the latter lady saw a figure noiselessly climbing the wide staircase opposite the door of her chamber. It was the figure of a lady dressed entirely in black, except for white kid gloves.

Speechless with horror, she recognized her friend, and fainted with a shriek as the apparition drew near her.

A few days later, she received a letter from Maud informing her of the death of the Barness. She hurried to Germany, where she learned that her friend had requested, on her deathbed, that she should be buried in black - with white kid gloves. The Baroness had died in Germany on November 9th, the date on which her ghost had been seen by her friend at Hampton Court.

After a costume performance of 'Twelfth Night' at Hampton Court Palace, producer-actor Leslie Finch told me that he was walking towards one of the gateways with Lady Grant, who has apartments at the palace, when he saw a grey, misty figure in Tudor costume approaching them, and he felt a sudden coldness.

He thought the figure must be one of the actresses, and moved to one side to let her pass. His companion looked oddly at him, and he discovered that Lady Grant had seen no figure at all but, as the phantom passed, she had also noticed a sudden cold draught of air.

During the 1966 season of *Son et Lumiere* [*an entertainment held by night at a historic monument or building, telling its history by the use of lighting effects and recorded sound*] at Hampton Court Palace, a member of the audience 'saw' the figure of Cardinal Wolsey (who built the palace) under one of the archways, and thought that an actor was taking part in the performance of sound and light - a fact that Christopher Ede, the producer, mentioned in his contribution to the 1970 programme.

*Mitre Hotel, Hampton Court, Middlesex*

## HASTINGS, SUSSEX

The castle is said to have been the scene of the first tournament in England, held for Adela, daughter of William the Conqueror. After the castle had ceased to be a stronghold, it was used as a religious house, and there were frequent reports of ghostly organ music being heard here.

A figure, believed to be Thomas Becket [*Archbishop of Canterbury from 1162 until his murder in 1170. He is venerated as a saint and martyr by both the Catholic Church and the Anglican Communion*], has been seen within the precincts of the castle on autumn evenings - never at any other time of the year. There are stories, too, of the sounds of rattling chains, and the groans of starving prisoners: perhaps some strange echo from the past.

It is said that on certain sunny, misty mornings, a huge mirage of Hastings Castle can be seen far out at sea on the horizon. This might be explained as a result of reflection and refraction of light - were it not that the castle appears again in all its former glory, with flags flying from the turrets.

*Queen's Hotel, Hastings, Sussex*

# *HEATHFIELD, SUSSEX

*[Warbleton Priory is now a Private Residence]*

Warbleton Priory, an ancient farmhouse near Rushlake Green, incorporated parts of an old Augustinian ecclesiastical building, and used to house two skulls, thought to be those of a former owner of the house - and of the man who murdered him.

In common with most houses that harbour skulls, there were vague stories of evil consequences for those who moved them from the house - of cattle drying up; of the person responsible being plagued with continual bad luck and strange noises - until the skulls were returned. There was also a bloodstain here that could not be removed.

Years ago, when one of the thick walls of the house was being knocked down, workmen are said to have found the two skulls.

When the first was discovered, it was buried. But the following morning, the skull is reputed to have worked its way out of the earth and was found on the doorstep of the farmhouse.

The skull was then placed in a box, and stored on the cross-beams of the house. Later, it was placed on a Bible in the front-room, where it remained for many years with tenant farmers coming and going. But when one attempted to take the skull with him:

- Screams sounded throughout the house.

- Thuds and knocks were heard.

- Doors and windows slammed and rattled.

- Horses showed signs of fright.

There was no peace until the skull was returned to Warbleton...

The second skull was also preserved here for many years, and then turned up at a farmhouse some six miles away, where the farmer is said to have been plagued with a whirlwind when he tried to bury it.

It is a good many years now since either of the skulls were at Warbleton, and I have been unable to trace any recent ghostly happenings hereabouts.

There was also a curious story associated with the rambling house. On certain moonlit nights, a pair of ghostly white hands were said to be seen fluttering at a small window high up near the roof.

The alleged bloodstain was still shown to visitors some years ago, and the floorboards seemed to be distinctly worn in that part of the floor where there was certainly a persistent stain of some kind.

*George Hotel, Battle, Sussex*

## *HEMEL HEMPSTEAD, HERTFORDSHIRE

'The King's Arms' has a room where guests have 'restless nights', the wife of the landlord told me a few years ago. And once, 'some manifestations' were experienced in the same room. There have been many unexplained noises, too, but the occupants were not distressed - 'far from it, we live very happily here', I was told.

*Breakspear Motor Hotel, Hemel Hempstead, Herts.*

The 'Bull' inn - old, dark and unusual - has been the scene, from time to time, of a curious and unexplained smell of burnt candles in one particular part of the bar. It may well be that there was a separate room or passage here at one time, for there have been many alterations over the years.

One occupant reported seeing a cowled figure bending over him while he was in bed. He was obviously sincere about this and troubled by the experience when I spoke to him. At the same time, he was honest enough to admit that others using the same room had not been disturbed.

*The Red Lion Hotel, Riverside, Henley-on-Thames, Oxon.*

## HENLEY-ON-THAMES, OXFORDSHIRE: KENTON THEATRE

In 1969, playwright Joan Morgan's play 'The Hanging Wood', based on the story of a local girl - Mary Blandy - who was hanged at Oxford in 1752 for poisoning her father, was produced here. As soon as rehearsals began, 'unusual incidents' took place:

- A large mirror 'jumped' off a wall.

- Lights were switched on and off.

- Doors were mysteriously opened and closed.

A figure of a girl was reported at the back of the theatre, watching the performances, although she was never seen to enter or leave the building. Whenever someone decided to discover who the girl was, the figure disappeared.

Once, when some members of the cast were discussing Mary Blandy, a cup jumped about six inches off a table and smashed on to the floor. Miss Morgan said that some years previously, when the trial of Mary Blandy was being re-enacted at Henley Town Hall, a similar unexplained figure was seen by a number of people, including herself.

*The Red Lion Hotel, Riverside, Henley-on-Thames, Oxon.*

## HEREFORD, HEREFORDSHIRE

A seventeenth-century haunted house in the centre of Hereford was towed a hundred yards along the street at the end of 1966 to become the showpiece of a new store on the High Street. The old house is once said to have belonged to an apothecary [*a person who prepared and sold medicines and drugs*] accidentally killed an apprentice, by mixing the wrong medicine for him - whereupon he committed suicide in remorse.

*Green Dragon Hotel, Hereford, Herefordshire*

## HERSTMONCEUX, NEAR EASTBOURNE, SUSSEX

There are many accounts of ghostly experiences at imposing and exceptionally well-preserved Herstmonceux Castle, which now houses the Royal Observatory. (This fifteenth century castle is no longer open to the public.)

Perhaps the best-known story concerns the 'White Lady' who has been seen swimming the moat. Several hundred years ago, when the castle was still the property of the Fiennes family (Sir Roger de Fiennes built the place in 1440), one of the young sons enticed a village maiden into the castle, and succeeded in getting her into bed.

However, she resisted his advances, and sought to escape by swimming the moat. But he dragged her back to the castle and eventually murdered her in what became known as 'the haunted bed'. The bed was still preserved a few years ago. The ghost of the terrified girl has been seen by local people, soundlessly and unsuccessfully swimming for her life.

One night in 1910, Colonel Claude Lowther, the owner at that time, met a girl he did not recognize in the courtyard. She was distressed, and stood there wringing her hands, which he noticed were white and shrivelled. He thought she must be a begging gipsy girl, but when he spoke to her, she instantly vanished. Another time, he saw a man in riding breeches and velvet jacket near the old bridge over the moat. The figure walked straight at Colonel Lowther, who was mounted on horseback, passed right through the horse's head - and disappeared.

The Drummer's Hall [*a chamber within the castle*] has long been reputed to be haunted by the ghost of a giant drummer from the days of Sir Roger Fiennes, and the figure is said to have been seen striding along the battlements above the Great Hall, beating a drum and sending showers of sparks cascading from his incandescent drum-sticks.

During the last century, a story was circulated suggesting that a member of the Dacre family, who was supposed to be dead, lived on in the castle in secret with a beautiful young wife. To frighten away the men who came to pay their attentions to the young 'widow', he dressed himself in a drummer's uniform, smeared his clothes and drum with phosphorus, and drummed his way along the battlements.

Another ghost at Herstmonceux is that of Grace Naylor, whose father George bought the property in 1708 - which originally contained exactly as many windows as there are days in a year, and as many chimneys as there are weeks. For some reason, that has never been revealed, her governess starved the girl to death in the room with the oriel window on the east side.

She was buried in the family vault at All Saints Church, Herstmonceux. But the sounds of her sobbing used to be heard in the castle, and occasionally a female figure would be encountered, floating about the corridors, and disappearing through walls.

Beautiful Georgiana Naylor lived at Herstmonceux Castle at the end of the nineteenth century, an independent, forceful and eccentric student of the occult. She daily rode a white ass to drink from an enchanted spring in the park, dressed in a white cloak embroidered with mystic symbols, while a tame white doe [an adult female in some animal species such as deer and goat] trotted at her side.

One day, some hounds fell on the doe, and tore it to pieces near the church. Georgiana left Herstmonceux, never to return. She died at Lausanne in 1806, and for years afterwards there were reports of her spectre riding a white ass in and out of the deserted rooms at the castle.

Finally, stories of the ghosts of Lord Dacre and a poacher have been current locally for centuries, and probably date from a fight between the young Lord and his friends, when they encountered three of Lord Pelham's keepers, while on a poaching lark.

The keeper haunts the field where he died from a blow from Lord Dacre's sword, and Dacre himself has been seen in the grounds of the castle wearing a rusty riding cloak and large brass spurs, and rising a fine chestnut horse.

There are reports of his having been seen in recent years, but whenever he is addressed, he turns and plunges into the moat and sinks in a cloud of mist.

*White Friars Hotel, Herstmonceux, Sussex*

# *HIGHER BRIXHAM, DEVONSHIRE

*['Black House' is believed to have become 'Black Cottage Guest House']*

The old and ominously-named Black House, used by the monks when they were building nearby St Mary's Church, has long had the reputation of being haunted, and for years local residents were reluctant to pass it at night. Not long ago, there were stories of various unexplained noises:

- A mysterious lighting-up of an upper room (once noticed by a police constable).

- The apparition of a man, possibly a monk, that used to be seen at one of the upstairs windows of the forty-two roomed house.

The owner, Miss Evelyn Joyce, will tell you that she thinks the ghost, if there is one, must be bored with being earthbound, and plays practical tricks on her. For she has been locked out of the house on more than one occasion.

Once, the bathroom door was found to have locked itself from inside, and a carpenter had to saw through locks and bolts to break in and release her. Unexplained noises - and particularly footsteps - have been reported both inside the fine house, with its wonderful carved staircase, and also in the garden where, nine feet under the present lawn, traces have been found of the cobbled stable yard of a much earlier building. There is a tradition that the clatter of a horse's hooves used to be heard here, sounding as though they were on cobblestones.

*Churston Court Hotel, Brixham, Devon*

HIGHER CHILTON FARM, SEE CHILTON
CANTELO, SOMERSET

## *HINTON AMPNER, NEAR ALRESFORD, HAMPSHIRE

The Tudor Manor House, demolished in 1793, was the scene of remarkable and unexplained happenings for some twenty years. The house is thought to have been built early in the sixteenth century, replacing a mediaeval building destroyed by fire. Sir Thomas Stewkeley lived here at the end of that century, and as a country seat, the sprawling 'E' shaped manor was later occupied by his descendants.

One of them, Mary Stewkeley, married Edward Stawell (later Lord Stawell) in 1719. Her younger sister, Honoria, lived with them, and when Mary died in 1740, an affair developed between Lord Stawell and his sister-in-law, who had continued to live at the Manor after the death of her sister.

There were stories of 'wild happenings', and a baby is supposed to have been born - and to have been murdered. Honoria died in 1754, and there is a plaque to her memory, in nearby Hinton Ampner Church.

Lord Stawell died in 1755, and very soon afterwards, a groom at the Manor declared that one bright moonlit night he had seen the 'drably dressed' ghost of the fourth Baron, his former master. Apart from servants, the furnished house was unoccupied for some years, except during the shooting seasons. Later, in January 1765, the property was let to the Ricketts family.

Mrs Mary Ricketts is the chief witness in this case, and it is worthwhile noting that she came from a distinguished family - her brother having been created Baron Jervis of Meaford and Earl St Vincent for his naval exploits.

Like George Washington, Mary Ricketts was regarded as being unable to tell a lie. In 1757, she had married William Henry Ricketts of Jamaica, and when his business took him to the West Indies - which was quite frequently - she stayed at home with their three children.

When the Rickettses moved into the Manor, they took with them an entirely new set of servants from London, who were complete strangers to Hinton Ampner and its tales. But almost immediately, the family and servants were disturbed by the continual noise of slamming doors, for which no normal explanation was ever discovered.

New locks were fitted to all the doors in the house, but the unexplained slamming noises continued, and six months after the Ricketts moved in, Elizabeth Brelsford, nurse to eight-month-old Henry Ricketts, plainly saw 'a gentleman in a drab-coloured suit of clothes' go into the yellow bedchamber, which was the apartment usually occupied by the lady of the house.

The groom, George Turner, maintained that he saw the same 'gentleman in drab clothes' one night. This would seem to be the identical figure seen in the house ten years earlier.

Later, the form of a tall woman, dressed in dark clothes which rustled like silk, was seen and heard one evening by four servants who were in the kitchen. Noises described as 'dismal groans' and 'rustling', were reported soon afterwards, most frequently in the vicinity of bedsteads.

A couple of years later, during one of William Ricketts' trips to Jamaica, his wife and all three of the children frequently heard the noise of footsteps and the rustling of silk clothes against the bedroom door. Sometimes the footsteps were loud enough to awaken Mrs Ricketts. Yet in spite of persistent searches, no physical explanation was ever found for these noises.

A couple of months later, Mrs Ricketts again heard footsteps, heavy and distinct. And about the same period, she reported hearing the sound of music and heavy knocks, which had no physical reality. About a year later, a curious murmuring sound was often heard throughout the house, like a wind beginning to rise - and a maid stated that she heard a great deal of groaning and fluttering in her bedroom.

Early in 1770, an old man living at West Meon called at the Manor, asking to see Mrs Ricketts. He explained that his wife had often told him the following: that in her young days, a carpenter whom she had known well, had related, how he had once been sent for by Sir Hugh Stewkeley, and on his direction had taken up some boards in the dining room, to enable Sir Hugh to conceal something beneath them. Afterwards, the boards were replaced.

In the summer of 1770, Mrs Ricketts, lying in bed in the yellow chamber, 'thoroughly awake' as she put it - for she had retired only a short while before - plainly heard the plodding footsteps of a man approaching the foot of her bed.

She felt the danger to be too near for her to ring the bell for assistance, so she sprang out of bed and fled to the adjoining nursery, returning with a light and the children's nurse. A thorough search revealed no trace of an intruder, or any cause for the noise she had heard. There was only one door to the bedroom - the one leading into the nursery. For some months after this experience, Mrs Ricketts was undisturbed in the yellow bedchamber until, having moved to a warmer room over the hall, she sometimes heard during the month of November, 'the sounds of harmony' and - one night - three distinct knocks. A little later, she often noticed a kind of hollow murmuring 'that seemed to possess the whole house', a noise that was heard on the calmest nights.

On April 2nd 1771, the sixteenth anniversary of Lord Stawell's death, a number of unexplained noises were heard at the house by Mrs Ricketts and some of the servants - including three heavy and distinct knocks. A month later, the disturbances increased, and by midsummer, they had reached a hitherto unparalleled level.

The sounds of a woman and two men talking were a frequent phenomenon at this time. These sounds were heard night after night. Usually a shrill female voice first, followed by two deeper men's voices. Although the conversation sounded close at hand, no words were distinguishable. Loud crashing noises and piercing shrieks followed, which died away as though sinking into the earth, and a nurse - Hannah Streeter - who expressed a wish to hear more, was thereafter troubled every night.

Mrs Ricketts' brother - the future Lord St Vincent - arranged to sit up with Captain Luttrell, a friend and a servant. Night after night, they heard loud noises, as of a gun being let off nearby, followed by groans. There were rustlings. Door-slammings. Footsteps. And other sounds, which convinced Captain Jervis and Captain Luttrell that the house was unfit as a residence for any human being.

Early in August, 1771, Captain Jervis left the house, and his sister and her children followed soon afterwards. The Bishop of Winchester allowed Mrs Ricketts to live at the Old Palace - the Manor of Hinton Ampner originally belonged to the Priory of St Swithun at Winchester (nine miles to the west), and was the particular prerequisite of the Almoner, whose title became attached to the place and gradually became corrupted to Ampner. Later, the Bishop of St Asaph offered Mrs Ricketts his house in London, where she lived before renting a house in Curzon Street.

There can be no doubt that the experiences at Hinton Ampner Manor House so terrified Mrs Ricketts that she had to leave the place - in particular, one curious experience of which she gives no details, merely saying: 'I was assailed by a noise I never heard before, very near me, and the terror I felt cannot be described.'

Towards the end of the Ricketts tenancy of the house, a reward of fifty pounds, then sixty, and finally one hundred, was offered for the solution of the disturbances. The money was never claimed.

A year after Mrs Ricketts and her family left Hinton Ampner, the Manor was let to a family named Lawrence, who endeavoured, by threats to the servants, to stifle reports of disturbances. Little information of the curious happenings undoubtedly experienced at this time leaked out, although it does seem that the apparition of a woman was seen. The Lawrences, who were the last inhabitants of the property, left suddenly in 1773, and the house stood empty, apart from its ghosts, for over twenty years, when it was demolished.

The Hinton Ampner case is exceptionally well documented in the form of contemporary letters from Mrs Ricketts to her husband in Jamaica, and to the Rev. J. M. Newbolt, Rector of Hinton Ampner. There are also letters from Mrs Ricketts' brother to William Ricketts, and various letters from servants to Mrs Ricketts. But perhaps the most moving evidence is contained in an account - written in 1772 - which Mrs Ricketts left for her children and for posterity. This is published in its entirety in Harry Price's *Poltergeist Over England*.

The fourth Baron Stawell's only daughter, who was created Baroness Stawell, married the Rt. Hon. Henry Bilson-Legge, and their grand-daughter - and only surviving child - married in 1803 John Dutton, second Baron Sherborne. The present owner, Ralph Stawell Dutton, F.S.A., is their great-grandson.

A new Hinton Ampner House was built about 1793, some fifty yards from the site of the old building, and this Georgian house forms the central part of the present building. During the demolition of the old Manor, a small skull was discovered under the floorboards in one of the rooms.

The present owner will tell you, as he told me when I was there in June 1970, that there were some reports of unexplained noises being heard in the new house, usually just before dawn, but between 1936 and 1939, the house was much altered, and in 1960 the main part was gutted by fire. Mr Dutton says there have been no apparently paranormal happenings in the present house.

*Swan Hotel, Alresford, Hants.*

## HINXWORTH PLACE, NEAR BALDOCK, HERTFORDSHIRE

*[Hinxworth Place is now a Private Residence]*

For years during stormy evenings in the autumn, strange noises have been heard here:

- Screams, followed by a thudding noise from the direction of the stairs.

- The sound of a baby crying.

- The sound of water gushing from the pump in the yard.

Major R. G. Clutterbuck, who has had connections with Hinxworth, suggested that the origin of the curious noises dates back many years to the time when some occupants left their small baby in the care of a young nursemaid while they went out one evening. The young boy of the house decided to frighten the girl by draping himself in a sheet and making weird noises. The frightened girl attacked the 'ghost' with a poker, and the boy fell down the stairs, screaming. He was found by the cook, who tried to restore the dying boy by putting his head under the pump - but to no avail.

*Ye Olde George and Dragon Hotel, Baldock, Herts.*

# *HITCHIN, HERTFORDSHIRE

Hitchin Priory was in the possession of the same family for four hundred years. The property incorporates part of the house of White Friars, and is reputed to be haunted each June by a cavalier named Goring, who was wounded in a skirmish during the Civil War.

Goring sheltered in a mansion known as Highdown House at nearby Pirton, where the small roof chamber he occupied over the porch is also reputed to have ghostly associations. When the Roundheads began to search the house, Goring changed his hiding place to a hollow elm (which is still standing), but he was discovered and killed on the spot - while his betrothed watched from an upstairs window.

Legend has it that each June 15th, he rides, headless, on a white horse, to the site of the cell in the grounds of Hitchin Priory.

The Priory is also said to have a ghost of its own: an unidentified 'Grey Lady' who has been seen in recent years outside the building, wearing a long grey dress but no coat, even on cold nights. What she is doing outside the former home of monks, is not known.

*The Sun Hotel, Hitchin, Herts.*

# *HOLYWELL, HUNTINGDONSHIRE

On the edge of the River Ouse, just beyond Holywell, stands the 'Ferry Boat Inn', which is haunted - for perhaps nine hundred years - by the ghost of Juliet, a young girl who loved a rough local woodcutter named Tom Zoul so deeply that it became a kind of sickness.

Tom preferred the company of his fellow-workmates to that of the tender-hearted Juliet. Neglected by him, she pined and languished and slowly her heart broke. One wild spring day, the grief became too much for her. Wearing a pink dress that Tom liked, she hanged herself on a tree beside the river. The date was March 17th.

As a suicide, she could not be buried in consecrated ground. She was laid to rest near the river that seemed to share her sadness. The grave was simply marked with a plain slab of grey stone.

Many years passed until the builder of the 'Ferry Boat Inn' came along, and decided to incorporate Juliet's gravestone into the flooring of the inn - for there are few quarries hereabouts and he was short of stone.

There is can be seen to this day, forming part of the inn's stone floor, and for many years, people have gathered here on each March 17th to watch for Juliet's ghost, which is said to rise from the flagstone, and drift out of the inn and towards the river.

A few years ago, no less than four hundred people turned up on the anniversary, and in 1955, the Cambridge Psychical Research Society sent a team of investigators equipped with electronic detection apparatus - but their instruments showed no abnormality.

This is a ghost which everyone knows about, but few have seen. 'There are certainly some very odd happenings here', the landlord told me in 1965, 'quite inexplicable; there is for instance the dog that will not go near the gravestone, and of course the local women don't come near the inn on March 17th.'

*Golden Lion Hotel, St Ives, Hunts.*

## HORDEN, DURHAM

In 1967, a minor and his wife living at number 4 Eden Street were so terrified by many 'ghostly incidents' (which they were totally unable to explain), that they called in their vicar, the Rev. T. Matthews. When his prayers did not end their problems, they decided to move and did so. The family were reluctant to talk about their experiences, but insisted that 'ghostly presences' had made themselves indisputably felt in the little house.

*The Three Tuns Hotel, New Elvet, Durham City, Co. Durham.*

## HOUGHTON, NEAR WALSINGHAM, NORFOLK

Sir Robert Walpole, (1676-1745), first Earl of Orford, statesman and perhaps the first effective Prime Minister of England, built the magnificent Houghton Hall on the site of his old ancestral home. But it is his sister, Dorothy Walpole, whose ghost - dressed in a brown brocade dress [*brocade is a rich fabric woven with a raised pattern, typically with gold or silver thread*], is reputed to haunt the house. She probably spent the happiest d days of her life here, and her ghost is said to have appeared to the Prince Regent, when he was occupying the State Bedroom - causing him to request a different room for the rest of his stay.

*The Red Lion Hotel, Fakenham, Norfolk*

# *HOYLAKE, CHESHIRE

*[The 'Royal Hotel' was demolished some years ago]*

The thirty-two bedroom Royal Hotel, facing the Irish Sea, and built in 1797, has an unidentified ghost in tweeds.

Some years ago, the proprietor informed me that there had been frequent reports of an unknown ghost in one particular wing of the hotel. Psychic investigator Harry Price spent several days and nights there in 1923, and decided that the manifestations were genuine, but that identity could not be established.

Twenty years later, a female employee reported seeing on several occasions, a male figure in knickerbocker tweeds and a cloth cap, walk down the corridor from the hall to the ballroom. She said that the rather slight form had an energetic and lively figure, and twice when she followed the solid-looking figure - it disappeared quite inexplicably. She realized afterwards that she had not noticed any sound accompanying the experience.

Some years later, after the hotel had changed ownership, a barman reported seeing a similar figure pass from the billiards room, across the room where the barman stood, and disappear along the same corridor. His description state: 'brown knickerbocker tweeds and cap.'

Years later still, a maintenance joiner on the staff repeatedly saw an unexplained figure in the same room, although his description did not entirely agree with that of the barman.

A few months later, unaccountable openings and closings of various doors in the hotel provided further food for speculation. At the time of their respective experiences, neither the barman nor the joiner were aware of reports of an unidentified figure seen many years before in the same part of the hotel.

*Royal Hotel, Hoylake, Cheshire*

# *HURLEY, BERKSHIRE

*[Only a remnant of the Old Priory ('The Cloisters'), and the gateways and cellars still remain of Ladye Place, a Tudor mansion that was pulled down in 1837]*

Ladye Place used to be an historic building standing in twenty acres of land, in this old world village when I knew Colonel Rivers-Moore, who bought the place in 1924. At the time, he hardly could have known that in the years to come, he would build up an impressive dossier of signed statements from responsible people who witnessed inexplicable happenings at this house - which used to be a Benedictine priory.

Colonel Rivers-Moore was interested in archaeology, and he began to dig, looking for early foundations, and hoping to find confirmation of a charter from the reign of King Richard II which gave Ladye Place as the burial place of Editha, sister of Edward the Confessor. He particularly wanted to find Editha's grave, for it was her ghost - the Grey Lady - that according to tradition, haunted his historic home.

Soon after excavation began Mrs Rivers-Moore's brother - a doctor - was staying at Ladye Place. He surprised his hosts one morning by telling them that he had encountered a ghostly monk in the house. Soon after another visitor said she had had some strange experiences which suggested a psychic presence.

Following seance messages, the Rivers-Moores unearthed part of the foundation of the Tudor house, and some human remains - but they were not those of Editha. Still, the digging continued, under the guidance obtained at seances, and at length a hard base was uncovered, surrounded by tiles, which could have formed the base of an early shrine.

Meanwhile, ghostly monks were seen more and more often at Ladye Place. One declared that he had practised black magic. Others were seen by visitors and friends, and it became a common occurrence for a monk to be seen, with arms crossed, in the cloisters.

But Colonel Rivers-Moore was primarily interested in archaeology, and after twenty years at Ladye Place, he had exhausted the ground of secrets - except for the resting place of Editha, which he may or may not have found. With the cessation of the digging, the ghosts went back to rest.

In 1947, Colonel Rivers-Moore put the place up for auction. He moved to Wargrave, and later to Scotland, where I saw him shortly before he died in 1965 - still firmly convinced that he was responsible for disturbing the ghostly monks of Ladye Place, and still sure that one day the grave of Editha would be found.

I didn't tell him that his beautiful house had been converted into three homes, and that his land was sold in lots - some of it for a market garden. Perhaps the ghosts had won their peace at last.

*Ye Olde Bell Hotel, Hurley, Berks.*

Bosworth Hall has a ghost that creaks and groans - and a bloodstain that has been damp for three hundred years.

Mrs Constable Maxwell's family have been at Bosworth since time immemorial, and although the house - so full of rambling corridors and twisting staircases - has been altered a good deal, the Roman Catholic atmosphere is still as strong as ever.

In Cromwell's days, masses had to be held in secret. One day - in those troubled times - Roundhead troops were heard approaching as the Jesuits were celebrating such a Mass. But they were prepared, and the priest leapt for the hide hole, which was entered from an attic.

My friend Granville Squiers, who made a study of secret hiding places, told me of this fascinating one which was large enough to accommodate two or three men comfortably and yet was also quite invisible - constructed as it was near the fireplace, but cunningly camouflaged by a cupboard with a rounded back and a false wall.

In his flight, the priest is thought to have knocked over the chalice of consecrated wine, or in his haste he cut himself. At all events, the dark, waxy stain has remained damp ever since. For the sceptic - an oddity. For the religious - a miracle.

Lady Lisgar, a Protestant widow who married Sir Francis Fortescue-Turville in 1881, is doomed to haunt Bosworth Hall forever, because she refused to allow a priest into the house to administer the last rites to a Roman Catholic servant. Mrs Maxwell recalls a doctor seeing her ghost when he stayed in the house when she was ill.

On his way upstairs from dinner one evening, he passed a strangely dressed woman on the stairs, and murmured a polite 'Goodnight' - but received no reply. When he enquired the next morning who the other guest in the house might be, he was told that there was nobody.

When he described the woman he had seen, Mrs Maxwell's mother recognized her ancestor. 'That was the ghost of Lady Lisgar,' she told the doctor, 'I beg you not to mention the matter to the children.'

The silent ghost of Lady Lisgar has been seen in the Bow Room, where she slept - and where she died - along corridors she knew and loved, on stairways and in passageways she helped to create. For she carried out many changes when she was at Bosworth. But wherever she is seen, Mrs Maxwell notes the date and the circumstances in the Black Book of Boswell Hall - and every Easter the rooms are blessed by a priest.

Guests complain that they are awakened by fearful groans and unearthly creaks, quite convinced that the house is full of ghosts. Once, a guest was thrown out of a canopy bed with considerable force, and landed on the floor. No need to ask that visitor whether Bosworth Hall is haunted!

*L'Auberge, Berridge Lane, Husbands Bosworth, Leics.*

## IGHTHAM MOTE, NEAR SEVENOAKS, KENT

A fourteenth-century manor house, eerie and isolated - but perfectly-reserved and occupied from the days of Queen Elizabeth I to the middle of the reign of Queen Victoria by the devout Roman Catholic Selby family.

Built at the period when castles were becoming obsolete, it became a mansion, fortified against vicious wandering bands of brigands. There is an escape route behind a chimney, and various hiding places. Secret religious services used to be held in the crypt. The chapel door has no less than five locks. In 1872, workmen discovered a fourteenth-century window and a blocked-up doorway in the tower, where many visitors have experienced an uncanny coldness.

When the doorway was broken down, they found a skeleton of a woman in a cupboard. She is thought to have been Dame Dorothy Selby. An anonymous letter in the Monteagle Collection of the British Museum warns Lord Monteagle not to attend the Houses of Parliament on November 5th, 1605.

It was through this letter that the Gunpowder Plot was uncovered. There is evidence to suggest that the letter came from Lord Monteagle's cousin, Dame Dorothy. Legend has it that she was walled up in the cupboard as a punishment by the partisans of the Plot. Some years ago, a bishop sought to exorcise the ghost in the tower, but the peculiar chill remains...

*Royal Oak Hotel, High Street, Sevenoaks, Kent*

## ILFORD, ESSEX

The old fire station on Broadway is said to have a ghostly fireman, complete with brass helmet. Firewoman Penny White reported seeing this figure - thought to be Godfrey Netherwood - a fireman in the 1890s who was interested in ghosts and hauntings. The same form was observed many times in the old building, but Penny White saw the figure under a stairway at the new fire station in Romford Road!

A careful search revealed no explanation.

*Cranford Private Hotel, Ilford, Essex*

## *ILFRACOMBE, DEVONSHIRE

The fifteenth-century Chambercombe Manor House has a haunted room which was discovered in 1865, when the owner noticed an extra window where there was no room. After a wall was broken down, a low, dark chamber was revealed with remains of tapestry still hanging on the walls, and Elizabethan black carved furniture almost falling to pieces.

Behind the curtains, the skeleton of a woman was found lying on the bed, and since then weird sounds have been heard at night from the vicinity of this room - hidden for so long. Today, the haunted room - situated between the Coat of Arms Bedroom (once used by Lady Jane Gray), and the low-beamed Victorian Bedroom - can be viewed through a hole in the wooden partition on the staircase.

A strange mystery that will probably never now be solved - perhaps it has some connection with the tunnel that ran from here to Hele beach, which was reputedly used by smugglers.

*Westwell Hall Private Hotel, Ilfracombe, Devon*

## INVERNESS, SCOTLAND

There is a vague local story of ghostly soldiers, led by an officer wearing a gold-laced hat and blue Hussar cloak, riding a grey dragoon horse. The phantom army suddenly vanishes and has never been identified.

*Royal Hotel, Inverness, Scotland*

JAY'S GRAVE, SEE DARTMOOR, DEVON.

## KILKENNY CITY, IRELAND

The vicinity of St John's Parochial Hall is said to be haunted by the ghost of a tall, thin woman using crutches who wears a long coat, no stockings, and has flowing white hair. A young nurse and a friend saw the figure twice one evening in May, 1969, when they were returning home from a dance.

'The Marble City' is one of the most interesting old towns in Ireland, with its dignified eighteenth-century houses, its castle, the River Nore dividing it in two, and its cathedral dedicated to St Canice - the sixth-century saint, from whom Kilkenny derives its name.

*Castle Motor Hotel, Ferrycarrig Bridge, Wexford, Co. Wexford, Ireland*

## KINGHAM, NEAR CHIPPING NORTON, OXFORDSHIRE

The century-and-a-quarter-old Langston Arms Hotel made news in 1964 when noises and a 'white shape' pestered the owner, the manager - and customers - for several months. The 'form' seemed to re-appear regularly every ten days or so, heralded by mysterious coughing noises and shuffling footsteps.

The figure was that of an elderly woman wearing a headdress which made those who saw 'her' think she must be a nun. She glided along certain corridors in the hotel, but never anywhere else. Once, she seemed to pass clean through a glass partition.

The Rev. W. Attwood-Evans was sceptical at first, but after hearing first-hand evidence from local people, changed his views, and investigated the history of the inn, but could find no record of a murder or suicide that might have accounted for the ghost.

*Langston Arms Hotel, Kingham, Oxon*

## *KNEBWORTH HOUSE, KNEBWORTH, HERTFORDSHIRE

The ancestral home of the Lytton family used to have a haunted room in the east wing where, according to tradition, 'Jenny Spinner' was imprisoned, and where she worked hard and long until her mind became deranged and she died.

Soon after her death, the sound of her spinning-wheel was heard, and this sound continued intermittently until the wing was demolished in 1811. The story has some foundation in fact, and 'Spinning Jenny' is mentioned in some of the old documents at Knebworth.

Roebuck Motor Hotel, Stevenage, Herts.

# LAMBERHURST, KENT

*[The Furnace Mill is now a Private Residence]*

In May, 1906, Mr J. C. Playfair of Furnace Mill discovered that all the horses in his stables had been turned round. Their tails were in their mangers, and their heads were where their tails should have been - while one horse was missing altogether! Eventually, it was discovered in a hay-loft, although the doorway was barely wide enough for a man to enter, and a partition had to be knocked down to get the animal out.

Other apparently inexplicable incidents included the movement of several heavy barrels, and locked and bolted doors opening by themselves. It is interesting to note that a young son was a member of the household, and that two watch-dogs guarded the premises - which could not be approached without the occupants being aware of the fact. Yet no adequate explanation was ever offered for these strange happenings.

Three miles to the west stand the beautiful ruins of Bayham Abbey, with its spectral monks, phantom voices, and ghost bells.

The Abbey was founded in 1200. An excellent idea of how splendid the building was can be obtained from the well-preserved ruins of the North Transept [*in a cross-shaped church, either of the two parts forming the arms of the cross shape, projecting at right angles from the nave*], the two Chapels and the Cloisters. There is part of a holy-water stoup here [*a vessel containing holy water generally placed near the entrance of a church*], and in a niche - the remains of an ancient tomb. The very air seems permeated with the past, and if Bayham is not haunted, it ought to be.

In fact, there are many stories of ghostly monks being seen

198

GAZETTEER OF BRITISH GHOSTS

here, sometimes a whole procession slowly wending its silent way amongst the ruins at midnight. Sounds of sweet music have been heard, and the noise of revelry. Voices chanting Latin. Bells faintly chiming. The smell of burning incense has also been remarked upon by visitors to this pleasant spot.

Nearby Scotney Castle, with its picturesque circular tower, rising from the edge of the lake or moat, has the ghost of a murdered man, dripping with water.

The story begins in 1259, when the castle was held by Walter de Scotney, steward to the Earl of Gloucester. He was induced by William de Valence to administer poison to the Earl and other nobles who were feasting as guests of the Bishop of Winchester.

The Earl's brother and some other guests died, but the Earl escaped, with the reputed loss of his nails, teeth and skin. Walter de Scotney was hanged at Tyburn, and his estates forfeited. The castle passed into the hands of the Darrells and in 1598 the Jesuit priest Father Blunt was concealed here by the Roman Catholic family.

When his hiding place was discovered, he escaped by swimming the moat. A member of the Darrell family, Arthur Darrell, had a fake funeral after he was outlawed, which he attended himself. In the eighteenth century, the Darrell family took to smuggling, and once entrenched themselves for three days to resist the attack of revenue officers.

It was another skirmish with the revenue authorities that gave rise to the haunting. For on that occasion, a Darrell killed one of the officers, and threw his body into the moat. The murdered man has been seen many times since, dripping with water, hammering at the great door of Scotney, seeking retribution.

*Wellington Hotel, Tunbridge Wells, Kent*

Until a few years ago, a haunted church stood like a sentinel near the Manor House, looking out over the desolate marshes. It is certainly the most haunted church that I have come across.

As soon as I heard about the curious happenings, I spent several hours with the rector, the Rev. E. A. Merryweather, who regaled me with the story of the strange experiences he vouched for. I examined the diary in which he had recorded the events at the time they had taken place. Later, he presented me with this diary.

I found Mr Merryweather to be a large, astute and kindly man - then in his sixties, level-headed and sensible - and with an infectious sense of humour, and a gift for looking on the bright side of things. Before coming to Langenhoe in 1937, he had spent most of his life in the North of England, and had previously experienced no psychic manifestations of any kind, nor was he interested in the subject - doubtless because he was at the church more frequently than anyone else, he had experienced himself much of the allegedly paranormal phenomena.

The first happenings for which he could find no explanation were typical poltergeist activity: door-slamming and paranormal locking.

Yes, it wasn't long before things happened that suggested to me that there was something odd about the place,' the rector said as I remarked on the date of the first entry in the diary: 'I visited the church on September 20th, 1937. It was a quiet autumn day. I was standing alone in the church, and the big west door was open. Suddenly it crashed to with such a force that the whole building seemed to shake. Doors don't usually slam to as if an express-train had hit them, when there is no palpable reason. This aroused my curiosity as to the cause.'

Twice during November 1937, the rector's valise, in which he carried his books and vestments, was found to be unaccountably locked while he was in the vestry. All efforts to unlock it proved entirely unsuccessful while in the vicinity of the church, although on each occasion, when he was outside in the lane, the valise unlocked without any difficulty. On the first occasion, a friend of the rector also witnessed this 'locking'.

There was little further to report until 1945, when, on Easter Sunday, there occurred the first of a number of incidents concerning flowers. Mrs Gertrude Barnes and her daughter Irene were helping Mr Merryweather decorate the church before the congregation arrived and had placed some flowers in a vase on a pew while attending to some other matter. A moment later, Mrs Barnes found the flowers removed from the vase and laid on the pew. Later, there were other incidents when flowers were moved and unaccountably appeared or disappeared.

During the autumn of 1947, Mr Merryweather called at the Manor House, and walked into - quite literally - a tactual phenomenon that is almost unique in the annals of psychical research. He was shown over the house by the late Mrs Cutting, and entered a charming front bedroom which Mrs Cutting said she did not use, as there was something queer about it. She preferred to sleep in the bedroom facing north, even though the view over the marshes was much less attractive.

She stayed in the room with Mr Merryweather only a few seconds, and the left him, saying as she went: 'I don't like this room.' Left alone, the rector, after admiring the grand sweeping view for a moment, turned from the window - and, as he told me - 'moved into the unmistakable embrace of a naked young woman'.

This singular tactual phenomenon lasted only a few seconds: 'one wild, frantic embrace and she was gone' as Mr Merryweather put it. But the rector was quite emphatic that he had this most unusual experience, and had no doubt whatsoever that it was just as he described it. There existed absolutely no doubt about it in his mind. Nothing auditory, visual or olfactory accompanied the experience.

Several times in 1948, while celebrating Holy Communion, the rector and members of the congregation heard thuds from the direction of the vestry door. Upon investigation, nothing was ever visible, and no explanation or cause for the noise was ever found. The thuds continued with some regularity for about a month, and were afterwards heard intermittently. Reference to the rector's diary shows that they were heard ten times between July and December, 1948.

On November 11th that year, while busy raking coal at the side of the church with an iron rod, the rector suddenly sensed that someone or something was near him in the deserted churchyard. He stuck the rod into the coal and, taking off his biretta [*a square cap with three flat projections on top, worn by Roman Catholic clergymen*], hung it on the end of the rod as a test. To his amazement, the hat began to revolve slowly in front of his eyes!

Five minutes later, he heard a voice in the empty church. For some time past, there had been a certain amount of hooliganism on the part of some boys staying at a nearby village. People had been attacked while out walking in the lonely lanes, so the rector, visiting his isolated church, decided to go armed, and selected a wicked-looking dirk or dagger - which his son had sent him from Cyprus.

He placed the dagger firmly in his belt beneath his cassock. After the biretta incident, Mr Merryweather went into the church, and as he was standing before the altar, he felt the dagger suddenly pulled from his belt, and as it was flung to the floor at his feet, he heard a female voice say, 'You are a cruel man.'

In answer to my question as to the direction from which this voice came, the rector said he thought that it came from the tower end of the church - that is, behind him, as he faced the altar.

On the 2nd of December 1948, the rector and a number of parishioners heard a series of unexplained noises which seemed to originate from the direction of a blocked-up door that used to be a private entrance to the church for the occupants of the Manor House.

The noises were described to me as resembling 'an old man's cough'. A moment later, a little brass credence bell rang of its own volition. Still later a loud 'crack' - as of a rifle - came from the same spot, and a pile of stained glass was found in the chancel [*the part of a church near the altar*].

During the months that followed, the credence bell rang several more times without anyone being near it. Lamps inexplicably swung (this happened for three days in succession. A lamp mysteriously burst into flames (and it had *not* been recently re-filled). Then, on August 21st 1949, the rector saw the apparition of a young woman in the church.

He was celebrating Holy Communion at the time. He turned round to read the gospel at the altar, and saw - upon looking down the church - the figure of a young woman, aged about thirty, wearing a white or grey dress, and 'flowing headgear' that reached over her shoulders. She walked from the north side of the church, near the window beside the tower, across the chancel, and disappeared into a corner in the south-west.

The wall seemed to open. She passed through. And then the wall closed again. He noticed, too, that she walked with a slight stoop. From the expression on her face and her attitude, he gained the impression that she was unhappy. She appeared to be about five feet six inches in height, and looked like a normal person. Nor was she transparent - although she made no sound.

During the severe earthquake of 1884, Langenhoe Church was badly damaged. The tremors lasted almost twenty seconds. Photographs of the west end of the church the morning after the earthquake show the devastation, but also clearly indicate a former doorway in the internal tower-wall, several feet to the right of the later doorway.

In view of this fact, it is interesting to note that Mr Merryweather insisted that the 'phantom girl' vanished into the tower wall and not through the later doorway. It was not until I began my research into the history of the area and located the photographs taken at the time of the earthquake that Mr Merryweather saw them for the first time.

During the rest of 1949, incidents included the smashing and disappearance of part of the vestry door handle, the unexplained locking of the same door, mysterious knocks, and footsteps inside the church.

I spent the night of September 24th, 1949 in Langenhoe Church with a friend who had become interested in psychical research - John C. Dening, then at the Foreign Office (later to become the Rev. John C. Dening).

I had a number of instruments which I set up, and I also scattered some 'controls' throughout the church and churchyard. I sealed the doors and windows, ringed a number of objects, and even left paper and pencils here and there - in case an entity should feel inclined to leave a message!

Objects that had moved or had been disturbed were under particular surveillance throughout the night. Powdered chalk was spread where the apparition had walked, and where footsteps had been heard. Threads were strung across the church at strategic points.

In fact, the psychical researcher's whole armoury was used in an effort to prove scientifically the 'existence' of a paranormal being in the church during the hours of darkness - if one put in an appearance.

Unfortunately, a thunderstorm raged during most of the night, and we may well have missed any auditory phenomena amid the claps of thunder and the sound of rain pattering on the roof. But I don't think we were in luck, for in the morning I found all my apparatus exactly as I had left them, and the instruments showed no abnormality.

Perhaps the most lasting memory of that visit was the magnificent view from the church tower across the marshes to Mersea Island at the moment when the autumn dawn was breaking.

Early in 1950, Mr Merryweather heard a female voice when he was near the south door. It made a sound resembling 'Ow!'. A few months later, a bricklayer - who had once been a local bell-ringer - was high up on the empty church, replacing tiles, when he heard the church bell chime twice - loud and clear.

Previously sceptical of the haunting, this experience caused him to modify his opinion considerably. Mr Merryweather, tongue in cheek, wondered whether the bell-ringing was a sly dig at the local bricklayer who was no longer a church bell-ringer.

In the autumn of 1950, an apparently paranormal odour joined the wealth of unexplained 'phenomena' at Langenhoe, when the rector visited the church on September 14th, and found that a strong smell of violets permeated the whole building - completely out of season.

Later the same month - while in the vestry - Mr Merryweather suddenly heard the voice of a young woman singing in the church. The sounds seemed to originate from the west end of the building. He described the singing to me as resembling Gregorian (plainsong) chanting.

As the singing stopped, it was followed by the sounds of a man's heavy footsteps, walking 'with slow and sinister tread' up the nave. This was too much for the rector, and he moved quickly into the church from the vestry. As he did so, the footsteps stopped abruptly - yet he could find nothing to account for either the singing or the footsteps.

Exactly a week later, the rector paid another mid-week visit. As he entered the churchyard, he was surprised to see two workmen, crouching in front of the west door - apparently looking through the keyhole!

As they became aware of his approach, they beckoned to him to join them and listen. Even as they stood up Mr Merryweather guessed the reason for the interest and, sure enough, the sound of singing came from the locked and empty church.

All three listened for a moment, and then the singing, seemingly in French, ceased. The rector unlocked the door and took the workmen inside, where they searched everywhere, even climbing the tower to satisfy themselves that there was no human being anywhere inside the church.

During the following months, a cupboard door was found open, although it was always locked before the rector left the church, as it contained his vestments. The one Sunday, the same thing happened - and then a further four times! Never again - either before or after, during the twenty-two years that he was Rector of Langenhoe, was this cupboard ever found other than securely locked.

On the 24th of December, 1950, the rector saw another apparition in the church - a figure that walked up the nave towards the chancel - a curious, vague form that suddenly appeared from nowhere, and proceeded to glide along the nave in front of him. The rector stopped in his tracks and watched the form - which seemed to resemble a man in a tweed suit. It disappeared into the pulpit.

On the 28th of January 1951, the white impression of a woman's hand was found on the vestry door. The rector had arrived at the church some fifteen minutes before, when the imprint had certainly not been there. He had gone into the churchyard to throw some dead flowers away, and when he returned, there was the full and clear imprint. This was also seen by Mr Merryweather's housekeeper and her daughter. It lasted for ten days, and then gradually faded away.

During a service on the 8th of July that year, the rector again saw the girl with the flowing headdress. She was dressed exactly as before, but this time she stood facing the credence bell, and the old entrance used years before by the inhabitants of the Manor House.

As he watched, she seemed to float towards the bricked-up door - disappearing through it. A few weeks later, as he arrived at the church one morning, he was surprised to hear voices from within. He told me that he had the impression that two or perhaps three people were holding a conversation in an undertone in the chancel. One man's voice sounded more distinct that the others, although no actual words were distinguishable. A heavy sigh followed. And then silence reigned.

On the 12th of October 1952, the rector saw yet another apparition in the church. He was singing Psalm CXIX verses 129-146, and had just reached the passage 'My eyes gush out with water because men keep not my law', when he felt someone was watching him, and saw the figure of a young woman, wearing a cream dress.

She had an oval face, and blue eyes, and gave the rector a 'strange, sad look', before she vanished - but the cream dress she was wearing seemed to linger for some time after the wearer had gone. Other incidents included:

- A 'popping' noise.

- The rattling of the church door handle.

- A loud 'bang'.

- More footsteps.

- The organ lid moved.

- The curiously quick burning of a candle.

Among several current local stories that may account for the haunting at Langenhoe - which is very ancient (there are witnesses of a veiled girl figure tracing back to the turn of the century - perhaps the most consistent one concerns a former rector, who is said to have murdered his illicit sweetheart.

If there is anything in this story, it might account for the figure appearing most frequently to another rector. Certainly, a number of the reported incidents can be made to fit such a theory - especially the whispering (between the sweethearts?) and the final sigh (the fatal move made, or the last breath of the victim?).

A dagger may have been the weapon used, and it could be suggested that the presence in the church of a similar instrument on the occasion when Mr Merryweather took the Cyprus dirk with him, may have revived memories and provoked the remark 'You are a cruel man'.

Alternatively, these may have been the last despairing words of the victim, recording perhaps forever, on the atmosphere. The thuds on the vestry door may have their origin in the victim's urgent summons to her lover (?) to admit her - little knowing that she was going to her death.

Mr Merryweather's experience as the Manor House may have been a repetition of the exhibition of a girl's conscious or unconscious need for love. And the temptation to which a former rector had been subjected. The appearance of a girl assumes significance when the passage of the Psalm heralding her coming is considered. While the smashing of the vestry door handle, the incidents concerning flowers and candles, the singing and the bell-ringing, may all have a symbolic meaning. The connection suggested by the door-slamming and the footsteps are all too obvious.

It is interesting to note that the whole area once formed part of an estate belonging to the powerful Waldegrave family. This included the church (the third to be erected on the site), a shooting-range, the Manor House, a former rectory, and several other houses and cottages - *all* of which have been the scene of alleged psychic disturbances.

I spent many hours with Mr Merryweather, during a period extending over twelve years - both at his home on Mersea Island, and in the vicinity of Langenhoe Church. I found him to be ready and willing to discuss the curious happenings that he had witnessed - open to questioning, and always eager to obtain corroboration or an explanation for the strange occurrences.

I believe he was genuinely puzzled by the things that happened to him, and if some of them were hallucinations - or unconscious mind phenomena - it was only in this single sphere that he experienced these manifestations.

Away from Langenhoe, his life was undisturbed in any psychic sense, and he led the quiet and satisfying existence of a country clergyman. Mr Merryweather retired from the ministry in 1959, and the living of Langenhoe was combined with that of a neighbouring parish. Haunted Langenhoe Church, a desolate and silent sentinel, stood for some years alone - with its ghosts - until it fell into decay, and was finally pulled down.

On one of my last visits to Mr Merryweather, he presented me with his private notes on the case, and a relic from Langenhoe Church: the beautiful little Credence Bell. I hope that it will ring for me one day without human agency!

*Red Lion Hotel, Colchester, Essex*

## LEICESTER, LEICESTERSHIRE

Mrs Jennie Morrison of Newbold, Verdon, used for the first time in January 1967, a cotton nightgown with lace trimmings - which had belonged to her great aunt who had, in fact, asked to be buried with it...

The aunt had died three years before, but Mrs Morrison's mother thought the nightdress too good to be used as a shroud, and she gave it to her daughter, who had it cut down and made it fit. She wore it once, and in bed that night, felt 'a tremendous force' dragging at her sleeve.

'The nightdress was being pulled so strongly that it nearly hauled me out of bed,' she said. She took the nightdress off, and threw it onto the landing outside the bedroom: then she heard a long drawn-out sigh, just like the sound that would be made by an old woman, and she is convinced that the sound came from her dead aunt.

'The nightdress is very pretty,' she said wistfully, 'but I'll never wear it again.'

*Bell Hotel, Leicester, Leicestershire*

Ghostly footsteps at night are reported to have frightened a dog which rushed, panic-stricken, from an empty room at 'Scudamore', Letchworth Corner, in 1946 - as Mrs E. M. Walker, managing director of Lloyds', the mowing machine manufacturers, will tell you.

She was alone in the house at about ten-thirty at night, and while downstairs, she heard a thud from the room above, followed by footsteps which appeared to cross the room towards the door. She hurried upstairs, thinking that someone had broken into the house, but there was no one there, and she discovered nothing to account for the noises she had heard.

Night after night, she heard the same sounds, and she began to think that her married son was right when he said it was probably old beams drying out, until the curious behaviour of her border collie, 'Bruce'. 'Bruce' used to go everywhere with Mrs Walker's cousin, Mr Edward Halford, but nothing would persuade it to enter Mr Halford's bedroom - the room where the noises came from each night at ten-thirty p.m.

Once, Mrs Walker tried hard to get the dog into the room. She held the dog's collar, and tried to force him inside, but the dog held back, struggling and growling, and once he was free, raced down the stairs and into the garden 'as if the devil were after him'.

Mrs Walker feels that the ghost paid its last visit to the house in 1947. She and her family decided that it was the spirit of the man who had three four-hundred-year-old cottages converted into the present house.

*Letchworth Hall Hotel, Letchworth, Herts.*

## LITTLE BURTON, SOMERSET

An early case of poltergeist activity was reported from 'old Gast's House' in 1677. The sound of washing was heard from upstairs by the occupants, and visitors who had a damp cloth thrown at them when they began to mount the stairs.

When they continued, another cloth was thrown at them. Arriving at the room where the sounds seemed to come from, they found a bowl of whitish water, some of it spilled over. The witnesses stated that immediately before they had come upstairs, the bowl had been downstairs in the kitchen, and could not have been carried to where it was now found - except through the room in which those present had been gathered.

The same night, a tremendous, thunder-like noise was heard, followed by a loud scratching sound in the vicinity of a bedstead. Then a violent hammering noise on the bed-head, so that the two maids occupying the bedstead cried out for help. When the investigators went into the room, a hammer lay on the bed, and there were many marks on the bed-head where the blows had landed.

The maids asserted that they were scratched and pinched by a hand that was inside the bedclothes, and which had exceedingly long nails. They were adamant that the hammer was locked fast in a cupboard when they went to bed. Later, objects were moved, more things were thrown at people, candles were put out, a hideous cry was heard, feathers were plucked out of a bolster, and some were thrust into the mouths of those lying in bed.

Two witnesses, James Sherring and Thomas Hillary, asserted that when they took up a position at the foot of the bedstead with a candle, they both saw a hand and wrist holding the hammer which kept knocking on the bed-head. One of the articles moved was a pole some fourteen of fifteen feed long, which stood in the yard. This was found upstairs in the house, on a bedstead. It was only with the greatest difficulty, and the removal of a window, that it was eventually taken from the house.

One night at old Gast's House, two granddaughters were in bed together - one aged twelve or thirteen, and the other sixteen or seventeen. Suddenly, they felt a hand in bed with them, which they tied up in a sheet and beat until it was as soft as wool, then placed it under a heavy stone - whereupon all was quiet for the rest of the night.

In the morning, the sheet was still there, held by the heavy stone, but when one of the girls declared that she would burn 'the Devil', she found the stone moved and the sheet wet. Stones were also thrown in a bedroom after a candle had been put out, and in the morning, there was a pile of them on the bed.

*Francis Hotel, Bath, Somerset*

# *LITTLE GADDESDEN, BERKHAMSTED, HERTFORDSHIRE

The Manor House of the Lucies was at one time known as 'The Priory', which suggests that the present house occupies the site of some religious building. There are many ghostly legends associated with the place. Perhaps the most convincing one concerned William Jarman, a churchwarden, who lived in the old house during the eighteenth century, and who committed suicide.

Some say he hanged himself inside the building. Others claim he drowned himself in the village pond which at one time used to be just across the Green from the Manor House.

A century or more ago, a fire destroyed much of the old house which Jarman knew, but nearby Ashridge House is still extant. Jarman killed himself because he was rejected by an unidentified heiress of Ashridge, which in the eighteenth century was the home of the Earls of Bridgewater. His ghost is reported to have been seen near the village pond.

There are also accounts of curious happenings involving lights at the Manor House. Years ago, candles would dip or be extinguished, and later the same thing would happen to electric lights. My friend Vicars Bell, author of a history of the parish, told me how he traced a witness who stated that many years ago, a former occupant and a visitor were chatting in the drawing room, when one after the other, the lights were extinguished.

The present occupant tells me that Jarman, who is said to have been so troublesome at one time that he was exorcized by 'bell, book and candle', is still reputed to make the lights burn low on a certain day each year, but for generations nobody has known which day!

In any case, the present occupant - Miss Dorothy Erhart - will tell you that there is nothing sinister about the ghostly presence, and most people regard him as a benevolent and friendly ghost - just as she does.

Gallows Hill, in the vicinity, has long been reputed to be haunted by the sounds of creaking and clanking that must have been a familiar noise when the long-vanished gallows stood hereabouts. There are reports of the apparition of an unidentified grey man seen to pass silently on dark nights.

*Rose and Crown Hotel, Tring, Herts.*

## *LITTLECOTE, WILTSHIRE, TWO-AND-A-HALF-MILES FROM HUNGERFORD, BERKSHIRE

This magnificent Tudor Manor House has a huge Great Hall with panelled walls and a grey and white stone floor. Its drawing room boasts of hand-painted Chinese wallpaper and an Aubusson carpet from the Palace of Versailles. The unusual, egg-shaped library is full of interesting and rare volumes. The Dutch Parlour has wall paintings by Dutch prisoners. There is a unique Cromwellian chapel. The historic and beautiful place is set in matchless scenery - and possesses several ghosts.

The best-known story dates from Elizabethan times, when the rambling and isolated seat of the ancient Darrell family was owned by 'Wild' or 'Wicked' Will Darrell, who is said to have murdered a newborn child in particularly horrible circumstances in 1575.

The charge is based on a statement made by a midwife - a Mrs Barnes of Great Shefford - who on her deathbed told a magistrate that she had been summoned one dark night to attend in secret a lady about to have a child. She was promised a large sum of money if she would do so.

She allowed herself to be blindfolded, and was taken by horseback to a house she did not recognize, where she delivered a young woman of a child. As soon as it was born, the child was snatched from her by a man and thrown into the fire where he held the infant down with the heel of his boot until it was quite dead.

The midwife was too terrified to say much at the time, although she had the presence of mind to cut a small piece of material from the bed curtains, and to count the number of stairs as she was led out, blindfolded again.

After her 'confession', suspicion centered on 'Wild' Will Darrell as the villain, and Littlecote as the house. Darrell was arrested. The connection with Littlecote was established by means of the correct number of stairs given by Mrs Barnes, and the corresponding hole in the bed curtains. But the account of the trial at Salisbury is confused. Littlecote was made over to Sir John Popham, the judge at the trial who took possession of the property on Darrell's death in 1589. Darrell was acquitted.

It was known that Darrell had several mistresses - including his own sister - and anyone may have been the unfortunate young mother. Or the mysterious birth may have been the result of his liaison with a Miss Bonham, whose brother was staying at Longleat at the time.

In 1879, a letter was discovered addressed to Sir John Thynne at Longleat, from Sir Henry Knyvett, which was written about the time of Mrs Barne's death, and substantiated the midwife's story.

It used to be said that bloodstains appeared from time to time in a mysterious way on the floor of the haunted chamber, and according to local tradition, the terrible crime is re-enacted by the ghost of the distracted midwife with the child in her arms. However, the original bed went to America, and the bed curtains are comparatively recent.

The ghost of the murdered babe is also said to have appeared suddenly in front of Darrell, when he was out hunting in Littlecote park, and so startled his horse that he was thrown and his neck broken. This place is known to this day as 'Darrell's Stile', and horses have been known to shy frantically at the spot. Also in the part - in front of the entrance gates where once the old Gate House stood - there is an ancient elm tree, known as 'Darrell's Tree'. Legend has it that the tree will flourish with the fortunes of the owners of the house.

Littlecote has belonged to the Wills tobacco family for fifty years now, and although the present owner, Major George Wills - who does not live there - will tell you that he has never seen a ghost, he is no sceptic. This may be due to the fact that his brother, Sir Edward Wills, saw a ghost in the passage beyond the Long Gallery.

In 1927, while sleeping in their room - which was the first up the few stairs from the Long Gallery - both Sir Edward and his wife were disturbed by the sounds of somebody or something coming up the creaking stairs from the Long Gallery. The third time Sir Edward heard the sounds, he quietly stepped out and saw a lady with a light in her hand which cast a shadow on the ceiling of the passage. Her hair was fair, she was not very tall, and wore a pink dress or nightdress.

Sir Edward followed the figure that disappeared into the room occupied by his younger brother - the present owner of Littlecote - he however slept through it all and knew nothing of the affair until told about it by his older brother. One curious thing about this ghost is that it appeared to open the door of the room into which it disappeared.

From time to time, terrifying screams have been heard in the small hours from the direction of the bedroom and landing that were the scene of the tragedy, while some say they have seen the apparition of the grief-stricken mother with a baby in her arms. Others maintain that the spot is haunted by the frenzied midwife. Another version speaks of Darrell himself. Where he appears, the floor can never be kept in repair, but constantly moulders away - no matter how often the wood is replaced.

When I was there in 1969, I was told of the apparition of a female figure dressed in brown - seen recently by one of the guides at Littlecote. The ghost, if ghost it was, walked along a closed-in, cloister-like passage, and out through a doorway and onto the lawns of the north side of the house.

Another guide heard footsteps in the Long Gallery. These were also heard by a student guide, where the two were alone in that part of the house. It was on the floor above this gallery that the Little Garrison - under Colonel Alexander Popham - was quartered during the Civil War.

One more of the guides at Littlecote maintains that she saw a woman standing by the herbaceous border in the garden. She disappeared completely a few seconds later. Clairvoyant Tom Corbett told me that he, too, saw a ghost in the garden - a beautiful woman whom he later recognized from a portrait in the house as Mrs Leybourne Popham - although why her ghost should appear, no one knows!

But at Littlecote, with its history and its atmosphere of the past, one might expect almost anything to happen.

*The Bear Hotel, Hungerford, Berks.*

# *LONDON, AMEN COURT, NEAR ST PAUL'S CATHEDRAL

It is worth going out of your way to find this delightful little court, with the handsome wrought-iron entrance gates, for it is one of the few places where it is still possible to see a piece of the old City wall on Roman foundations that divides the garden of the court from former Old Bailey property. R. H. Barham, author of *The Ingoldsby Legends* lived here when he was a minor canon of St Paul's.

The tall, dark wall that has clearly been extended over the years, bordered part of the old Newgate prison graveyard, and the path immediately on the other side of the wall was known as Dead Man's Walk, for here the hanged criminals were buried in quicklime, after they had used the path to pass to and from their trials. Over the years, there have been persistent reports of:

- A dark shape crawling along the top of this wall at night.

- The scrape of his boots.

The occasional rattle of his chains is also said to break the uncanny silence that seems to hang around this fateful spot. A clergyman saw the figure several times back in 1948.

*Three Nuns Hotel, London, EC3*

## *LONDON, BANK OF ENGLAND

It is not generally known that the Bank of England in Threadneedle Street has a ghost - an apparition that many people have seen wandering about the Bank garden. It is known as the Black Nun.

The story of the haunting goes back to 1811, when Philip Whitehead - a former employee of the Bank - was arrested for forging cheques, and was condemned to death at the Old Bailey. This tragedy caused Whitehead's sister, Sarah, to lose her reason, and for some twenty-five years - the rest of her life - she daily journeyed to the Bank, loitering there and looking for her brother.

Some people think she gave the name of The Old Lady of Threadneedle Street to the Bank. She died suddenly, and was buried within the Bank premises, the the old churchyard, which afterwards became the Bank garden. Here her figure has been glimpsed on many occasions over the years.

Great Eastern Hotel, London, EC2

## LONDON, BERKELEY SQUARE

Colonel A. Kearsey, visiting a relative in the square, was shown into a room where - by the light of the bright fire burning in the fireplace - he saw a woman in a long dress and broad-brimmed hat, sitting in an armchair.

She was sobbing bitterly, and when he went forward to ask whether he could help, she rose from the chair and - without looking at him - passed through the heavy curtains and disappeared through the shuttered windows. Later, he learned that his hostess's children had reported hearing sobs in that room, while a previous owner had told him that at one time, a woman who lived there who had left her husband for another man. She had cried a great deal. After she left, she never returned to the house, but it seemed that her ghost did.

*Grosvenor House Hotel, Park Lane, W1*

## *LONDON, 50, BERKELEY SQUARE

The most famous of all London's hauntings. The house - now occupied by the Maggs Brothers, the well-known antiquarian booksellers - was said to have possessed, years ago, a haunted room in which the ghost caused at least two deaths, in convulsions, for people foolhardy enough to attempt to sleep there.

Victorians would not have dreamt of visiting London without a look at 'the haunted house in Berkeley Square'. Lord Lyttelton spent a night in the haunted room, comforted by the company of two blunderbusses loaded with buckshot and silver sixpences, the latter being protection against the powers of evil. He later reported that during the night, he fired at an entity that leapt at him from the darkness - that something fell to the floor 'like a rocket', and then disappeared. He had also traced a woman who went out of her mind after spending one night in the house.

Among the many unsubstantiated but persistent stories associated with the building, is the account of a little Scottish child that was either tortured or frightened to death in the nursery, and whose pathetic little wraith - wearing a plaid frock, sobbing and wringing its hands - was said to appear periodically in the upper part of the house.

There is the story too, of a young lady who lived in the house at one time with her lecherous uncle. To escape his attentions, she threw herself out of a top room window, and her ghost is said to have been seen - apparently clinging to the window ledge and screaming.

Perhaps the most famous story concerns a curious white-faced man with a gaping mouth, whose appearance is said to have terrified two fog-bound sailors who stumbled one night into the house, which stood empty at the time.

During the night, they were first disturbed by the sound of muffled footsteps mounting the stairs. Something entered the room they were occupying, and when one of the sailors, in an effort to escape the horror creeping towards them, fell through the window, his partner succeeded in escaping, and was found in a state of collapse outside by a passing policeman. His companion's dead body was found in the garden, but the policeman found no trace of the horrible creature that had so terrified the two tough sailors.

During the 1870s, the occupants of neighbouring houses told of:

- Loud cries and noises emanating from the locked and empty building at night.

- The sounds of heavy furniture being dragged across bare boards.

- Bells ringing.

- Windows being thrown up.

- And stones, books and other articles being hurled into the street below.

At one time, the haunted room was said to be kept locked, and there were stories of a lunatic who died there. Others spoke of a housemaid found lying in the haunted room in convulsions. She died the next day in St George's Hospital, refusing to give any account of what she had seen, because it was 'just too horrible'.

A visitor volunteered to spend a night in the room on condition that help would be forthcoming if he should ring. He did, and they rushed to his aid. He was found exactly where the housemaid had lain, his eyes fixed upon the same spot. Neither did he ever reveal what he had seen - for he was dead.

Today, the house stands much as it was in the days of horse-drawn carriages, and when I called there in June 1970, I learned that the Maggs had a lease on the whole property since 1939. Nothing really untoward, I was told, has happened there in recent years, though throughout the Second World War, fire-watchers used the building night after night.

The haunted room was pointed out to me on the top floor. The middle window is the one from which the sailor is said to have fallen or been pushed. It seems that he was impaled on the spiked railings still bordering the pavement.

All the rooms in the property are used by the Maggs, who regard the various ghost stories as vague and ancient, as indeed they are. But a hundred years ago, anything might have happened in the murky, gas-lit square.

*Grosvenor House Hotel, Park Lane, W1*

## *LONDON, BIRDCAGE WALK, ST JAMES'S PARK

Several sentries of the Coldstream Guards, when they were stationed at Wellington Barracks, reported seeing the ghost of a headless woman walking between the Cockpit Steps in Birdcage Walk towards the lake in St James's Park.

One guardsman, in his signed statement, reported that it was about one-thirty a.m. when he noticed the figure of a woman 'rise from the earth at a distance of about two feet before me'. He was so alarmed that he momentarily lost the power of speech as - wide-eyed - he watched the figure, dressed in a red-striped gown with red spots between each stripe, for about two minutes, before it vanished.

Another guardsman reported hearing shrieks and shouts at night from an empty building behind the Armoury House. In his subsequent sworn statement, he said the voice shouted: 'Bring me a light! Bring me a light!' - the voice dying away on the last word.

Thinking that someone must be ill, the soldier tried to locate the origin of the cries, and shouted the phrase. Then he heard noises which sounded like sashes of windows being hastily lifted up and dropped from different parts of the dark and empty building.

Twenty years before, a sergeant in the Coldstream Guards murdered his wife in a house near the barracks - he cut off her head and threw her body into the lake in St James's Park.

*Hotel Meurice, Bury Street, St James's, SW1*

Walpole House in Chiswick Mall - a fine seventeenth-century property - was the home of Barbara Villiers, Duchess of Cleveland, and mistress of King Charles II.

She lived here during the latter part of her life with her grandson Charles Hamilton, the son of one of her daughters by the Duke of Hamilton. The young man's father was killed in a duel by the wicked Lord Mohun.

She died in her sixty-ninth year, from dropsy [*a condition characterized by an excess of watery fluid collecting in the cavities or tissues of the body*], which had 'swelled her gradually to a monstrous bulk'. At one time famed for her beauty, her accommodating manner and lack of morals caused many a scandal, and Charle II acknowledge five of her many children. She must have led a sad life here after the years of pleasure, and probably often walked up and won the shallow stairs in the high heels she always wore, gazing wistfully out of the tall windows of the drawing room. It is said that she would raise her hands to the moonlit sky on occasions, begging for the return of her lost beauty.

It is over two-hundred-and-fifty years since Barbara Villiers died, but at certain times, the tap-tap of her heels is said to be heard on the stairway, and on stormy, moonlit nights, her form has been seen at the window of the drawing room - wringing her hands.

The 'Old Burlington', Church Street - a four-hundred-year-old former Elizabethan ale house, purchased by Mr Richard Strickley in 1963, has a household ghost: Percy, who wears a wide-brimmed black hat and cloak. He had also been seen by previous occupants, who described him as 'good-humoured and harmless'. In the courtyard, highwayman Dick Turpin is said to have once leapt from an upstairs window to evade the Bow Street Runners - the predecessors of the Metropolitan Police.

*Anna Hotel, London, W6*

## LONDON, COCK LANE, SMITHFIELD

In 1762, a little terraced house (long since disappeared), was the scene of a reported haunting, which set the whole country talking, and intrigued such personalities of the day such as Dr Samuel Johnson, Oliver Goldsmith, Horace Walpole, various ecclesiastical luminaries - and even the Duke of York.

In 1759, the house was occupied by Richard Parsons, the hard-up parish clerk of St Sepulchres, Mrs Elizabeth Parsons and their eleven-year-old daughter, Elizabeth. The troubles began when Parsons let rooms to a William Kent, whose young wife had died in childbirth five years before. Kent's sister-in-law, Fanny, joined him.

They lived together at Cock Lane, and made wills in each other's favour - a fact which may be significant in light of later events. Parsons borrowed money from Kent which he was unable to repay, and after Kent sued his landlord, he and Fanny moved to fresh lodgings in Clerkenwell, where Fanny died in 1760. But before they left Cock Lane, the little house is said to have been the scene of mysterious happenings, which made it one of London's most famous haunted houses.

The affair started when Kent went to the country one Saturday to attend a wedding, leaving Fanny, who - not wishing to sleep alone - asked little Elizabeth to share her bed. Violent bumps, rappings, knockings and scratchings began almost immediately and kept Fanny awake.

The noises were centred on and around the bed. Next morning, Fanny complained to Mrs Parsons, who told her the noises must have come from the cobbler next door, who sometimes worked all night. However, when Fanny found the noises continued the following night - a Sunday - this theory was discarded. She was terrified by the noises, and thought they foretold her death...

She did in fact die eighteen months after leaving Cock Lane, and during this period no manifestations were reported. But soon after her death, fresh disturbances broke out around the bedstead of little Elizabeth Parsons, who is reported to have trembled and shivered uncontrollably at the activities of the 'ghost'.

The scratchings and bumps even followed Elizabeth when she visited neighbours, and as word spread of the curious happenings, crowds of sightseers thronged the narrow street to gaze at the 'house of wonder', and to pester the Parsons with interminable questions.

By the time-honoured code of one rap for 'yes', two for 'no', and three for 'uncertain' or 'don't know', Mary Frazer - the Parsons' servant girl, established contact with an entity who answered questions. The Parsons were told that it was indeed Fanny who was responsible for the noises. Fanny said she had been poisoned by William Kent, who had given her arsenic, and she hoped he would hang!

At one stage, the 'ghost' promised to accompany little Elizabeth to the vault of St. John's Church, Clerkenwell, where Fanny was buried (after dying of smallpox), and strike the coffin to convince witnesses of authenticity of 'Scratching Fanny'. However, when the little girl's hands were held, it was noticed that all the noises stopped, and no manifestations were produced in the vault of St John's.

After attending one of the seances, Oliver Goldsmith published a pamphlet on the affair, which was in effect a defence of Kent, who was being increasingly annoyed at the charges being levelled at him. The authorities now stepped in to make enquiries, and to hold tests.

Nothing happened until, at the third 'test' seance, with little

Elizabeth slung in a hammock, feet and hands extended wide, she was told that unless something *did* happen, her father would be committed to Newgate Prison, whereupon the frightened child was detected secreting a small board and a piece of wood inside of her dress.

This was really the end of the matter - except that William Kent indicated Parsons and his wife, the servant Mary Frazer and several others, of conspiring against his life and character. They were duly found guilty, and had to pay several hundred pounds to Kent. In addition, Parsons was condemned to the pillory [*a wooden framework with holes for the head and hands in which offenders were formerly imprisoned and exposed to public abuse*], and to a year in prison (although the populace - convinced of his innocence - collected money for him).

His wife also went to prison for a year, and Mary Frazer for six months. Later, Elizabeth Parsons is said to have 'confessed' that she had caused all the noises deliberately.

Dennis Bardens adds an interesting note to this curious case. Years later, in 1845, a coffin - believed to be that of 'Scratching Fanny', was opened, and it was found that there was no discoloration, mouldering, or any of the usual disintegration of the body - a state of affairs well in-keeping with the administration of arsenic.

*Great Eastern Hotel, London, EC2*

## *LONDON, DRURY LANE

The Theatre Royal possesses the most famous of all theatre ghosts - the 'man in grey', a daytime spectre which has been seen dozens of times at matinees during the last two hundred years, in the vicinity of the upper circle, sometimes occupying a seat, but more often wandering along the gangway from one side of the theatre to the other, where it disappears into a wall.

The figure was seen by the late W.J. McQueen Pope, the theatre historian, who showed me the exact spot where he had observed the tall, upright figure with tricorn hat and long grey cloak, not once - but several times.

Here, about a hundred years ago, a small room was discovered containing a skeleton of a man with a dagger between his ribs. He is thought to have been the victim of a vicious manager of the theatre in the eighteenth century. At all events, the ghost is regarded as foretelling a successful production at the theatre, since it has often been reported either before or during the early days of many successful runs at Drury Lane. It has never been associated with a failure.

The Green Room at the Theatre Royal was the scene of a murder some two hundred years ago, when actor Charles Macklin - in a fit of anger - killed another actor in front of the fireplace, which can be seen to this day. Macklin was never punished for his crime, and a ghost with a thin, ugly and heavily-lined face, answering to his description, has occasionally been seen near the theatre-pit.

This theatre is also haunted by the ghost of much-loved Dan Leno and Stanley Lupino is among those who have claimed to see the unforgettable face of the comedian in a dressing room which the player had used during his lifetime.

*Strand Palace Hotel, Strand, WC2*

St Dunstan's Church was (and perhaps still is) haunted by ghostly monks - sometimes singly, and sometimes walking in procession up the central aisle.

When the red-brick church was built a hundred years ago, a stately mansion called Friar's Place stood close by. During the Middle Ages, a chapter of St Bartholomew's the Great of Smithfield existed here. In those days, monks - singly, and in procession - probably walked where now the big church of St Dunstan's stands.

It is now twenty years since I first visited St Dunstan's at the invitation of the incumbent, the Rev. Hugh Anton-Stevens, and heard from him and his secretary, the full story of the remarkable experiences of many people at the church. Mr Anton-Stevens considered his secretary to be one of the best psychics in the country; he believed that she was the medium through whom some of the manifestations occurred.

I learned that a former curate, the Rev. Philip Boustead, always maintained that he had seen ghostly monks in the church in the 1930s. Mr Anton-Stevens had been vicar only a short time (he went there in December, 1944), before he realized that there was something very strange about the church, and that ghostly monks did indeed walk there.

'There is no doubt,' he told me, 'that on many evenings, up to a dozen monks can be seen walking in procession up the central aisle, and into the chancel [*the part of a church near the altar*] of St Dunstan's. They wear golden brown habits, and are hooded. Apart from myself, three other people - unknown to each other - have seen these figures from time to time. Most interesting, I feel, is a violet-hooded monk who keeps apart from the others, and with whom I have had a number of conversations.'

The vicar put me in touch with a member of his congregation, who saw the procession of ghostly monks three times from the vestry, during evening discussion groups. When glancing at them from the corner of the eye, they were quite clear, I was told. But they seemed to disappear when looked at directly.

There has long been a theory that the human eye is a deterrent to psychic phenomena, and it is interesting that the vast majority of poltergeist-propelled objects have been seen in flight - and when ending their flight or movement - but very rarely is there good evidence for objects seen to commence movement.

One November evening, a reporter spent some hours in the church in an attempt to establish whether or not the ghostly monks walked. He dropped off to sleep in the quiet of the church, but soon found himself awake again - and was absolutely certain that he was not dreaming. There, walking slowly towards him, were six monks in grey hooded gowns. The reporter, Mr Kenneth Mason of the *Daily Sketch*, stood up to bar their way - but they passed right through him!

A churchwarden - previously sceptical of the ghosts, saw a monk himself in the church one evening; the church organist heard music he could not account for, and 'felt a presence' in the empty church. Mr Anton-Stevens, after publishing an article on confirmation in the parish magazine - which he claimed was dictated by the violet-hooded monk, became distressed by the resulting publicity.

Although for the rest of his life (he died in 1962) he always maintained that the ghosts of St Dunstan's had objective reality, he did not encourage active investigation, and he talked less and less about the remarkable experiences he had. The late psychic investigator Harry Price decided, after extensive research, that the reports were based on fact, and that the procession of ghostly monks appeared in four-year cycles.

*Carnarvon Hotel, Ealing Common, London, W5*

## LONDON, EATON PLACE

One of the best authenticated of London's many ghosts is that of Admiral Sir George Tryon. On June 22nd 1893, Lady Tryon was giving one of her 'At Home' parties at her house in Eaton Place.

The London season was in full swing, and the cream of Edwardian high society chatted and moved among the elegant furniture. Dandies in tight-waisted frock-coats. Military gentlemen in colourful uniforms. Ladies in resplendent frills, laces and jewels. Suddenly, there was a hush in the conversation, as a commanding figure in full naval uniform walked across the place - the guests drawing aside to let him pass - and vanished! He was recognized as Sir George Tryon by everyone present.

At that precise moment, the body of Admiral Sir George Tryon - just dead - was lying in the wreckage of his flagship, H.M.S. *Victoria*, at the bottom of the Mediterranean. The cause of the collision - which resulted in the loss of Admiral Tryon and most of the crew of the *Victoria*, is one of the great naval mysteries.

The Mediterranean Fleet was steaming along in two columns at the time when Lady Tryon was welcoming her guests. Admiral Tryon led one column, Admiral Markham in the *Camperdown* the other. For no reason that has ever been discovered, Sir George Tryon suddenly signalled to the two columns of battleships to turn inwards on each other at a given point.

His officers and those of the *Camperdown* were amazed. It seemed that a serious accident could not be averted, unless the order was retracted - but Sir George was adamant, and in due course, the two lines of ships turned towards each other: the

*Camperdown* heading straight for the *Victoria*.

Sir George seemed to realize too late the follow of his previous order, and he now commanded 'full steam astern'. But, before the manoeuvre could be executed, the *Camperdown* sheared into the *Victoria*, and the flagship sank quickly.

One of the surviving officers reported that as the ship went down, he heard Sir George cry out that it was all his fault and, with a young midshipman standing beside him - a lad who refused Sir George's order to jump to possible safety overboard - the Admiral went to his watery grave.

At the same moment, he also appeared in full uniform, with a set and haggard face, in his wife's drawing room, hundreds of miles away in London.

*Hotel: 99, Eaton Place, London, SW1*

# *LONDON, GARLICK HILL, OFF QUEEN VICTORIA STREET

The Church of St James, built in 1326, destroyed by the Great Fire, and rebuilt by Sir Christopher Wren (1632-1723), was the burial place of no less than six Lord Mayors. It now has an unidentified, mummified body - and a ghost.

The mummified corpse of a young man was found under the chancel [*the part of a church near the altar*], and is now preserved in a glass-faced receptacle in the vestibule. The body was discovered before the Great Fire of London, and buried in a glass coffin near the altar. Nobody knows who the man was. He may have been the first Lord Mayor of London, or an embalmed Roman general, Richard Rothing, who built the church in King Edward II's reign. Or even Belin, a legendary King of the Britons. Today he is known as 'Old Jimmy Garlick' and, according to reports, he sometimes takes a stroll round the church.

An american lady visited the place with her two sons, and when the elder boy looked up a staircase to the balcony, he saw the figure of a man, wrapped in a winding-sheet, standing erect, with his hands crossed on his chest. The figure resembled a dried-up corpse, and the terrified boy ran back to his mother and dragged her out of the church and into the street.

During the Second World War, 'Jimmy' had a narrow escape when a bomb shaved his case in 1942, and penetrated into the vaults below the church, but fortunately, it did not explode. After that, 'Jimmy' was reported to be seen in the body of the church more frequently, and other manifestations, including noises and movements of objects, were said to take place. But there are no recent reports of similar happenings.

The mortal remains of 'Jimmy' have been a relic of the church for five hundred years, and although he is getting thin on top, he retains his skin, his fingernails, and his teeth - and seems good for another five hundred years!

*Howard Hotel, Norfolk Street, Strand, London, WC2*

## *LONDON, THE GARGOYLE CLUB, SOHO

*[The Gargoyle Club is now the Dean Street Townhouse]*

One of the oldest clubs in Europe, the site of the Gargoyle Club once housed a musketry school belonging to Charles II, and at one time Nell Gwynne lived in the same building.

Many people, including the owners, staff, members and visitors have reported unusual experiences. Dylan Thomas - the poet - told me he found the atmosphere fascinating, but would never spend a night there on his own for anything in the world.

Several witnesses have seen a woman dressed in period costume, a grey shadowy figure in a high-waisted dress with a large flowered hat accompanied by an overpowering odour of gardenias, drifting rather than walking across the floor, and disappearing at the lift shaft - a rather incongruous visitor among the strippers who work here! Others say they have seen a tall figure, cowled and shrouded, on the pavement near the Meard Street entrance to the club.

Regent Palace Hotel, Piccadilly Circus, London, W1

One of the sights of University College - built in 1828 - is the embalmed body of Jeremy Bentham, the law reformer and natural scientist, whose ghost haunts the main corridor.

It was part of Jeremy Bentham's will that his body should be used for the purpose of improving the science of anatomy, and this was done when Bentham - the prophet of utilitarianism and a reformer - died in 1832.

Afterwards, the skeleton was re-erected, padding was used to stuff out Bentham's own clothes, and a wax likeness - made by a distinguished French artist - was fitted to the trunk. Seated on the chair which he usually occupied, with one hand on his constant 'companion', his walking-stick called Dapple, and wearing his famous white gloves. With a five-pound note and a pack of playing cards in his pocket, he was enclosed in a moth-proof mahogany case, with the folding glass doors, and deposited at University College, where he can be seen to this day.

Legend has it that the great eccentric was mummified against his wishes, and the unexplained noises heard from time to time at the College are said to be Bentham rapping on the doors and windows of his cage with his walking-stick to frighten the officials of the College into having him sent away and buried.

He is housed in the cloister near the main entrance, and one evening Mr Neil King - Mathematical Master at the University College School - then accommodated in the College buildings, heard the tap-tap-tap of Jeremy's walking-stick in the nearby corridor.

He walked towards the open door to take a peep, not really expecting to see anything, but there was Jeremy, complete with white gloves and walking-stick! He walked right up to Mr King, and when he reached him, made a sudden dart forward, and seemed to throw himself bodily at the teacher - but there was no sensation of impact.

Another time, a sound of flying wings and the displacement of books in one particular classroom were attributed to the ghost of Jeremy Bentham, and the sound of his footsteps and tap-tap-tap of his walking-stick have, according to reports, been heard many times.

*Hotel Russell, Russell Square, London, WC1*

## LONDON, HAMPSTEAD

An early Georgian terraced house - formerly occupied by television personality Peter Cook, his wife Wendy, and small daughters Lucy and Daisy - is reputed to be haunted by the ghost of H.G. Wells [*who is thought to have once lived at 17 Church Row*]. The ghost of the great visionary novelist and sociologist who used to live at the house has been seen and heard walking around in what became known as the nursery wing.

*Clive Hotel, Primrose Hill Road, London, NW3*

## LONDON, HAMPSTEAD LANE

In 1947, the manager of 'The Gatehouse' public house collapsed after seeing an apparition here, and was taken to hospital suffering from shock. He later left the premises on the advice of his doctor. A spokesman for the owners gave the reason as 'overwork'. The ghost of a white-haired smuggler who was murdered here after an argument over money was clearly seen by medium Trixie Allingham, who visited the pub and found the gallery a 'cold, evil place'.

*Sandringham Hotel, Holford Road, London, NW3*

## *LONDON, HAYMARKET

At the Haymarket Theatre, there is a certain dressing room which was always used by John Baldwin Buckstone, about a hundred and twenty years ago. Here the ghost of the gentle, kindly actor-manager has been seen from time to time - he is said to rattle doors and open and close them, and his footsteps are repeatedly reported to have been heard.

More than one employee has seen the figure of a man in the theatre which has disappeared as they watched. One man identified John Buckstone form a photograph. In 1880, soon after Buckstone's death, his ghost is said to have been seen in Queen Victoria's box, where he was often present during his lifetime - and from where Dame Flora Robson quite recently thought she saw the ghost on stage.

The ghost of Buckstone is not a frightening one. Mrs Stuart Wilson, Chairman and Managing Director of the theatre, will tell you that no one could be frightened of him. He returns because he loved the old theatre so much, and because he was so intensely happy here. When she hears a rattling at the door, or when it unaccountably opens, Mrs Wilson says 'Come in, love', or 'Hallo, you are so welcome'. For she, like everyone at the Haymarket, would hate to offend this inoffensive ghost.

*Cavendish Hotel, Jermyn Street, SW1*

## LONDON, HORNSEY, FERRESTONE ROAD

The Hornsey 'rachety' ghost received considerable publicity in January 1921, when for several weeks, unexplained happenings puzzled the occupants and visitors to the house.

The events began with the sound of loud explosions, almost like small bombs, which greatly startled the Frost family, then occupying the premises. The noises seemed to originate from lumps of coal which exploded both in coal buckets and in the grates [*a metal frame for holding fuel in a fireplace or furnace*] of the house. The days passed, and still the 'explosions' occurred. A new delivery of coal made no difference. Coal was found upstairs, and then proceeded to be projected in all directions, although it was never seen in motion: glass globes, vases and china were smashed.

One day, the family - which included three children: Gordon, Bertie and Muriel - were at tea, when two of the tea-plates rose seemingly unaided into the air, and then dropped back again, without breaking.

A step-ladder also was lifted into the air and lowered again. Two glass dishes flew off the sideboard and broke when they fell to the floor. A book lifted itself from a shelf, dropped to the floor, and there twirled round and round before lying still and flat. Once, Mr Frost saw one of his sons lifted into the air - chair and all. He caught hold of the chair, and replaced it on the floor, but five minutes later, the same thing happened again. A police inspector stated that a piece of coal which he picked up to examine, broke into three pieces in his hand, and then vanished!

A vicar - the Rev. A. L. Gardiner, visited the house, and saw a lump move from its place on a shelf and fall. But instead of falling straight down to the floor, it moved outwards into the room for a couple of feet, and then dropped lightly. Mr Gardiner stated after his visit: 'There can be no doubt of the phenomena: I have seen them myself.' Another visitor was Dr Herbert Lemerle, who stated that he was present when a clock vanished mysteriously.

The strange events - which Harry Price regarded as 'well-attested'), began on January 1st, 1921. Little Muriel was so terrified by the disturbances, that she died on April 1st. The boy Gordon was frightened into a nervous breakdown and was taken to Lewisham Hospital. It was said at a public meeting held on May 8th 1921, that the phenomena always occurred in the presence of one of the young boys, and that the ghost of their father's sister - who had died a year previously - had been seen by one of the brothers.

*The Orchard Private Hotel, London, N12*

## *LONDON, KENSINGTON PALACE

This royal palace - purchased by King William III in 1689 - is haunted by the anxious face of King George II, looking out of the window, over the main entrance.

Queen Victoria was born here, and so was Queen Mary - consort of King George V. King William III, Queen Anne and King George II, the last sovereign to use the palace, all died here.

The home of two exiled kings, WIlliam III and George II, there still seems to be an air of expectancy and sadness here, where two hundred years ago the ailing King George II would frequently gaze from the window of his room and think of the Germany he had left.

In October 1760, the irritable and choleric king was dying. He would often raise himself to look out of the window and up at the curious weathervane, with its conjoined cyphers of William and Mary, hoping for winds from the right quarter to speed the ships carrying long-overdue despatches from his beloved Hanover.

He died on October 25th 1760, before the winds changed, and they say that when there are high winds from the west, a ghostly face peers from the old windows up at the weathervane - just as it did all those long years ago.

[See also Underwood's *Queen Victoria's Other World*]

*De Vere Hotel, Kensington, London, W8*

## *LONDON, THE CHURCH OF ST MAGNUS
## THE MARTYR, BY LONDON BRIDGE

Evidence has been collected of an unidentified robed figure having been seen here in daylight through the years. Many visitors - especially those from Eastern countries, sense an unusual atmosphere as soon as they enter.

The church was built by Sir Christopher Wren in 1676, on the site of a previous church destroyed in the Great Fire of London - one that had been founded before the Norman Conquest in 1066. Among those buried in the old church was Henry de Yevele, master-mason to Kings Edward III, Richard II and Henry IV. One of the architects of Westminster Abbey, and sculptor of the tomb of the queen of King Richard II, he died in the year 1400.

A former rector - the Rev. H. J. Fynes-Clinton, M.A. - told me he had no doubt whatever that the church was haunted by a robed figure which he thought was probably a former priest of St Magnus. His former verger (church attendant), and an ex-soldier who was very reliable and unimaginative, once found himself within four or five feet of a priest or monk, one Sunday evening after service.

Everyone had left, and he had locked the door. The lights were all on, and he was just putting things away in a cupboard behind a side altar, when he saw the figure immediately in front of him. He was on the point of asking how he had got in, when it bent down and seemed to be looking for something on the floor, so the verger enquired: 'Have you lost something - can I help you?' The figure straightened up, turned and smiled at the verger, and then just faded away in front of his eyes.

A former verger's wife told the rector that she had twice seen a short, black-haired priest wearing a cassock, kneeling before the Blessed Sacrament in the Lady Chapel. Each time when she spoke to it, the figure disappeared.

Later, a church worker was in the vestry one afternoon doing needlework, when a priest in a cassock walked into the room - a modern addition built on the site of a much older building. It circled the table in the middle of the room, and then disappeared through a wall.

Four years later, she saw the same figure in similar circumstances. This time, she was sitting at the table in the vestry room one Saturday afternoon, working on embroidery for the church, when she suddenly became aware that someone in a thick woolen cassock was standing by her side.

She saw the ribbing of the woolen material quite clearly. But when she looked upwards, she could see no body or face. She suddenly felt very frightened, and walked out of the room without looking back.

On the third occasion that she saw the figure, she was at early Mass one Sunday morning. As she turned her head to make her contribution to the collection, her eye caught a movement behind her. She turned round and saw a priest wearing a cassock walk up the nave and turn into a seat behind her. She took him to be a real person, and expected him to go and get a surplice and help as they had no server at the time. When he did not do so, she glanced round, and found that he was not behind her.

When she asked the verger about the priest who had come in during the collection, she was told that no one had entered, nor had anyone been moving at that time, and no one had occupied the seats behind her.

- An electrician working in the church asked who the priest was who watched him so intently, and who seemed to be there one minute and gone the next.

- A choir-man ran up from the crypt one Easter looking very frightened, and said he had passed a robed figure on the stairs, and who had disappeared - into one of the old walls.

An interesting point concerning the stooping figure seen by the verger is that the spot where this took place is exactly over the grave of Miles Coverdale - the sixteenth-century English translator of the Bible. He was a friar and Bishop of Exeter, and all the witnesses of this apparition have agreed that the figure they saw wore a cowl or monastic hood.

*Howard Hotel, Norfolk Street, Strand, London, WC2*

One part of the palace - which looks like a country house - is reputed to harbour a 'horrible ghost': a small man, his throat slit from ear to ear, and with his mouth hanging open, sits up in bed, the head propped precariously against the wall, and the body and bedstead drenched with blood.

The awful spectre is said to have its origin in a murder that took place in the haunted room on May 31st, 1810. The debauched Duke of Cumberland - son of King George III - after a night at the opera, retired to his bedroom. Soon afterwards, shouts and the sounds of a scuffle were heard. But those sounds were not unknown in the Duke's quarters. And the servants took no action.

The Duke had two valets - Yew and Sallis - and at length, after things had quietened down, the Duke called for Yew, who found the Duke standing in his room, 'cool and composed', but with his shirt-front covered with blood, and his sword lying on the floor - bloodstained.

The Duke explained that he had been set upon and severely wounded, and asked the valet to fetch his physician - Sir Henry Halford. Sir Henry arrived within minutes, and found that none of the Duke's wounds were serious, and that in fact the only real wound was a deep cut on the Duke's sword hand.

Almost two hours had passed since the Duke had returned to the palace, and now, with the wounds dressed and the room rearranged, the Duke said to Yew: 'Call Sellis.' Yew's sworn statement states that he went to Sellis's room and there found the valet lying perfectly straight in the bed - the head raised against the headboard, and nearly severed from the body.

A razor - covered in blood - was found in the room, but too far from the body to have been used by Sellis himself, or to have been thrown away by him in such a condition.

The Duke, already hated in London, was now openly booed in the streets, and he no longer dared to show his face at the opera. At the inquest, he stated that Sellis had tried to murder him, and had then committed suicide. Which seemed unlikely, in view of the fact that Sellis was a small, weak fellow - while the Duke was a gross, beefy man.

The truth seems to have been that the Duke had an affair with Sellis's daughter, who either had a child by him, or committed suicide because of his conduct. In order to silence Sellis, His Royal Highness, seizing the poor man as he was in bed, and holding him by the hair, had cut Sellis's throat with his sword. Then he had probably gashed himself with a razor which he had thrown down on the floor before returning to his own room.

Originally, it was King Henry VIII who had acquired the palace for the Crown, pulling down the old leper hospital and building a manor for himself and Anne Boleyn. Another well-known ghost story associated with the palace concerns two notorious women of the Court, who were rivals for the affections of King James II: the Duchess of Mazarin, and Madame de Beauclair.

The two women - living in retirement - had become friends. They often talked about the possibility of a future life, and agreed that whoever died first would, if possible, communicate with the other from beyond the grave.

At length, the Duchess of Mazarin died, and Madame de Beauclair waited in vain for a message from her friend. As the months passed, she grew sceptical, and declared that there was no life after death. She had a heated argument on this subject with a friend who was surprised, some time later, to receive a message from Madame de Beauclair entreating her to come at once if she wished to see her alive. The friend was unwell, and hesitated - whereupon she received a still more urgent message - accompanied by a gift of jewelry, imploring her to come immediately.

She hurried to St James's Palace, where she found Madame de Beauclair seemingly in the best of health. But she was told that within a short time, Madame would be dead. She had been visited by her dead friend - the Duchess of Mazarin - she affirmed. The ghost of the Duchess had walked round her room, 'swimming rather than walking', had stopped beside a chest and, looking at Madame de Beauclair, had said: 'Between the hours of twelve and one tonight, you will be with me.' The midnight hour was close at hand. As the clock began to strike.

Madame de Beauclair exclaimed, 'Oh! I am sick at heart!' - and she was dead within half an hour.

There ought to be other ghosts at St James's Palace: perhaps the ghost of King Henry VIII's daughter, 'Bloody' Mary, who died here. Or handsome Prince Henry, King Charles I's adored elder brother, who also died here in spite of the medicines sent to him by Sir Walter Raleigh from the Tower. Or King Charles himself, who spent the last few days of his life there, leaving the palace early on that January morning in 1649, to walk across the park for his execution in Whitehall.

There are fourteen crosses on the cobbled stones of an inner courtyard, worn but still visible. They mark the graves of fourteen leprous maidens who were buried here when the palace was a hospital for 'maidens that were lepers, living chastely and honestly in divine service'. They, too, appear to sleep undisturbed.

*Hotel Meurice, Bury Street, St James's, London, SW1*

# *LONDON, TOTTENHAM

Tottenham Museum is housed in Bruce Castle where, each November 3rd, the ghost of Costania - Lady Coleraine - runs screaming through a certain room at dead of night.

Bruce Castle is a late Elizabethan manor house once owned by Sir Rowland Hill (1795-1879), the originator of the penny post. So it is a happy choice for a museum of postal history. Three hundred years ago, the jealous Lord Coleraine is said to have kept his beautiful wife locked here, in the room that is now haunted by her screaming ghost. In desperation, she threw herself to her death from the balcony, but still her screams and other uncanny sounds are occasionally reported from this impressive buildings near the parish church.

Some years ago, Mr C. H. Rock, B.Sc., A.L.A., the Curator of the Museum, informed me that he had traced a lady who used to live opposite Bruce Castle a sa child, and she claimed to have heard the screams on November 3rd several years running.

In 1949, thirteen watchers held an all-night vigil on the anniversary of the Lady Coleraine death, and when several of the watchers heard footsteps, the spiral stairs and echoing corridors were immediately searched, but the lady did not put in an appearance on that occasion.

At one-thirty a.m. however, all the ghost-watchers noticed a strange chill. But the thing that particularly interested Mr Rock - who joined the watchers - was the peculiar behaviour of a reliable clock, situated immediately above the haunted chamber, which totally failed to strike the hour of one a.m., although it struck midnight and the hours after one a.m. quite normally.

*Pembury Hotel, Stamford Hill, London, N4*

## *LONDON, THE TOWER OF LONDON

Built by William the Conqueror, this venerable collection of buildings is closely connected with the tragic side of English history, having been a fortress, a palace, a prison, an arsenal - even a mint and a menagerie - although it is best remembered because of a long list of state prisoners lodged here, so many of whom were executed within its walls.

Its tragic deaths and violent happenings can cause hauntings, then surely the Tower should be ghost-ridden and, indeed, there are convincing reports, extending over many years, of curious and inexplicable happenings.

A remarkable story is told by Edward Lenthal Swifte - a Keeper of the Crown Jewels (a post to which he was appointed in 1814), who resided at the Tower with his family until his retirement in 1852.

One Saturday night, in October 1817, he was having supper in the sitting room of the Jewel House - then in the Martin Tower - along with his wife, her sister, and their young son. (The Jewel House was thought by Swifte to have been the 'doleful prison' of Anne Boleyn). The doors and windows of the room were closed and shuttered that dismal winter's night. His wife was about to take a drink with her food, when she stopped with the glass halfway to her mouth, and exclaimed: 'Good God! What's that?'

Keeper Swifte looked in the direction of his wife's gaze, and saw a 'cylindrical figure, like a glass tube', about as thick as one's arm, hovering between the ceiling and the table. Its contents appeared to be a dense fluid - white and blue - incessantly mixing and mingling within the cylinder.

The shape remained in one spot for about two minutes, and

then slowly moved towards Swifte's sister-in-law - apparently following the shape of the table. It passed in front of Swifte and his son, then behind his wife, pausing for a moment over her right shoulder. (There was a mirror opposite, in which she could watch its progress.) Suddenly, Mrs Swifte's nerve broke, and she collapsed onto the table, her hands covering her head and shoulders as she shrieked out, 'Oh, Christ! It has seized me!'

Swifte immediately picked up a chair and struck at the mysterious object, which promptly disappeared. Subsequent questioning revealed that while Swifte and his wife had seen the object clearly, neither his son nor his sister-in-law saw anything.

A few days later, one of the sentries at the Jewel House maintained that he saw a figure, which reminded him of a large bear 'issuing' from under the door of the Jewel Room! He thrust at the form with his bayonet, which struck the door, and the sentry promptly fainted. He was carried senseless to the main guard-room, where he revived to some extent - but his nerves were completely shattered, and a couple of days later, he died.

Sir George Younghusband, a later Keeper of the Crown Jewels, stated that a sentry on duty at the Jewel House (in his time, still in the Martin Tower), declared that he often saw the ghost of one of the earls of Northumberland pass up and down the narrow walk along the edge of the ramparts running on each side of the Martin Tower; a walk known to this day as 'Northumberland's Walk'. Other sentries also saw the ghost, and the sentries on duty were doubled.

The Bloody Tower, where the little princes and Sir Thomas Overbury were murdered - where Sir Walter Raleigh was imprisoned - where Judge Jeffreys died - was built by King Henry III and his several ghosts. Guido ('Guy') Fawkes, of the

Gunpowder Plot fame, was 'examined' here, and there are records of agonized groans emanating from the place long afterwards, when no human being was in the former council chamber.

As might be expected, there have also been stories also of the pathetic little ghosts of the two murdered princes: King Edward V, acclaimed before he was thirteen, although he never lived to be crowned - and his younger brother, Richard, Duke of York, smothered on the orders of Richard, Duke of Gloucester - afterwards King Richard III.

Their ghosts have long been reputed to walk, hand in hand, about the palace that became their tomb. Their bodies were hastily buried - first in the basement of the Wakefield Tower, and then at the foot of a staircase leading from the White Tower to the Chapel of St John.

The ghost of Anne Boleyn has been seen at the Tower of London, as well as several other places. Here, her ghost has been seen in the vicinity of the White Tower, and Tower Green. Sometimes she is seen - and her footsteps heard. Sometimes she remains invisible.

In 1933, a sentry, hearing approaching footsteps, called out a challenge and saw, floating towards him, the headless body of Anne Boleyn, which he recognized by the dress she wore - before he deserted his post in terror. Because that spot was well known to be haunted, he was only reprimanded.

When Field-Marshal Lord Grenfell (a Member of The Ghost Club) was a lieutenant at the Tower, a similar appearance frightened a guard outside the King's House, where Anne Boleyn spent her last night on earth - in human form.

He declared that a headless woman had suddenly appeared in front of him, wearing a dress similar to that which he had seen in portraits of Anne Boleyn, and when he had received no answer to his challenge, he fixed his bayonet and approached to find the weapon made no difference to the advance of the headless woman. He fainted with shock, and was charged with being drunk on duty. But at the court martial, eh told his story, and when other sentries testified to similar experiences, he was acquitted.

Anne's ghost has also been seen inside the church within the Tower precincts, the Chapel of St Peter-ad-Vincula (Saint Peter in the Fetters), where her bones lie before the high altar. Years ago, a captain noticed a light in the church, and asked the sentry on duty outside what the cause was.

The sentry said he did not know, but he often saw this eerie light - and heard strange noises. The officer procured a ladder, and when he looked into the church, saw a procession of men and women in Elizabethan dress walking slowly down the central aisle with noiseless tread, headed by a figure that was unmistakable: it was Anne Boleyn. After having paced the chapel several times, the procession and light, for which no origin could be seen - vanished.

Perhaps the most striking ghostly manifestation is that of the execution of the wicked Countess of Salisbury, daughter of the Duke of Clarence, beheaded by order of King Henry VIII. The harrowing scene of her execution is said to be reenacted on the anniversary of her death - the ghostly Countess being seen and heard - screaming with terror - as she is chased by the phantom executioner who, axe in hand, finally overtakes her and hacks off her head with repeated blows.

In the small chapel in the Wakefield Tower, there were reports in the past of the ghost of King Henry VI having been seen there. The persistent stories of his having been stabbed to death as he knelt at prayer, may have some foundation, but I have no record of this particular ghost being seen for many years now.

The ghost of Sir Walter Raleigh is supposed to have been seen from time to time at a spot near The Bloody Tower known as 'Raleigh's Walk', although he was executed at Westminster Old palace Yard.

The most recent happenings at the Tower, for which there appears to be no logical explanation, are unexplained footsteps, a shadowy form which disappeared near the Wakefield Tower, and a remarkable account from a high-ranking officer at the Tower who saw what he described as a puff of smoke emerge from one of the ancient and long disused cannon.

It floated over the ground, and appeared to sit on top of a wall. If such an account had not come from an authoritative source, it could be dismissed as a trick of the light - instead, it remains one more curious incident at the haunted Tower of London.

*Three Nuns Hotel, London, EC3*

*[Now used for government receptions and is closed to
the public except on rare open days]*

Some years ago, jewels consisting of about one hundred and fifty gold, and enamelled necklaces, pendants, rings, stones and ornaments, enclosed in a decayed wooden box, were discovered by workmen near St Paul's Cathedral, during excavations for building a warehouse. They were taken to the house of an official of the London Museum, who kept them in his study for a fortnight, informing the Treasury of the find.

The jewels arrived about six in the evening on a warm June night. By ten p.m., although the night was still warm, the official and his wife and daughter experienced a sensation of coldness, and found themselves shivering in the room where the jewels had been placed.

The next day, a friend who was interested in the occult called, and they discussed the matter with him. While he was in the room containing the jewels, he startled the family by stating that he could see, standing by the precious stones, a tall, thin man dressed in Elizabethan costume. The man seemed angry, and the student of the occult heard or sensed the apparition say words to the effect that the jewels were his, and by what right had they been brought there?

Several years later, after the jewels had been placed officially in the London Museum - then housed at Lancaster House - a professional medium, who knew nothing of what had happened two or three years before, was visiting the museum official at his home, when he declared that he could see a tall man standing by the side of the official's daughter, who did not like the girl, and who might try to do her harm.

His description exactly tallied with that of the occult student. The daughter has assisted her father in cleaning the jewels while they were in the house. Another incident concerned a spiritualist who fainted when she was shown the jewels at the London Museum, and on recovering, stated that she had seen blood on a gold necklace among the jewels, and that she had sensed that the woman who wore it had been murdered.

*Hotel Meurice, Bury Street, St James's, London, SW1*

## LONDON, VINE STREET POLICE STATION

[*The police station closed in 1997 and the building was
demolished in 2005 for redevelopment*]

A grim, one-hundred-year-old building, haunted by the ghost of a police sergeant who committed suicide in the cells at the turn of the century, and who is still reputed to pound with heavy footsteps the station corridors.

Locked cell doors have been found unaccountably open. Papers and documents in one of the offices have been discovered scattered and disarranged. One senior detective said in December 1969, that he had been thoroughly scared on two occasions. Each time he had felt the presence of someone else when he was alone in a room. He had made no official report - for fear of being laughed at...

*Three Nuns Hotel, London, EC3*

## *LONDON, WESTMINSTER CATHEDRAL

A sacristan on night duty in the locked cathedral, in July 1966, reported seeing a 'black-clad figure', which disappeared as he watched.

A spokesman at Cardinal heenan's London residence stated that 'an extensive search of the cathedral inside and outside, failed to yield any clue, and police dogs did not find any scent. Officially, we do not support the theory that it was a ghost, but I have heard it mentioned.'

The figure disappeared in the direction of the high altar as the sacristan approached…

*Eccleston Hotel, Victoria, London, SW1*

## *LONDON, WILTON ROW, NEAR MARBLE ARCH

A fashionable public house has long been said to be haunted by a ghostly grenadier.

The 'Grenadier' was once an inn that served as a mess for officers of regiments stationed nearby. The name of the alley that runs beside the pub - Old Barrack yard - recalls the time when soldiers drilled here. In those days, one of the bars was situated where the cellars are now, and the present bar served as a dining room for the officers.

The story goes that during a game of cards, an officer was caught cheating, and rough justice was handed out by his companions - a little too rough, it seems, for he was flogged on the spot and staggered down the stairs to the cellar, where he died. His ghost is said to haunt the pub to this day.

The fatal game of cards is supposed to have taken place during the month of September, and it is during this month that the disturbances at the 'Grenadier' reach their climax. I remember Roy Grigg - a previous licensee - telling me that while he had reservations about the grenadier story, he had no doubt whatever that the place *was* haunted - especially during each September.

His Alsatian dog always showed every sign of being terrified during this period, growling and snarling at no visible presence, and often trying to scratch and dig its way into the cellar. This curious behaviour of the dog was confirmed by all the occupants of the 'Grenadier' at that time.

One September, Roy Grigg's nine-year-old son, lying in bed with the door open, saw what he described as a 'shadow' of someone on the landing. As the boy watched, the shadow grew larger and larger, then became smaller - almost as though someone were approaching the bedroom - then retreating, undecided whether or not to enter.

Not long afterwards, Mrs Grigg was changing in her bedroom at midday. Believing herself to be alone in that part of the house, she had not troubled to shut the door. Suddenly, when she was half-undressed, she became aware that a man was climbing up the stairs towards her bedroom.

She quickly covered herself, but when she turned to confront the figure, there was nobody there. As far as can be established, no human being was in fact on the stairs at the time. Certainly Mrs Grigg, who obviously knew all the men in the pub at the time, did not recognize the person she glimpsed through her bedroom door.

A year later, the proprietress of a Hammersmith public house, having a drink in the bar of the 'Grenadier', distinctly saw a man going up the same stairway. A 'man' who seemingly vanished as easily as the one seen by Mrs Grigg.

Mr Grigg told me too about a Roman Catholic friend of his whom he had known since childhood, who stayed a night at the 'Grenadier', and slept in a bedroom about which he had heard disturbing stories. He therefore hung a rosary over the bed to safeguard his undisturbed sleep.

Instead, he found himself suddenly awake in the middle of the night, and sensed - rather than saw - someone or something standing at the foot of his bed. The figure seemed to be trying to touch him, but almost as soon as he was aware of the presence, it disappeared.

The present landlord Geoffrey Bernard is equally sure that peculiar happenings occur at the pub. Things he is totally unable to explain:

- Knocks, raps.

- Lights switched on during the night.

- Taps turned on.

- Objects moved.

These and other phenomena he related during the course of a film made there when I took the BBC to the 'Grenadier' for a programme broadcast on All Hallow's Eve. Bernard's teenage daughter - with whom I had a long talk - told me she sometimes was very frightened at night for no apparent reason. Occasionally, she saw shadows she could not explain.

There were other factors that suggested to me that this young lady may be the focus of the phenomena then occurring at the 'Grenadier'. When I asked her what she did when she had these feelings or saw something she could not explain, usually soon after she had gone to bed, she replied very sensibly that she put her head under the bedclothes and went to sleep!

*The Berkeley Hotel, Wilton Place, London, SW1*

# *LONG MELFORD, SUFFOLK

*[Underwood's account is based on his first investigation in 1944.
He revisited 'The Bull' of many occasions, and reflects upon it again
fifty years later in* Nights in Haunted Houses (1994)]

At one time, the ancient and picturesque Bull Hotel was reputed to be haunted by a poltergeist that threw things about.

This mellow sixteenth-century hostelry was originally a mansion built by a rich 'woolman' in the days when the little town was the centre of the cloth-making industry. The old courtyard at the back is particularly interesting, with part of the gallery that at one time surrounded the yard - still preserved.

After receiving reports of various unexplained happenings at the Bull, I approached the manager at that time - a Colonel Dawson, late of the Indian Army. He invited me to spend a night or two there.

On arrival, Colonel Dawson told me that the mysterious happenings began at a time when he had a young nursemaid looking after his children. When she left, nothing untoward happened for a time. But after a new girl took her place, strange things began to occur again.

There is a theory that a poltergeist obtains its energy from an adolescent, and certainly there is usually a young person present in such cases. The Bull manifestations were interesting because it appeared that the 'geist' was able to attach itself to more than one adolescent. Perhaps the fact that neither girl was at the Bull during my visit accounted for the absence of paranormal phenomena at that time.

Mr Whayman - the head-waiter - told me that he had several times een objects in flight. Once a heavy copper jug was hurled across the dining room in his direction. At another time, a copper urn - which normally stood on a Dutch dresser, and was safe-guarded by a ledge - flew through the air as he entered the room, landing on the carpet just behind him. Still another time, the same jug was found lying in the middle of the room, having presumably moved there when nobody was present in the room.

One of the first apparently unaccountable incidents concerned the movement of some dining-room chairs. One morning, they were found grouped round the enormous fireplace, as though people had been sitting there all night. Next, a flower vase was found on the floor in the same room. At the time, both these incidents were regarded as being due to lack of attention on the part of members of the staff.

About six months later, Colonel Dawson and his wife were having lunch in the dining room, when they heard a loud 'click', and the door leading from the hall into the dining room opened of its own accord. The Dawsons noticed that the room felt suddenly cold.

It was in the entrance hall of the Bull in July 1648, that a yeoman - Richard Everard - was murdered by Roger Greene. The heavy oak door leading from the hall to the dining room was reported to open unaccountably on many subsequent occasions.

One night, when he was alone at the inn, Colonel Dawson heard distinct footsteps pass his bedroom door. He quietly brought his dogs upstairs, and as soon as they reached the passage outside his bedroom, they bristled with fright, absolutely refusing to go along the passage.

It was some time before they could be quietened down. Some months later, a visitor heard footsteps outside her bedroom door, early one morning, followed by a knock on her bedroom door. Thinking it must be her early-morning tea, she called out. 'Come in.' By way of reply, she heard a terrific crash, as though a tray with teapot, jug, cup and saucer and other crockery had been dropped, and she hurriedly got out of bed to help. When she opened the door, nobody was there - nor was there any sign to account for the noise she had heard. Later, she established that no one else in the hotel had heard the crash.

I was shown a pewter coffee pot, kept in the dining room on a little shelf guarded by a ledge. Once, I was told, this pot had jumped off the six-inch deep shelf, some six feet from the ground, in the presence of nine people having breakfast. It is not unusual for a building three centuries old to have a little dust here and there, and this particular shelf was no exception.

Colonel Dawson told me that he examined the shelf immediately after the pot had 'jumped', and discovered the slight layer of dust on the shelf had only been disturbed in a clean circle where the pot had stood. There was no displacement of the dust consistent with the pot sliding to the edge of the shelf and then falling over the ledge. So it had to be deduced that the pot had literally 'jumped'.

Two small fires - typical poltergeist activity - were experienced at the Bull. The first occurring in the lounge situated just across the hall from the dining room. A smell of burning from the empty room heralded the discovery of a small hole burning in the carpet, five feet seven inches from the fireplace - where no fire was burning at the time.

The other incident also took place in the lounge. This time there was a fire burning there in the heavy fire-basket. After a loud bang had been heard, this fire-basket was found in the centre of the room. It was only with some difficulty that it was replaced in its proper position.

I experienced no unusual happenings during my visit to the Bull, and Colonel Dawson invited me to pay a return visit at a future date, in the hope of witnessing some paranormal activity. But soon afterwards, the disturbances ceased as unaccountably as they bag, and as far as I know, nothing untoward happened there for a long time now.

[*The Bull Hotel was the hotel where Harry Price stayed whilst carrying out his initial investigations at Borley Rectory, which itself used to stand a mile or two to the south west, just over the border in neighbouring Essex*]

*The Bull Hotel, Long Melford, Suffolk*

# *LUDLOW, SHROPSHIRE

The eleventh-century castle at Ludlow has a ghostly 'White Lady' - and a mysterious breathing noise.

Historic Ludlow Castle, in its strong strategic position on the Welsh border, was the last Shropshire fortress to surrender to the Parliamentary Army in 1646. It had been the seat of the Lord President of Wales, and began to fall into decay - in 1689.

The 'White Lady' haunting is said to date from the days of King Henry II, when Ludlow was the scene of many Border clashes. A maiden by the name of Marion de la Bruyere was among the few retainers left at the castle on one occasion, in the absence of its custodian - Josce de Dinan.

Marion had an admirer who was attached to the enemies of Ludlow, and she was in the habit of lowering a rope, when the opportunity occurred, to enable the night to visit her at night. This time, he did not come alone, and while Marion was greeting him, he purposely left the rope dangling. Within a short time, a hundred men had swarmed into the castle, and Ludlow was in the hands of the enemy. Realizing that she had been betrayed, Marion snatched her lover's sword, slew him, and then threw herself over the battlements of the Hanging Tower to her death on the rocks below...

For many years, the ghost of 'Marion of the Heath' was said to be seen in the vicinity of the Hanging Tower, wandering among the ruins on dark nights. Now, all that seems to remain is a curious gasping or breathing sound, that seems to originate halfway up the Garderobe or Hanging Tower.

This is thought to be either the expiring gasps of the knight who betrayed the innocent Marion. Or Marion's deep breathing as she struggled to kill her deceiver. At all events, there appears to be no denying this aural phenomenon, for which no entirely satisfactory explanation has yet been discovered.

A few years ago, I was in touch with Mr. J. Didlick - a Ludlow man - who heard the noise several times. He told me that the sounds might be likened to those made by someone in very deep sleep, but he particularly remarked on the loud and distinct quality of the noise, which he felt originated high up on the ancient battlements.

On the first occasion he heard the noise, he was so puzzled that he returned home and asked his wife to accompany him back to the castle, taking care not to tell where what he had heard. But as soon as they reached the spot where he had heard the very heavy breathing, Mrs Didlick stopped and remarked on the curious noise which seemed to come from the castle walls. She was very reluctant to stay anywhere near the spot, and subsequent questioning established that she had heard precisely the same noises as her husband.

Mr Didlick told me that he had since heard it on several occasions and, each time - although he had searched carefully - he had been unable to discover any material cause. A nest of young owls was a popular suggestion. But Mr Didlick assured me that this theory could be discounted, as owls do not nest in January, and no traces were found to suggest that owls habitually visited the spot.

A suggestion that the wind might be responsible was not accepted by Mr Didlick, who maintained that on two occasions when he has heard the noise, there has been no wind whatsoever...

Another witness explored the possibility of night birds - either animal or human - being responsible. He maintained that the breathing was too restrained to originate from a human being, and too human to come from an animal or bird. A young man and his girlfriend also heard the noise, which they describe as 'wheezing'. They became frightened and ran from the spot beneath the Hanging Tower.

During the Second World War, a family were evacuated to Ludlow from Liverpool, and spent four months in part of Ludlow Castle. Soon after they arrived, odd things happened:

- Raps and bangs which they could not account for.

- And the mysterious opening and closing of doors.

When I was there not long ago, I talked to one of the officials, and he told me that he was always getting reports of odd happenings in and around the castle.

Ludlow's parish churchyard and rectory are also reputed to be haunted. At the rectory, a tall, elderly woman with grey hair dressed in a long, dull-coloured robe, has been seen from outside the house when the place has no occupants.

Sometimes, shuffling footsteps have been heard by those living there. A similar figure - an old woman in a drab dress - has been seen wandering among the tombs, and disappearing among the ancient headstones. No one knows who she is or what she wants.

*Feathers Hotel, Ludlow, Salop.*

## LYME REGIS, DORSET

*[Trent Manor is now a Private Residence]*

Nearby Trent Manor House contains a hiding-place used by King Charles II. A legend tells of ghostly horses' hooves thundering past, on the old highway, on certain nights of the year. They are said to have originated in the mysterious disappearance of a coach and horses, driver and passengers, who all vanished from the face of the earth one dark and stormy night.

*Three Cups Hotel, Lyme Regis, Dorset*

## *LYMPNE, NEAR HYTHE, KENT

Lympne Castle has been a Roman fortress - an Anglo-Saxon outpost, a Danish stockaded camp, a Norman castle, a home of the Archdeacons of Canterbury (including Thomas a Becket), a Tudor fortified residence, a farm, and the haunt of smugglers and a look-out in the Second World War. It also has several ghosts, including one seen by a previous tenant - Mrs Henry Beecham - sister-in-law of Sir Thomas Beecham.

Ancient documents and local folklore tell of six Saxons fleeing from the Normans - a flight perpetuated perhaps forever because their ghosts (the Normans discovered their hiding place, and they met an 'untimely ' end), have been seen inside the castle.

Another ghost is that of a Roman soldier who, on watch in the east tower, accidentally fell to his death. Appropriately enough, his footsteps are heard mounting the tower steps... but they never come down.

The present occupants are Mr and Mrs H. Margery, who will tell you that they have heard mysterious footsteps and other noises, which they are simply unable to account for.

*Clifton Hotel, Folkestone, Kent*

## LYTCHETT-MATRAVERS, NEAR POOLE, DORSET

There are several haunted houses in this village of Norman origin, where Sir John Maltravers, involved in the murder of King Edward II, lied buried in the churchyard of St Mary the Virgin. The ancient Church Path - once used by survivors of the plague, when they abandoned the doomed village in the valley - is still the shortest way from the present village to the church.

It climbs a hillside, skirts a wood, and then - at the angle where it bears sharply left - we find Whispering Corner. In daylight - and at night-time, anxious and urgent voices have been heard here - as though several people were urgently discussing some pressing subject. But the words are always indistinguishable.

*Sandacres Hotel, Poole, Dorset*

Capesthorne Hall, near Macclesfield, is the ninety-eight roomed home of Sir Walter Bromley-Davenport. Perhaps significantly, all the unexplained happenings here have been reported from the original portion of this ancient towered and domed mansion, and none from the middle section of the house, which was rebuilt after being destroyed by fire in 1861.

Sir Walter himself saw 'a line of shadowy, spectre-like figures descending the steps into the family vault' in his private chapel, and briefly glimpsed a grey form gliding along a corridor in the house.

On a still, windless night in 1958, Sir Walter's son William was startled by the sound of the bedroom window rattling near his head, and awoke to see a detached arm reaching towards the window. Since then the place has been known as 'The Room with the Severed Arm'.

William Bromley-Davenport promptly got out of bend to discover the source of the disturbance, but the arm disappeared as he approached. He opened the securely fastened window, and looked down at the deserted courtyard - a sheer drop of thirty feet below.

Other witnesses of strange happenings here include Sir Charles Taylor, M.P., who saw a 'lady in grey' hurrying past the foot of a staircase in the west wing as he was going up stairs. His attention was attracted by the 'swish' of her long skirts, and he noticed that she floated rather than walked. Another Member of Parliament spent a sleepless night in a bedroom where the door kept opening and then banging shut for no apparent reason.

*Bulls Head Hotel, Macclesfield, Cheshire*

## MANCHESTER, LANCASHIRE

A house in Cheetham was the scene of curious happenings in 1964, including reports of:

- A child's cries.

- 'Mournful whistling'.

- A dressing table moving across a bedroom.

- A pram which hook noiselessly while the baby inside slept peacefully.

- Apparitions of an old woman and 'a black figure'.

The family tried to planchette, and seemed to contact a dead man who referred to a baby that had been murdered. In response to the messages obtained, a search of the house revealed a narrow strip of calico [*a type of cotton cloth, typically plain white or unbleached*], sheeting in a chimney: copies of newspapers dated 1922, and a pencilled music score - which read similar to the mysterious whistling...

Later, small bones were discovered beneath the kitchen floorboards, but when these were handed to the police, the family were informed that they appeared to be those of a cat or a rabbit!

'The Rover's Return', a fourteenth-century curio shop in Shudehill - says owner Mr Francis Shaw - is haunted by a killed Jacobite ghost, who often appears at the foot of Mr Shaw's bed. The apparition is described as having auburn hair, wearing buckles on his shoes, and carrying a dirk.

The ghost seemed to be gazing at a portrait of Bonnie Prince Charlie, and Flora Macdonald and Mr Shaw gained the impression that it was one James Stewart, who came to

Manchester with Prince Charlie, and was stabbed to death in this old house.

Mr Shaw's partner - Mr Robert Stark - an ex-R.E.M.E. [*Royal Electrical and Mechanical Engineers*] man, said that once when he slept alone in the house, there was a loud crash from the direction of the cellar, as though a stack of bottles had fallen down. But when he went to investigate, there was no sign of any disturbance.

*Mitre Hotel, Manchester, Lancs.*

# *MARKYATE, NEAR ST ALBANS, HERTFORDSHIRE

The curious name of Markyate Cell for the wonderful old house here, is derived from the hermitage built by Roger - a monk of St Albans in the early twelfth century. After Roger had been on a pilgrimage to Jerusalem, he settled as a hermit at Markyate, and the care of the Abbot of St Albans. He died about 1122, and was buried in St Albans Abbey, where his shrine was visited by King Henry III, in 1257.

In 1118, Christina - a member of a wealthy Anglo-Saxon family in Huntingdonshire, fled to Markyate to become one of Roger's hermits, when her parents attempted to force her into a marriage against her will. Her presence was kept a close secret, for fear of the Bishop of Lincoln's intervention, and she was enclosed in a cell measuring only a span and a half. For four years she sat on hard stone - there being insufficient room to stand - and suffered extremes of heat and cold, of hunger and thirst.

Under these rigorous conditions, she acquired - apart from physical ailments - a great reputation for sanctity, and in due course, she succeeded Roger as head of the meritage. Christina was renowned for her embroidery, and in 1155, samples of her work were sent to Pope Adrian IV.

The priory survived until the dissolution of the monasteries in the sixteenth century, when much of the building was pulled down, but some of the material was incorporated in the new house built by Humphrey Bourchier - Master of the King's Past-times.

Bourchier's widow Elizabeth married George Ferrers in 1541, and much of the Tudor house is still evident, despite extensive alterations in the nineteenth century. One can discern the general Tudor style of the house from its courtyard. Many of the windows are Tudor, too. And so is much of the actual stonework. While the garden - at once peaceful and expectant, is laid out in perfect Tudor style.

During the seventeenth century, the lady of the house was Catherine Ferrers: 'the wicked Lady Ferrers', who was married at the age of thirteen to a sixteen-year-old member of the aristocracy names Fanshawe. The marriage was not a success. Perhaps it was the disillusionment of a broken union. Or maybe just the loneliness and frustration that first caused Catherine Ferrers to take to crime. But there can be little doubt that it was the excitements of the chase, and not the financial and other rewards, that came her way when she changed into a highwayman's costume and practised the art of her choice upon the late travellers in the surrounding countryside.

She had a secret room built into the kitchen chimney, reached by a concealed stairway, and there she kept her three-cornered hat, her buckskin breeches, and riding cloak. It was down this secret stairway (which can still be seen today), that she would steal to mount her coal-black horse - to hold up and kill without hesitation, travellers and coachmen on their journeys north and south.

One night, during the course of a robbery, she was wounded on nearby No Man's Land, and although she managed to struggle home, she expired outside the door which let to the secret stairway. Now the secret was out, but the doorway was bricked up, and remained so for over a century and a half...

Shortly after her funeral, stories began to circulate in the surrounding countryside that her ghost had been seen abroad, riding hell-for-leather on horseback over the treetops. While others declared that they had seen her spectral figure swinging in the branches of an old oak tree, under which she is thought to have buried the proceeds of her robberies.

In 1840, there was a bad fire at Markyate Cell, and some of the men working to put out the blaze asserted that they distinctly saw the ghostly Lady Ferrers beneath a branch of a large sycamore tree near the house. After the fire, Mr Adey - the owner at the time - decided to open the bricked-up doorway, but found great difficulty in enlisting workmen locally.

For it appeared to be common knowledge that the place was haunted, and that unaccountable sighs and groans were frequently heard there. At length, workmen had to be obtained from London, and when they opened the doorway, they found that the narrow stone staircase led up to a heavy oak door, which they broke down, only to find afterwards that the door opening by means of a concealed spring. The room, however, held no secrets - only spiders and bats.

There seems to be good evidence that the ghost of Catherine Ferrers has been seen in the vicinity of Markyate Cell. Either riding her black horse, appearing near the branch of a tree, or sitting or standing in the garden. Once, she was seen by a number of people at a parish tea. At other times near the kitchen and in other parts of the house.

Mr E. A. Sursham and his wife - the occupants when I was there in 1966 - told me that their own daughter had seen the figure of an unexplained woman in the garden. The figure disappeared under curious circumstances.

*The Noke Hotel, St Albans, Herts.*

## MARSHWOOD VALE, BETWEEN BROADWINDSOR AND LYME REGIS, DORSETSHIRE

*[Bettiscombe House is now a Private Residence]*

The lonely Queen Anne mansion, in the shadow of the hills, is called 'The House of the Screaming Skull', because of the yellowed skull preserved here. And because of the manifestations that are said to have occurred when it was removed from Bettiscombe House.

The story was first related in print by J. S. Udal - a High Court judge and collector of folklore, who in 1872, told of the human skull that had been at Bettiscombe for many years. He added that, according to tradition, if it were to be removed, the property itself would rock to its foundations, and the person responsible would be dead within a year.

One legend says that the skull is that of a Negro brought to England by Azariah Pinney (from whom the present owner, Michael Pinney, is descended), and who declared, just before he died, that he would never rest until his body was buried in his native land.

According to another, the skull is that of a black servant who was murdered. Still another says that the skull was brought to England by Azariah Pinney, and belonged to a faithful old black servant, who died in his master's service abroad.

The fourth suggests that the skull is that of a young woman who died at Bettiscombe. Some say after a long illness. Some say she was murdered. Near its traditional resting place, there is a priest's hiding-place - immediately under the roof, which might be connected with the mysterious skull.

Azariah Pinney was the son of the Rev. John Pinney, who died in 1705, and lies buried at Bettiscombe. Both Azariah and his brother John joined the ineffectual Monmouth rebellion, and were found guilty of high treason by Judge Jeffreys in 1685.

John was hanged and Azariah shipped to the West indies as a slave. It may be that years later, he brought back this memento of a trusty servant, whom he had names 'Bettiscombe'. At all events, it is said that soon after the black servant was buried in the local churchyard, screams were heard - animals on the farm died, crops failed - and the house seemed to rock. But after the body was exhumed, and the skull taken back into the house - all was quiet.

Among the stories associated with the skull, one states that years ago, a tenant threw the skull into the duck pond opposite the house, and a few days later spent hours raking the pond until he found the skull. For he had been much disturbed by noises of all kinds during its absence, and was only too glad to have it back inside.

Another tale tells of the skull being buried nine feet deep, and working its way back to the surface. It is said to have been heard screaming at the turn of the century - screams that reverberated throughout the house, and were heard by villages and farm workers. In 1914, the skull is said to have sweated blood.

In 1963, the skull was examined by a professor of Human and Comparative Anatomy at the Royal College of Surgeons, who decided that the skull was probably a female aged between twenty-five and thirty, rather small, but a normal European one.

*Stile House Hotel, Pound Street, Lyme Regis, Dorset. [Now a grade II listed building]*

Meopham - where a headless monk is reputed to walk between the Georgian public house and the village church a few hundred yards away across the road. The ghost's path leads between two pillars, but whether these have any significance for the headless apparition or indeed, why the monk is headless and why he walks, no one seems to know. There are however reports of the figure having been seen within the last few years.

The old Manor House was haunted during the 1930s, and Mr G. Varley - during the six months he was there - saw the ghost on several occasions. Once, terrified, he threw a poker at the figure - which still didn't move! The cellar door used to be opened several times a day, and once, Mr Varley was in the lounge when the ghost opened the door.

He and his family were always hearing footsteps and mutterings, nearly every night. Psychic investigator Harry Price conducted a broadcast from this haunted house, and obtained evidence of a sharp fall in the temperature. One member of the broadcast team who slept in the house heard unaccountable footsteps.

*King's Head Hotel, Rochester, Kent*

## *MERSEA ISLAND, ESSEX

The ghost of a Roman centurion has long been said to haunt The Strood. Some accounts say the lonely figure is joined by other legionaries, and a clash of swords is heard across the quiet saltings.

I remember an elderly inhabitant telling me of how she thought she had once walked with a ghostly centurion from Mersea Barrow, on the East Mersea Road, to the Causeway. She described the steady tramp of a soldier's feet beside her. She met a friend who also heard the regular and heavy stamping sounds. But Mrs Jane Pullen of 'The Peldon rose' was not in the least frightened: 'Those old Romans do you no harm,' she would say.

In February 1970, two naval men were driving over The Strood when something loomed up suddenly in front of their dipped headlights. Something dark, upright, with vertical and horizontal white lines across it - perhaps the metal skirt of a Roman tunic.

It was a very clear night, yet they were on to whatever it was almost before they realized, and then they were through it - there was no bump. The thing seemed to have no definite shape, but resembled a human figure surrounded by a white mist. Both men are seasoned members of the Royal Navy - and so are well used to observation at all times of the day and night.

The unidentified figure of a woman - dressed in a smock and wearing a tall hat, with a stick tucked underneath her arm, has been seen sitting on a wall at the corner of the Colchester Road and High Street - there were reliable reports that she was seen in November, 1966.

*Red Lion Hotel, Colchester, Essex*

## *MIDDLE CLAYDON, NEAR AYLESBURY, BUCKINGHAMSHIRE

Delightful Claydon House - built in 1766 and standing in its own open parkland - has several ghosts, including Sir Edmund Verney, the King's Standard Bearer at the battle of Edgehill in 1642, who walks here looking for his hand - which was buried in the family vault.

When Cromwell's men captured Sir Edmund, they demanded that he give up the colours, but he refused, saying: 'My life is my own, but my Standard is the King's'; so he was killed. But when the Roundheads came to take the Standard from his hand, they could not unlock his death grip, and they cut off his hand with its signet ring.

Later in the battle, the Standard was recaptured by the King - with Sir Edmund's hand still grasping it. Sir Edmund's body had been buried in an unknown grave, but his hand was sent home and interred in the family vault at Claydon. The ring was removed, and is now in the possession of the present baronet - Sir Harry Verney, who showed it to me when I was there in 1962, and allowed me to examine the exquisitely beautiful jewel.

Sir Harry and Lady Rachel recounted the history of Claydon as we wandered through this magnificent house, with the quite exceptionally fine staircase. Its iron balustrade depicts a continuous garland or ears of corn, so delicately wrought that they rustle when anyone walks up the stairs. Sir Harry presented me very kindly with a letter from his sister - Miss Ruth Verney - about the ghost she saw on the Red Stairs here.

As with so many haunted houses, there are convincing reports of unexplained footsteps at Claydon. A forester's wife, who still lives on the estate, has told of hearing very heavy footsteps in the corridor above her when she was at Claydon House in 1923, looking after the children - while everyone else was away.

She knew that there was no one in the house at that time - apart from herself and the children, who were within sight. The footsteps stopped at what she judged to be the trapdoor entrance to the priest's hole, but when she went up there, no one was in sight. Years later, exactly the same experience befell her sister, who returned home shaking with fright, after hearing heavy and distinct footsteps in the empty house.

Sir Harry told me of John Webb, the level-headed and practical estate carpenter, who assisted with the demolition of the enormous ballroom that was pulled down some years before. He had been working among the rubble when he chanced to look up, and saw a strangely-dressed man standing nearby, looking sadly at the devastation. When the carpenter called out to the man - for he knew the stranger did not belong to the big house - the figure disappeared. There was no cover whatsoever at the spot where the stranger had stood...

In giving me his sister's account of the apparition she had seen at Claydon, Sir Harry mentioned that this was probably the same figure that other people had seen whilst staying at Claydon. I cannot do better than quote Miss Verney's letter verbatim:

'I was born in 1879, and it must have been about 1892 - when I was thirteen - that I ran up the Red Stairs at Claydon House, and turned left and left again on the first landing, and then took a few steps towards the Cedar Room.

'I noticed without surprise that a man was half-way down from the upper floor. After I got nearly to the front door of the Rose Room, I quite suddenly thought, "But who was he?", and I ran back to look. He was gone, and there hadn't been time for him to reach the top or the bottom of the flight.

'I saw him on the third step of the second flight, and he was coming down: he was tall and slender, and wore a long black cloak, beneath the hem of which peeped the tip of his sword. He carried a black hat with a white feather gracefully curled round the crown. That was all I saw. Mother said he was just where the secret stair had been.

'There was a curious little sequel, which may or may not have been merely a coincidence. Some time later, a little school-friend was coming to spend the weekend. She was of course all agog to see the ghost - but in the interval, we both forget him completely.

'We were going up to the top of the Red Stairs, and as she put her foot on the third step, she said: "By the bye, *where* did you see the ghost?" Alas! He has never come back. Other people have seen ghosts and heard unaccountable noises. Andrew Lang, sleeping in the Rose Room, was much honoured to be awakened one night to see a lovely lady in grey - but she quickly vanished into the wall of what had been a secret room.'

Sir Harry Verney keeps an open mind on the question of ghosts, and although he hasn't encountered the wraith of Sir Edmund, wandering about the little chapel at Claydon and within the house, looking for his lost hand, I am sure he would treat his ancestor courteously and sympathetically - should he ever do so.

*White Hart Hotel, Buckingham, Bucks.*

## MINEHEAD, SOMERSET

In 1636, there lived at Minehead a family named Leaky. A respected shipowner, his wife and small daughter, and his widowed mother. Mrs Leaky senior was a much-loved old lady with a large circle of acquaintances, some of whom - at times - would lament the fact that one day death must separate them from their beloved but ageing friend.

To this, the old lady would reply that while she might be missing from the convivial gatherings which she also enjoyed, should her friends meet her after her death, they would in all probability rather they had not seen her.

In due course, the old lady died, and was accompanied to her grave by many of her loyal friends. Not long afterwards, there were stories that old Mrs Leaky had been seen about the town and near the house of her son. Stories that were treated with respect after the experience of a Minehead doctor who recounted that, on his way back to town after a country visit, he had met an old gentlewoman whom he had helped over a style.

He found her hand uncommonly cold, which made him eye the woman more closely, whereupon he observed that, in speaking, she never moved her lips - nor her eyes. Somewhat perturbed, the doctor deliberately refrained from helping the old lady over the next style.

She went ahead of him and sat upon it, effectively barring his passage. He turned aside to a gate, only to find her sitting upon that, and his strange game went on for some time, until at last the doctor managed to get by, and reached the outskirts of the town where the 'spectre' gave him a kick in the breeches, telling him to be more civil to old ladies in future!

From then on, she became more vicious. All the good nature for which she had been so beloved disappeared. She seemed to haunt her son's ships, distracting and scaring the crews as the ships neared port, so that many vessels went aground. Often, it is said, she would appear at the masthead and whistle in an eerie and blood-chilling manner, whereupon a storm would arise and wreck the ship.

Owing to this peculiarity, she became known as 'the whistling ghost'. Before long, her son's fortunes diminished, and now she appeared night and day, in and about the house where she had lived. At night, her daughter-in-law would often wake to see the apparition in the bedroom, and although she always woke her husband immediately, the figure invariably disappeared before he saw her.

The climax came one terrible night when the ghost strangled the five-year-old Leaky child. Her parents heard a terrible scream from the child's bedroom: 'Help! Help! Father, father, grandmother is choking me …' Before the anguished parents could reach the child, she had been murdered.

On the morning of the funeral of the little girl, the distraught mother was tidying her hair when she saw - in the looking-glass - her mother-in-law, looking over her shoulder. Almost paralysed with fright, the poor woman murmured a prayer, and then turned to face the horror, and implored the apparition in the name of God to say why she plagued the family so.

In reply, the ghost told her to go to Ireland and visit her uncle, the Lord Bishop of Waterford *[there is an entry for 'Waterford' in this volume]*, who was to be told that unless he repented of the sin (which she said he knew all about), he would be hanged.

The horrified and distraught mother asked what sin, and was told: murder. Apparently, when he lodged at Barnstable and was married to the sister of the ghostly Mrs Leaky, he had a child by her daughter, which - after baptizing it - he had strangled, smoking it over a pan of charcoal 'that it might not stink', and then buried it in a chamber of the house.

All this was found to be true, and after the bishop did his best to atone for his sins, the ghostly Mrs Leaky was seen no more.

*Carlton Plume of Feathers Hotel, Minehead, Somerset*

## *MINSDEN, NEAR HITCHIN, HERTFORDSHIRE

Almost hidden and practically forgotten, the ruins of Minsden Chapel - a fourteenth-century chapel-of-ease [*a church building other than the parish church*], have long been reputed to be haunted by a ghostly monk.

As long ago as 1690, Minsden was reported to be 'totally ruined, stripped, uncovered, decayed and demolished', but Reginald Hine - the Hertfordshire historian - leased the ruins for his lifetime, and cautioned 'trespassers and sacrilegious persons take warning, for I will proceed against them with the utmost rigour of the law, and after my death and burial, I will endeavour, in all ghostly ways, to protect and haunt its hallowed walls.'

After Hine's tragic death, his wife made of the ruins a memorial to her husband, and the picturesque walls and arches seem to have been rescued from oblivion at the eleventh hour.

Minsden is traditionally associated with Alice Perrers - mistress of King Edward III, who is charged with stealing her royal lover's rings while he was on his deathbed. She infatuated the old King by 'occult spells' manufactured by her physician, who was regarded as a 'mighty sorcerer', but eventually he was arrested on a charge of confecting [*make (something elaborate or dainty) from various elements*] love philtres [*a drink supposed to arouse love and desire for a particular person in the drinker*] and talismans [*an object, typically an inscribed ring or stone, that is thought to have magic powers and to bring good luck*].

All Hallows Eve, the night when ghosts are reputed to hold sway and be able to return and be visible, is the night of the year when Minsden's ghosts manifest, and there are many stories of horses and dogs behaving as though they see or sense something invisible to their human companions as they climb towards Minsden Chapel on that night.

Elliott O'Donnell told me that one All Hallows Eve, he heard sweet music here, and thought he caught a glimpse of a white-robed figure standing in one of the archways.

It seems that the ghostly manifestations usually begin with the tolling of the lost bells of Minsden, and as the sounds die away, the figure of a monk is seen under the ivy-covered arch on the south side. Walking with bowed head, he silently mounts steps no longer visible, and disappears. After a moment, the strains of sweet and plaintive music fill the air, but almost as soon as the hearer is aware of the sounds, they cease, and all is quiet again.

Reginald Hine gave me permission to spend the night of All Hallows Eve at Minsden some years ago. During the course of a preliminary visit with my brother and a friend, both my friend and I - although ten yards apart - heard, just for a moment - a snatch of music we could not account for. My brother meanwhile, only a step behind me, heard nothing.

We met no ghost during our vigil on All Hallows Eve [*although there was 'a white cross which seemed to glow with an unnatural brightness for a few seconds before fading, only to reappear a few seconds later. It was a... Latin Cross and appeared on what had been part of the wall of the chancel. I suppose it could possibly have been a trick of the moonlight, as a full moon was shining down through the trees at the time'; Peter Underwood,* No Common Task (1983), *p.53*].

Hine never saw the ghost of Minsden, although he did see one at Stanegarth (as he reports in his *Confessions of an Un-Common Attorney*), and he recalled that experience vividly when I talked to him about ghosts. He believed in ghosts for the best of reasons: because he had seen one.

*The Sun Hotel, Hitchin, Herts.*

Cleve Court - a handsome, red-brick, early Georgian house bought by the lawyer Sir Edward Carson in 1920, stands off a quiet road. A great advocate, he is particularly remembered for his merciless cross-examination of Oscar Wilde in 1895. On becoming a lord of appeal in 1921, he was given a life peerage. He died here in 1935, and his body was taken to Belfast for a State funeral. Lady Carson, who often told me how she loved the house from the first time she had seen it, lived at Cleve Court until she died a couple of years ago.

Lady Carson was as clear-sighted and practical a person as anyone I have met, and she was utterly convinced that Cleve Court was haunted:

- There were noises at night-time, though never during the day.

- Footsteps that sounded like a woman wearing high heels.

- Taps on doors, as though someone were seeking admission.

- Dragging sounds that disturbed visitors.

- Noises of drawers being opened and closed, although nothing physical was ever interfered with.

Lord Carson tended to dismiss the curious noises, but there were occasions when even he was quite mystified. The time, for example, when Lord and Lady Carson were in their bedroom and a light knock sounded on the door. He called out 'Come in', but no one did - and there was nobody outside; the Carsons were alone in the house at the time.

Soon after they moved in, an old man in the village told them that a previous owner, many years ago, had been a tyrant who kept his wife locked up. She finally died, childless, although her greatest wish had been to have a son or daughter.

It was soon after they had heard this story - to which they did not give much attention - that the Carsons began to notice, whenever children were in the house, a mysterious 'grey lady' was often seen. Patricia Miller, a great niece of Lord Carson, asked her mother who the lady was who stood by her bed - a lady she had seen before, to whom nobody ever talked.

Joanna Wilson paid a return visit to Cleve Court when she was about eight years old. She remembered seeing a lady there 'who walks in and out of rooms and whom nobody speaks to', and she wanted to know whether the lady was still at the house. A grandson, Rory Carson, visited the house when he was fifteen in 1965, but refused to sleep in the old part of the house. A large dog couldn't be made to say in the room, either.

It was soon after Lady Carson herself saw the 'grey lady' in 1949 that I first met her. She told me of her own experiences. She had been awakened about one-thirty a.m. by her spaniel, Susan, who needed to be let out. Lady Carson put on a dressing-gown and, leaving a light on the landing by her bedroom, took the dog downstairs.

As she passed a switch on the stairs, she accidentally turned the light off, but continued down the stairs, and stood waiting for Susan to return indoors. When she did so, the dog immediately began to run back up the stairs, then suddenly stopped dead in its tracks.

Lady Carson switched on the lights and found the dog whimpering and shivering and looking up the stairs. There, on the landing, a grey-coloured lady was floating noiselessly down towards them. When the figure reached a half-landing, it turned and disappeared through an open door into the old part of the house.

Lady Carson described the figure minutely. Although she could not see the face clearly, she was certain that it was a young woman who wore a very full grey dress that reached to her feet. A pale grey lace cape on her neck and shoulders, and a white ribbon in her hair. The form appeared to be quite solid, but Lady Carson knew by the silence, and by the behaviour of her dog, that she was seeing a ghost, and she was terrified. She told me she had never been so frightened of anything in her life. She felt ice-cold, and began to shiver, until the figure disappeared from sight.

After reports of Lady Carson's experience appeared in print, a former housemaid at Cleve Court wrote to her. The letter related that when she was fifteen years old, she had been busy early one morning in the old part of the house, when she had heard footsteps coming along the passage. She had looked up, expecting to see one of the other maids, but saw instead a lady in an 'old-fashioned dress'. As the girl got up and prepared to leave the room, the grey lady waved a hand and went away.

Cleve Court is now the home of the Hon. Edward Carson, a former Member of Parliament and Lord and Lady Carson's only son. He was hardly a year old when the family moved to Cleve Court, and when he was six, he told his mother that he did not like the lady who walked in the passage outside his room. Lady Carson, who knew this could be no 'normal' lady, asked her son what she looked like. 'I don't know,' little Edward replied, 'I've only seen her walking away.'

Some years ago, Mrs Edward Carson heard footsteps approaching down a passage as she came out of a bathroom. The footsteps seemed to pass her, although she saw nothing. This was the same year that Lady Carson saw the 'grey lady'. She used to say that the apparition was never seen again, and footsteps were never heard after that night. But an ex-hospital sister - who knew nothing of the ghost of Cleve Court - will tell you that she, too, heard footsteps pass her bedroom door very late one night. And perhaps if there were children now at Cleve

Court, the 'grey lady' might appear again.

*San Clu Hotel, Ramsgate, Kent*

The thirteenth-century Stanbury Manor has, or had, a haunted chest that is thought to have come to England with the Spanish Armada.

A few years ago the owner, Mr T. A. Ley, told me that when he bought the chest from an antique shop, the proprietor said he was glad to get rid of it. For there was something queer about it. He had found that he could never keep anything hanging on the walls near the old cedar chest, which was heavily carved on the lid and the sides with such grisly subjects as dismembered limbs and headless bodies.

At Stanbury Manor, Mr Ley first had the chest placed in the armoury until a permanent place could be found for it, and there the first unexplained incident took place. The morning after the chest had been delivered, Mr Ley had occasion to pass through the place. And as he did so, six guns fell off the wall together. He told me that the guns were hung on stout wire, which was not broken, and none of the hangings had come out of the wall.

The chest was next moved to the Leys' bedroom. The same evening, when Mr Ley was assisting his wife in the next room, hanging curtains on a four-poster bedstead, a picture fell off the wall and hit him on the head, although he was at least eighteen inches away from the wall at the time. An odd thing about this incident is that although the picture was a heavy one, Mr Ley hardly felt it strike him - it was perhaps a gentle warning of what *might* happen.

Next day, Mr and Mrs Ley were working in the same room when three more pictures fell off the walls. Two days later, four more pictures came down in the drawing room, which is immediately beneath the Leys' bedroom - where the chest still stood.

Both Mr and Mrs Ley were present at the time. One of the pictures went backwards through some stout pine panelling into a secret passage, which shows the force that was exerted on that occasion. Next day, one more picture came down in the drawing-room. None of the wires were broken, but most of the pictures that fell were damaged.

Two days later, Mr Ley had news of the death of a near relative, and he wondered whether there was any connection between the falling pictures and the death, for there were no further disturbances associated with the chest.

A former curate of Newlyn West recognized the photograph of the Morwenstow 'poltergeist chest' (as the press dubbed the case), and related the following story concerning it. Many years ago, there lived in the village two ladies who owned the chest. They were elderly, and both stone deaf.

They used to communicate with each other by writing notes. They lived like recluses, and were rarely seen by the local people. During their long lives, they had gathered a great deal of junk which they believed to be a valuable collection of antiques. When they decided to put these objects up for sale, the curate went along to examine the articles, but found it very difficult to do business with the old ladies as they wrote their usual notes and expected him to do the same.

On making enquiries afterwards, the curate learned that when the sisters were young, they had gone to visit some friends, and as they arrived late at night, the retired, without unpacking their trunks - which they had placed on a chest by the window in their bedroom.

In the morning, when they awoke, their attention was immediately drawn to the chest. Although weighted down by the heavy trunks, the lid was slowly opening... The two sisters got out of bed and went over, looked inside the chest, and 'what they saw was so horrible that they were both struck deaf on the spot'. They would never reveal what they saw. The two old ladies are long dead - but the story still persists locally.

When I heard this story, I immediately recalled the account of a haunted chest told be a hard-headed surgeon in the Midlands. The bedroom allocated to him when he went to visit a friend was spacious - but dreary, and a large carved chest stood in one corner.

Soon after his arrival, moved by some unexplained impulse, after examining the outside of the chest, he raised the lid. Inside he saw a man lying with his throat cut. With an exclamation of horror and surprise, the surgeon let the lid fall, but almost immediately reopened the chest.

To his great astonishment, it was completely empty. When he mentioned this curious experience to his host the following morning, the latter stared at him in amazement, and told him that a former occupant of that room had in fact committed suicide, and his body was found in the chest in the condition described.

If it was the same chest, was a sight such as the surgeon saw horrible enough to strike two young ladies deaf? One wonders whether on re-opening the chest the ladies, too, found it empty - a fact that might well account for their never revealing what they had seen.

*Grenville Hotel, Bude, Cornwall*

## NEWMARKET, SUFFOLK, HAMILTON STUD LANE

In 1927, a native of this East Anglian town famous for its racecourse, declared that she had seen the ghost of the great jockey Fred Archer, mounted on his favourite grey horse, emerge from a copse, gallop noiselessly towards a woman and her daughter (who both saw the apparition), and then vanish mysteriously.

The woman was familiar with the winner of more than 2,000 races, and was adamant that the figure was Archer - who had then been dead for some forty years. The affair caused something of a sensation, and other local people came forward to say that they, too, had seen the phantom horse and rider in the vicinity of Hamilton Stud Lane - and also on the heath.

Archer was an outstanding jockey who won the Derby five times, but he was known to have a violent temper, and to be intolerant of rivals. He had been greatly depressed by the death of his wife within a year of their marriage. Within two years, he was dead himself, and lies in the same grave with her. His ghost is thought to be responsible for a number of unexplained mishaps on the Newmarket Course, where there have been many instances of horses swerving or slowing or stumbling for no apparent cause.

In 1950, jockey Charlie Smirke said he could not explain why his mount - the Aga Khan's horse Kermanshah - fell in a race at a spot where another horse had fallen the previous year. But jockeys and spectators have, on occasions, seen a white formless shape hovering in the air at this spot at about the height of a horse's head.

*White Hart Hotel, Newmarket, Suffolk*

## NEWTON-LE-WILLOWS, NEAR
## WARRINGTON, LANCASHIRE

Here the ghostly tramping footsteps of the 'chok'd Battalion' are said to be heard sometimes during the month of August. The sounds are reputed to have originated with the Highlanders caught by Cromwell's men here, in August 1648, and summarily hanged on nearby trees [*these manifestations appear to relate to the Battle of Winwick (also known as the Battle of Winwick Pass and the Battle of Red Bank), that was fought on August 15, 1648. It is significant for being the last battle of the Second English Civil War, where Oliver Cromwell defeated a mainly Scottish royalist army, removing the last hope of assistance for the captive Charles I, who had been held at Carisbrooke Castle on the Isle of Wight since November 1647 (after escaping from Hampton Court Palace, where he had been under house arrest after surrendering to the Scots in May 1646 after defeat in the first Civil War). Charles was executed, and the Commonwealth of England established (as a result, Charles II became the new king of Scotland, leading to the Third English Civil War in 1651)*].

*Patten Arms Hotel, Warrington, Lancs.*

## *OXFORD, MERTON COLLEGE

There have long been stories of a room which cannot be slept in. In 1966, the Warden told me that when he was an undergraduate at Merton in the 1920s, he had been told about a haunted room. It was rumoured that a service of exorcism had taken place here, but this particular room has now become part of the Library, and no longer appears to have any ghostly associations.

St John's College. The ghost of Archbishop Laud is said to roll his head across the floor of the Library of the College where he was educated and elected Chancellor of the University of Oxford. Three years later, he was made Archbishop of Canterbury, but in another seven years, he was impeached for high treason by the Long Parliament, and was executed at the Tower of London, in 1645.

*Randolph Hotel, Oxford, Oxon.*

# *PENCAITLAND, EAST LOTHIAN

*[Fountain Hall House is now a Private Residence]*

Fountainhall House - or Penkaet Castle, one of the most interesting mansions in Southern Scotland, is haunted by the ghost of King Charles I, by the ghost of John Cockburn - an owner of the property centuries ago, and an alleged murderer - and by the ghost of Alexander Hamilton, a beggar who was hanged...

The sixteenth-century house is full of interest. Its treasures include a crusader's helmet, a Spanish treasure chest, and part of the chair used by Mary, Queen of Scotland - when she abdicated her throne. The late Professor Holbourn acquired the property in 1923, and I am indebted to his widow, Mrs M. C. S. Holbourn for details of the purported local paranormal activity.

The picturesque rubble-built structure, with its external

staircase leading leading from the courtyard, and an interesting circular tower, was at one time owned by Sir Andrew Dick Lauder. He is reported to have been terrified there as a child when he saw an apparition near one of the fireplaces in an upper room.

The manifestations associated with King Charles I seem to have begun when a four-poster bedstead that was once occupied by the king (and bears a reproduction of his death-mask), was moved into the house after being presented to Professor Holbourn by his students.

In 1924, a relative took a visitor to see the room, and found the bedclothes disarranged, as if the bed had been slept in - although Mrs Anderson, who was responsible for keeping the room tidy, insisted that she had personally left the room - including the bed - perfectly tidy.

Shortly afterwards, another visitor - looking into the room for the purpose of taking a photograph of the historic bedstead, also found that the bed seemed to have been slept in. He found that the photograph he eventually took was under-exposed, and returned to take another. Once again, the bedclothes on this haunted bed were found in a disarranged condition.

On this occasion, Mrs Anderson - after making the bed - had taken the precaution of locking the two doors giving access to the room, and making sure that the windows were secured. In addition, two bricks were placed against the main door. Next day, the bricks were found to have been moved, and although the doors were still locked, and the windows closed, the bedclothes were disturbed yet again.

When a party of students spent a weekend at Penkaet to rehearse a play, all except one were awakened during the early hours of the morning by strange sounds. Two of them sleeping in the room containing the haunted bed noticed what they described as 'a ghastly stain' on the wall, while weird noises went on. Yet in the morning, when all was quiet, they could discover no trace of the mysterious stain.

Miss Avis Dolphin, a survivor of the *Lusitania* disaster, lived at Penkaet Castle for some years the the Holbourns. One night in 1925, while occupying the King Charles Room, she came to Professor and Mrs Holbourn's bedroom - which was situated directly below - to say that someone was moving about downstairs.

Professor Holbourn got up, but by the time they got downstairs, all was quiet. However, as they were returning upstairs again, the both heard - as they reached the first floor - unmistakable creaking noises, as of a person tossing and turning in the King Charles bed so recently vacated by Miss Dolphin. On another occasion, Miss Dolphin felt a light touch on her neck as she climbed upstairs in the dark.

She described it as if someone drew the tip of one finger across her throat. About the same period (and certainly in the same year), Mrs Holbourn saw a faint shining light in several of the passages, which she was never able to account for.

In 1935, an elderly lady was recovering from an illness at Penkaet, and occupying the King Charles bed. Mrs Holbourn's brother was using the bedroom directly below at that time, and one morning he awakened Mrs Holbourn to say that - judging by the sounds he had heard - the old lady must have fallen out of bed, and was knocking for help. On reaching the room, Mrs Holbourn found her friend sleeping soundly.

Sounds of heavy footsteps were frequently heard echoing through the house, together with the noise of heavy furniture being moved about - right from the day the Holbourns moved in. The following year, when friends occupied the house while Professor and Mrs Holbourn were visiting the Island of Foula, they complained of loud shrieks and groans heard during the night. The doors, which were always securely closed at night, were often found open in the morning - even though some had been locked quite securely. One girl refused to sleep in the house after just one night.

After a time, the noises and disturbances became less violent, and whenever a continuous rattling or tapping was heard, one of the Holbourns would call out: 'Now John, that's childish. Stop it.' The noise usually ceased! Such a well-behaved ghost as John Cockburn soon became known as 'the perfect gentleman', but some of the other disturbances were not so easily stopped.

One Christmas Eve, the family and guests, after singing carols, were gathered around the fire in the music room. Everyone present watched amazed as a piece of oak, carved with the family crest, emerged from its place on the wall, paused for a moment, and then returned to its normal position.

Since then, a number of objects have moved apparently of their own volition, including large and heavy furniture:

- Once, an antique cabinet - too heavy to be moved by one person, was found shifted right away from its usual place. A brass jug and basin (brought by Mrs Holbourn's grandfather from Turkey), were placed on top of a cabinet - the jug on its side.

- A bath was filled when nobody turned the tap on or off.

- A strange piece of soap unaccountably appeared in the bathroom.

- A glass case containing a model of the castle cracked and broke in several places when nobody was near it.

- Clocks and watches stopped when placed near a certain wall.

And there was the still unexplained apparition of a small man dressed in a cloak. He was seen by Mrs Holbourn's daughter-in-law to emerge from a cupboard, and walk the whole length of one room, before disappearing into a solid wall.

Many years ago, a local beggar who dealt in wizardry called at Penkaet, but received a brusque welcome from the lady of the house, who chanced to open the door, which was soon shut in his face. In revenge, the spiteful Hamilton resorted to witchcraft and, returning to Penkaet at dead of night, bound the bars of the gate 'with murderous intent'.

Two days later, the lady of the house - Lady Ormiston, and her eldest daughter, were dead - struck down by a mysterious illness. But Hamilton did not escape. He was brought to trial, and after confessing to being responsible for the two deaths and other felonies, he was hanged on Edinburgh Castle Hill. On certain nights of the year, his ghost is said to return to Penkaet, to repeat his wicked deed - but happily it no longer has any effect.

*George Hotel, High Street, Haddington, East Lothian, Scotland*

# *PENRITH, CUMBERLANDSHIRE
## (NOW PART OF CUMBRIA)

*[Eden Hall was demolished many years ago - but the
'West Lodge Lodge' to it remains]*

Just outside Penrith stands Eden Hall, the home of the Musgrave family since the reign of King Henry VI. It is the scene not of a ghost, but of a legend - perhaps the most famous of all family legends: the 'Luck of Eden Hall'. The grand house owes its name to the river flowing through the park, and is renowned for its lovely gardens as much as for the present, rebuilt structure.

The 'Luck' is said to have come into the possession of the family before history was written, in those magical days when 'fairies were common and were seen by everyone'. The story goes that in those far off times, a butler at Eden Hall went to draw water from St Cuthbert's Well, near the house, and came upon a company of fairies holding a revel around a curiously designed and painted glass.

The butler snatched it up, whereupon the fairies tried to wrestle it away from him - but realizing that the mortal was more than a match for them, eventually withdrew, leaving him with the glass and vanishing, after warning him: 'If that glass either break or fall, Farewell the Luck of Eden Hall.'

The glass, six inches tall, is a beautiful example of enamelled and engraved glassware, of a yellowish-green colour, patterned in an almost Moorish style, in blue and white enamel - heightened with red and gold. It is perhaps rather large for fairies, and the more sceptical experts who have examined it consider that it may have once been used as a chalice, and probably came from Spain.

When I last heard, the 'Luck' was securely locked away in a

strong room at the Hall, with the key deposited at the Bank of England.

*Edenhall Hotel, Penrith, Cumb.*

'The Dolphin Inn' stands on the waterfront, and was the headquarters of Sir John Hawkins in 1588, when he was enlisting Cornishmen to fight the Spanish Armada. Judge Jeffreys is reputed to have held court here, in what is now the dining room.

The prisoners were kept in the cellars, where the old kitchen range and lavatory remain to this day. More concrete proof was found a few years ago during repairs, that the inn had been used by smugglers. In the old days, Penzance was the first call for ships coming from the Americas, and it is thought that tobacco was first smoked in England at this tavern, and that potatoes were first eaten here.

Some years ago, during the course of redecorating one of the bedrooms, a door was discovered that led to a small secret closet in the roof. This too had probably been used by smugglers, either as a hiding place, or to secrete their contraband.

As befits such an historic building, the inn has a ghost: an old sea captain dressed in laced ruffles and a three-cornered hat - who died here. I learned when I was here in 1969 that he has not been seen in recent years - but that his footsteps have been heard...

Both the landlord and his wife will tell you that they have heard a heavy and measured tread across the ceiling. It always comes from the direction of the upper part of the tavern, and passes over the bar towards the back part of the building. The sounds never return.

Once, a visitor heard the footsteps, and drew the attention of the landlord's wife to them, saying that he thought he was the only visitor staying at the inn at that time. He was told that he was the 'only human visitor'.

*Rose Hill Private Hotel, Marazion, Penzance, Cornwall*

## PETERBOROUGH, NORTHAMPTONSHIRE

*[Woodcroft Manor is now a Private Residence]*

Nearby Woodcroft Manor was the scene of bitter fighting during the Civil War, when Dr Michael Hudson - a King's Chaplain - took off his clerical clothes and dressed as a soldier, in order to collect about him a band of determined men who succeeded in harassing Cromwell's troops on many occasions.

At length, they met an overwhelming contingent of the Protector's army, and were forced to retreat to Woodcroft Manor, hotly pursued by the Roundheads. Fighting gallantly and bravely against hopeless odds, they were forced to draw back one by one through the rooms of the manor, and then up the staircase, and eventually out onto the roof.

Each man gave his life dearly, but it was all to no avail, and soon Hudson was the only defender capable of putting up a fight. This he did - until he was driven back against a low roof-wall, and then over it. His sword dropped into the moat below, while Hudson clung to the edge of the wall.

Still he refused to surrender. An officer cut off his fingers, and with a cry, he fell to his death - into the night - and the inky moat below...

And still, on summer nights - they say - the clash of steel is heard, and the cries of 'Mercy! Mercy!' - perhaps the last words of the defenceless chaplain that have become impressed forever upon the atmosphere.

*Great Northern Hotel, Peterborough*

*[Old Mint House is now a Private Residence]*

The fourteenth-century Old Mint House has a small bedroom that is long reputed to be haunted by a girl in sixteenth-century costume who died there.

Although the house was built in 1342, the interior was much altered by Dr Andrew Borde, Court Physician to King Henry VIII, in 1542. Today, the twenty-eight roomed mansion is full of interesting nooks and crannies, and next to the Oak Room is the smallest room of all - the Haunted Chamber.

Many people claim to have seen the spectre of the girl who died in agony in this room. A few years ago, the owner told me that his father had seen her, and so did a local clergyman. I heard about a man who volunteered to spend a night in the room, which has only one door, and a single small window.

He was disturbed during the night by a metallic sound, which seemed to come from the direction of the little window. When he looked, he saw a face pressed against the outside of the diamond-paned glass. As he involuntarily cried out, something passed through the wall into the room, and stood by his bed.

He could distinctly see the figure of a young woman in an old-fashioned close-fitting bodice, with tight sleeves, and a dress that was very full at the hips - with a small ruff around the neck. After a moment, the apparition moved back towards the window, and the 'ghost hunter' took the opportunity of dashing out of the room! When he returned with witnesses, the figure had vanished, but he did establish that the window had not been tampered with, and some threads that he had fastened across were still intact.

In 1686, the Mint House was rented by Thomas Dight - a London merchant. Here he installed his young mistress. One evening, he visited the house unexpectedly, and surprised the girl in the arms of a strange man, whereupon Dight, in jealous fury, had his young mistress's lying tongue cut out.

He then had the young people carried to what had been the minting chamber where, at his command, his servants bound the girl, forcing her to watch as they suspended her naked lover in chains from the ceiling, and built a fire on the stone floor beneath him.

There she had to witness the unfortunate man's slow torture - by heat and smoke, until death put an end to his agonies. At night, the body was carried down to the town bridge, and cast over the parapet to be carried out to sea. The girl, still tied hand and foot, was thrust into that little room, and left without food or light to die a lonely, painful death.

Afterwards, her body was buried nearby. The crime may never have been revealed had not Thomas Dight recounted the whole story to friends in a confession he made shortly before he died in 1601.

The ruins of nearby Pevensey Castle - the last stronghold of the Britons after the Roman legions had been withdrawn, and the scene of the first battle of the Norman Conquest - for William the Conqueror landed in Pevensey Bay in 1066 - are reputed to be haunted by several military ghosts.

The eerie sounds of fighting have been heard at night in the vicinity of the ancient walls. It is said that on occasions, an endless procession winds its way across the marshes - from the sea to the castle. Armour and weapons glint in the moonlight - although no sound is heard - as the ghostly army, led by William Rufus (who once fruitlessly attacked the old castle for six days), silently disappears into the moat.

There is a story, too, of the ghostly Lady Jane Pelham, walking on the castle walls at night. She successfully defended the castle in the fourteenth century against an army of Kent, Surrey and Sussex men, while her husband was away in Yorkshire.

*Granville Hotel, Bexhill-on-Sea, Sussex*

# *PLUCKLEY, ASHFORD, KENT - KNOWN AS THE MOST HAUNTED VILLAGE IN KENT

*[Rose Court is now a Private Residence; The Old Mill is destroyed, and located new 'The Pinnocks', a Private Residence; 'Greystones' is a Private Residence, and Surrenden Dering Manor has since been demolished]*

There is a haunting associated with the church of St Nicholas that involves the beautiful Lady Dering, who died several hundred years ago. Her husband - wishing to preserve her loveliness - decreed that she should be attired in a rich gown with a red rose on her breast. Her body was placed in an airtight lead coffin. This coffin was encased in a second and a third, both of lead.

The three coffins were then enclosed in an oaken one, and the quadruple casket buried in the Dering vault, below the Dering Chapel, in the south-east part of the church. In spite of all these encumbrances, Lady Dering is said to walk in the churchyard on certain nights, resplendent in her finery - the red rose at her breast. The story was for a long time a closely guarded secret, and there have been suggestions that she may have been as wicked as she was beautiful.

- Unexplained lights have been reported in the upper half of the stained glass window by the Dering Chapel.

- A woman's voice has been heard in the churchyard.

- Peculiar knocking noises echo in the Dering Chapel at night-time.

The ruins of Surrenden Dering are said to be haunted by a White Lady, another former Lady Dering. Still another member of this 'haunting' family is referred to as the Red Lady - a sad, wistful figure, who walks in the churchyard searching for the baby she lost.

The mellow house named Greystones has a ghostly monk. While Rose Court is haunted by a former owner whose voice has been heard calling her dogs - as she called them so often during her lifetime. The old mill is said to be haunted by a former miller who walks when the moon is full, searching for his lost love.

Opposite 'The Black Horse', is a lane where a schoolmaster once hanged himself, and his ghostly form has been seen swinging from one of the overhanging trees. The ghost of a gipsy, huddled in a shawl, and smoking a pipe, has been glimpsed by people taking a late walk on autumn nights near the crossroads by the little stone bridge.

Nearby, you can see the remains of a hollow oak tree where a highwayman met his death - he was cornered here, and a sword was run through him, pinning him to this very tree. Occasionally, it is said, the whole grisly episode is re-enacted, but without a single sound disturbing the moonlit night. Among other local ghosts are:

- The phantom coach-and-horses, which are said to clatter through the village on certain nights.

- The figure of a soldier that walks through Park Wood.

- A man who fell to his death at the brickworks near the station and still screams.

- The unidentified figure of a woman in the church, in modern dress.

*The George Hotel, High Street, Ashford, Kent*

# POLING, NEAR FELPHAM, SUSSEX:
## ST JOHN'S PRIORY

*[St John's Priory is now a Private Residence]*

A substantial part of the ancient Commandery of the Knights Hospitallers of St John of Jerusalem are incorporated in this old house, and there is said to be a vault outside the chapel walls which contains the tombs of some twelfth-century knights.

On three occasions, six people have heard the unexplained sounds of chanting here. Many residents of the house have frequently reported hearing ghostly music and voices - sometimes growing louder, as if a procession were approaching.

One authority verified the chanting as ancient Gregorian music - the type used at funeral services. A visitor had just entered the house when he heard the chant of men's voices. He closed the door, listened for a moment, and then the sounds died away. He described the experience as the most surprising and ghostly one of his life.

*Norfolk Arms Hotel, Arundel, Sussex*

## POOLE, DORSET

The 'Crown Hotel' in Market Street was reported to be the scene of strange happenings not long ago. They included a single note played on a piano by an invisible hand, and the sound of a body being dragged across the floor.

Two young men who heard the piano 'playing' in an upstairs stable, went to investigate, and found the room empty. Later, a 'fluorescent mist' was said to have drifted down the staircase, floated across the courtyard, and out of the hotel entrance. The 'mist' was described as about the size of a child's head.

An Australian staying at the hotel decided to prove that the story was the result of imagination, and painted five crosses on the door of the haunted room, closed the door, bolted it, and went down to the courtyard to watch. To his horror, the door opened of its own accord as he stood there, watching.

Landlord Alan Brown said that most of the mysterious noises started when the stable room was altered, although there had been unexplained sounds in the past from this part of the house - including one which sounded as though a body were being dragged across the top floor.

*The Crown Hotel, Market Street, Poole, Dorset*

## *POTTER HEIGHAM, NORFOLK

The famous old three-arched bridge here - known to thousands of yachtsmen and sailors who frequent the Broads, has long been reputed to be haunted by a striking and recurring manifestation.

The story goes back to the eighteenth century, when Sir Godfrey Haslitt married the beautiful Lady Evelyn Carew, on May 31st 1742, in Norwich Cathedral. But the wedding had been brought about - so goes the legend - by the bride's contract with the devil, who demanded his price immediately after the wedding.

On the stroke of midnight, the bridge was seized at the hall and carried, struggling and screaming, to a waiting coach with four coal-black horses stomping and snorting in the night air. Taking the terrified girl with them, the occupants of the coach - who looked like skeletons, tore down the drive and raced away down the road towards Potter Heigham.

Few people were aboard, but those who were saw a luminous coach dash past, swaying from side to side, its wheels glowing with phosphorescence and sparks flying from them as they sped over the road - driven by a skeleton.

Arriving at Potter Heigham bridge, the coach swung across the narrow roadway, smashed against the wall of the bridge in the centre, broke into a thousand pieces, and was flung - coach, horses, occupants and all - over the parapet and into the River Thurne below.

And each midnight of May 31st, it is said, the phantom coach repeats its fatal journey. Well-known yachtsman Charles Sampson told me that he saw the arresting spectacle in 1930 with two friends, and that he knew two other people who had seen it. When I was there a few years ago, I located several local inhabitants who said they knew people who had seen the phantom coach, but I was unable to trace any first-hand witnesses.

*Central Hotel, St Georges Road, Great Yarmouth, Norfolk*

## RAYNHAM, NORFOLK

Raynham Hall is the home of the famous 'Brown Lady' ghost.

Captain Marryat, the novelist, saw the ghost when he stayed at the house, occupying the room where a portrait of the Brown Lady hangs on the wall. Her identity is unknown. It was while he was walking along the corridor towards his room one evening, that Captain Marryat saw the apparition...

The Brown Lady grinned at im in a 'diabolical manner'. As he happened to be carrying pistols, he discharged one straight at the figure - at point-blank range - hoping to prove whether it was a ghost he saw, or someone playing a trick. The figure disappeared immediately, and the bullet, which he always swore passed through the figure, was found embedded in a door behind where she had appeared.

In November 1926, Lady Townshend, staying at Raynham Hall - the seat of the Townshend family, stated that her son and a friend met the Brown Lady on a staircase. Later, when they saw the portrait, they both declared that this was the woman they had met - although they had never heard the ghost story.

The late Marchioness of Townshend told my friend Dennis Bardens that she had seen the Brown Lady several times, and in his *Ghosts and Hauntings*, he recounts the story of Colonel Loftus and a man named Hawkins, who saw the figure of a woman in period dress in an upstairs corridor.

Later, she was seen again by the Colonel. This time face to face. He described an aristocratic-looking lady, dressed in brocade [*a rich fabric woven with a raised pattern, typically with gold or silver thread*], her hair in a coif [*a woman's close-fitting cap, now only worn under a veil by nuns*], and her features lit by an unearthly light - and, empty eye-sockets where her eyes should have been!

In 1936, two photographers took a series of photographs of the interior of Raynham Hall for *Country Life*. One of them, Captain Provand, had taken one shot of the ancient staircase, down which the ghost is said to have walked, and was preparing to take another, when his assistant - Mr Indra Shira - remarked that he could see a shadowy form on the stairs.

As the form glided down the stairs towards the photographers, another exposure was taken, and when the photograph was developed, the shadowy form of a hooded female figure was discernible. The original photograph is in the *Country Life* photographic library, and experts who have examined it and the place are satisfied that there was no trickery.

*Victoria Hotel, Holkham, Norfolk*

## READING, BERKSHIRE

A four-roomed house in Oxford Road was reported to harbour the hazy figure of a grey-haired old lady a few years ago.

The occupants, MR and Mrs Edgar Morley and their son and two daughters - then aged seventeen, eleven and nine respectively - had only been at the house a week when Mrs Morley saw the figure in the kitchen. After a few minutes, it vanished as she watched. She told her husband of her experience, and they both laughed about it - until she saw the same figure shortly afterwards, and subsequently no less than ten times during the following three months.

Alan Morley also saw the figure, and Mr Morley - a down-to-earth traffic warden - sensed rather than saw the form, while the two younger children became so frightened that they slept on a mattress in the living room.

A previous occupant of the house, elderly Mrs Davies, died here in 1961, and her description seems to fit exactly that of the ghost. Always just before it was seen or sensed, there was an overwhelming scent of flowers which vanished after the ghost disappeared.

*Great Western Hotel, Reading, Berks.*

# *READING, BERKSHIRE.

*['The Roebuck' is now a Private Residence]*

The Roebuck Hotel, on the Thames, is haunted by:

- Mysterious footsteps, which pace the corridors late at night.

- Unexplained hammering on doors.

- Disarrangement of furniture, and by opening locked doors and windows.

Mr Alex Wolfenden - the landlord - said in February 1966 that 'the house is definitely haunted. Nobody has actually seen a ghost, but there have been some very strange things happenings, particularly in the Admiral's Room, which is never occupied, and I certainly wouldn't sleep there myself.'

The Admiral, after who the room is named, died at the Roebuck over two hundred years ago, in obscure circumstances - possibly being burned to death. There were four rooms in the oldest part of the ancient oak-beamed hotel that were permanently unoccupied, because the landlord thought guests would be frightened by things that happen there.

The Roebuck Hotel, Reading, Berks.

## *RICHMOND, SURREY

The old Palace of Richmond was long said to be the scene of scandalous happenings, some concerning Queen Elizabeth I - who died here on March 24th 1603, after having lain in a stupor for days on the point of death.

A persistent and curious story was current at the time, to the effect that the ghostly figure of the great queen was repeatedly seen pacing the rooms of the palace, while she was still alive but unconscious. Years later, there were stories of the old gatehouse - one of the few surviving remnants of the palace, being haunted.

It was from a window over the gatehouse that the Queen's ring was thrown, after she died, to a waiting horseman, who sped the news to Scotland that James I was King of England - that the reign of the Stuarts had begun.

*Richmond Hill Hotel, Richmond Hill, Richmond, Surrey*

# RINGCROFT, GALLOWAY, SCOTLAND

*[The Ridge-top houses have long since been demolished]*

Commonly known as the Ringcroft Disturbances, or the Ringcroft Poltergeist, these allegedly paranormal happenings took place in 1695. They are thoroughly attested and authenticated in a nineteen-page report published at the time, and signed by the ministers of five neighbouring parishes, by the lairds of Colline and Milhouse, and by other persons of repute who were eyewitnesses of the remarkable events.

There were a number of young children in the Ringcroft household of Andrew Mackie, but all of them seem to have been under observation at the time of the occurrence of important phenomena. The disturbances began in February, although the house had long had the reputation of being haunted.

The first inexplicable incidents took place at night and outside the house, when Mackie discovered that all his cattle had been let out from their sheds - their tethering ropes were broken. The same thing happened the following night, when one of the beasts was found tied to an overhead beam, so that its feet scarcely touched the ground.

A great quantity of peat was then found to have been brought into the house. For several days, stones were thrown all over the place - but never on a Sunday, and mostly at night - although sometimes in daylight too.

A blanket and stool were combined into a shape resembling a sitting person. Pot hooks and hangers disappeared, and were found days later in a place that had already been searched. After an interval, there was more stone-throwing, and it was noticed that the stones seemed only about half their normal weight. They were now appearing more frequently - and on

Sundays, too - and more especially when members of the household were at prayer.

A month after the disturbances commenced, they ceased abruptly, and the family thought that their troubles were over. But 'it' returned, 'more violent than ever', after seven days of peace. Stones were again thrown, and more often, and they seemed to be heavier, for 'they hurt more when they hit'.

A staff was wielded invisibly, and hit witnesses several times on the shoulders and sides. People in bed were disturbed. Knockings sounded on doors and furniture. Things became so bad that some of the occupants were driven out of the house.

Mackie himself was hit on the forehead, pushed at the shoulders, and felt something like nails scratch the skin on his head. Sometimes too, people were dragged along by their clothes - including the local miller, who cried out for help.

One night, the children had their bed clothes removed, and they were beaten about the hips - the sound of the beatings being distinctly heard by other occupants of the house, and sounding as though done by a man's hand. At the same time, various objects were seen by many witnesses to move about the house of their own accord.

A voice saying 'Hush! Hush!' was now heard at the end of each sentence when the family were at prayers. Each time the dog, hearing the unfamiliar voice, would bark and run to the door. Sometimes, whistles and groans were heard. Fires were started. Lumps of burning peat were thrown at the family while they were at prayer. 'Fire-balls' fell in and about the house, but fortunately, they vanished as soon as they fell. Very hot stones were found in the children's beds, and they were still too hot to handle nearly two hours later.

The local magistrate arranged for the examination of every person who had ever lived in the house built twenty-eight years before. During these enquiries, some human bones were found buried just outside the building, giving rise to the suggestion that a murder had been committed in the house, and the body buried outside.

It was thought that the uneasy spirit of the victim might be the cause of all the trouble. A test, often used in witchcraft trials, where suspects were made to touch the bones, achieved no result, and the next five local ministers attempted to lay the ghost with a service of exorcism.

But no sooner had they started, when stones were thrown - apparently from nowhere, not only at the ministers at prayer, but all over the house. Some of the witnesses were levitated by something gripping their feet: the five ministers all attested to this phenomenon.

During the days that followed, more stones and other objects were thrown about the house. Children were pulled out of bed. Sheep were tied together. Furniture was set on fire. Whistles and groans were heard. The house itself was set on fire seven times in one day. And a 'black thing' without shape - but like a cloud - was first seen in a corder. It increased in size so that it seemed to fill the whole house...

Next day, May 1st, 1695, the disturbances ceased as mysteriously as they had begun.

*Hamilton Arms Hotel, Girvan, Ayrshire, Scotland*

## *ROCHESTER CASTLE, ROCHESTER, KENT

For nearly a thousand years, the Norman castle keep of this impressive ruin defied the ravages of time, and of battles. Designed by Gundulf the Good, it was built in 1098, and has seen many stirring times. On Good Friday, in the year 1264, Simon de Montfort - Earl of Leicester - besieged the castle, which was defended by Ralph de Capo, a crusader.

Inside with de Capo was his betrothed, the lovely Lady Blanche de Warenne. Among the men under Simon de Montfort was one Gilbert de Clare, a knight and a rejected suitor of the Lady Blanche. When the siege was raised, de Capo left the castle to pursue the retreating rebels, and de Clare, seizing his opportunity, disguised himself in a suit of armour resembling that worn by de Capo and entered the castle.

Inside, he sought out Lady Blanche high up on the southern battlement, watching the flight of the insurgents. Looking back at the castle, de Capo saw his lady struggling in the hands of a man he knew must be an enemy. Being a renowned archer, he seized a bow and arrow from one of his men, and sent an arrow speeding towards the stranger molesting his beloved.

The arrow sped true to its mark, but glanced off the armour de Clare was wearing, and pierced the breast of the Lady Blanche, mortally wounding her.

That same night - according to reports - her ghost walked the battlements in a white robe, her raven hair streaming in the breeze, the fatal arrow still embedded in her bosom. On the anniversary of the tragedy, she is still said to haunt the battlements of the old castle, bewailing the sad fate of having been killed by her lover. I traced two people who claimed to have seen her on different occasions.

A variation of this story tells of de Clare pursuing the Lady Blanche around the battlements, and of her hiding within the round tower, where she was found by her old suitor. According to this tale, it was here that de Capo spotted him and shot the fatal arrow. Yet another version suggests that rather than risk capture, she threw herself off the top of the round tower, and so met her death by suicide.

At all events, there seems little doubt that she died a violent death, and it seems difficult to dismiss all the odd happenings at Rochester Castle - including unexplained footsteps in this part of the ruin - as figments of the imagination.

The Old Burial Ground of St Nicholas, in the former moat of Rochester Castle, is reputed to be haunted by a white bearded figure. This is the churchyard where Charles Dickens wished to be buried, and he may have been laid to rest here - the spot he loved best in his beloved Rochester - had not the burial ground been out of use at the time of his death, and had not the nation thought to honour him by burial in Westminster Abbey.

Yet perhaps the great novelist had his way in the end, for there are many reports of a spectre seen here at night. A spectre that takes the form of an elderly man with a beard, slowly and lovingly wandering among the tombs of long-forgotten men and women who dwelt at Rochester.

There is a story, too, that at Christmas time, when the 'moon-faced clock' over the Corn Exchange strikes midnight, the ghost of Dickens returns to this spot, which he immortalized in *The Mystery of Edwin Drood*. Reports of this apparition began to circulate within a few years of Dickens's death in June, 1870

*King's Head Hotel, Rochester, Kent*

# *ST ALBANS, HERTFORDSHIRE

*[Battlefield House has since been demolished]*

Battlefield House in Chequer Street, an Elizabethan half-timbered building with a modern shop front, has foundations of a very early building made from flint and stone, similar to that used for the wonderful Abbey nearby. It was probably one of the buildings belonging to the Abbey at one time.

Here, noises resembling galloping horses, and the clash of armour, are alleged to have been repeatedly heard over the years. It is interesting to recall that the house stands on the reputed site of the Battle of St Albans - one of the fierce encounters of the Wars of the Roses.

A previous occupant found the house a friendly one - free from ghosts and ghostly phenomena, but he frequently had the feeling that he was being watched. Although he instinctively looked round to see who it was, there was never anybody present. On the other hand, when he had guests in the house, they would often complain of feeling unhappy in the house, and of noticing a brooding eeriness about the place.

There seems to be good evidence that over the years, unaccountable noises resembling the clash of weapons on armour, galloping horses and the chanting of monks, have been heard here.

St Albans is named after a Roman soldier convert, who suffered martyrdom here in the year 303, the first Christian martyr in England.

Nearby Salisbury Hall, an old moated manor house was built in the seventeenth century, and purchased secretly by King Charles II for Nell Gwynne, whose ghost is one of the visitors from the past to this historic house.

Beneath the black and white floor in the hall, there is a Tudor floor of bricks, and beneath that again, a floor of stones even older. What lies beneath *that*, nobody yet knows. It does not seem unreasonable to think that on this site there has been a building of one sort or another for many centuries.

During the Civil War, Salisbury Hall was used by King Charles I as headquarters and armoury. In 1668, King Charles II found another use for it. That year he had started his affair with orange-seller Nell Gwynne, an association that lasted until the King's death sixteen years later.

It was for Nel the he purchased Salisbury Hall. Today, you can still see the little oak-beamed cottage overlooking the moat, a property known as Nell Gwynne's Cottage - where one of the intimate and moving incidents of history is reputed to have taken place.

It is said that Nell, concerned for the future of one of her children by Charles, after he had refused the boy a title, held the child out of the window of the cottage, dangling him over the moat and threatening to drop him until Charles called out: 'Pray, spare the Duke of St Albans!'

The ghost of pretty Nell has been seen at the Hall, both on the staircase, and in the panelled hall by, among others, Sir Winston Churchill's step-father, George Cornwallis-West. He told of seeing the young and beautiful figure of a woman standing in the corner of the hall.

She looked intently at him, and then turned and vanished into the adjoining passage. He followed at once, but could find no trace of the 'lovely girl'. Weeks later, he was looking at prints of Nell Gwynne, and realized how much she was like the figure he had observed. Cornwallis-West had always been very sceptical about ghosts - until he encountered Nell Gwynne at Salisbury Hall.

343

The present owners of the Hall - charming Mr and Mrs Walter Goldsmith, will tell you all about the ghosts there, and some of the fascinating history of the beautiful house and gardens. The Edwardian era gave the Hall a revival of its great days, for Lady Randolph Churchill had married George Cornwallis-West.

They had bought the property, and the society of the day came to the house: Dame Nellie Melba, Italian actress Eleonora Duse, King Edward VII himself. To write his speeches in the garden, young Winston Churchill would also come to visit his mother and stepfather.

Mrs Goldsmith told me about the haunted bedroom. About the unmistakable footsteps she has heard in the passage outside her bedroom door. The passage where the sounds appear to originate now ends in a bathroom, but once, it led into the old Tudor wing of the house - destroyed in 1818.

Thinking the footsteps must be those of her husband, Mrs Goldsmith waited for them to return, expecting him to look in on her - but they did *not* return. In the morning, her husband told her that he had slept all night without stirring. Soon afterwards, the Goldsmiths were visited by the daughter of Sir Nigel Gresley, who lived at Salisbury Hall for fives years before the Second World War. She asked Mrs Goldsmith whether she had heard the ghostly footsteps, and said they were always being troubled by strange footsteps in the night when they were there.

Mr Goldsmith told me he had found a reference in an old book - found within the house - to a cavalier, who had died unpleasantly at the Hall and whose ghost, complete with a sword sticking through him, used to be seen frequently.

The bedroom over the entrance hall is also haunted. Here, children have been disturbed over the years by 'something' standing by their beds, not once but on many occasions. A governess, spending a night in the same room, saw 'something terrifying' come out of the wall near the fireplace, and stand by the bed. She would never spend another night in the house.

In the top storey of the house, there are four rooms, their ceilings sloped to the contours of the roof. In the smallest, there is a secret chamber, made in the thickness of the wall, and leading up among the rafters - a 'Priest's Hole', where a hunted fugitive could be hidden and fed.

In one of these roof rooms, there is said to have been a suicide. Altogether, Salisbury Hall is a fascinating place. A labyrinth of secret passages, sliding panels, and hidden rooms, But even on the brightest summer days, the shadows somehow lengthen strangely in the mellow hall, and one is glad to walk in the peaceful gardens.

*The Noke Hotel, St Albans, Herts.*

## *ST IVES, CORNWALL

A recently built house was haunted by the sound of footsteps made by high-heeled shoes. They used to pass along one particular passage, halt outside one particular door, and after a moment, a loud knock would sound, apparently form the direction of the door.

The footsteps never receded. There never was a second knock. Nor did the door ever open. Though perhaps other doors in the house did. At all events, there were the sounds of doors opening and closing at other times - and occasionally, the sounds of footsteps heard mounting the stairs, but these were never heard descending.

According to local tradition, phantom bells have long been heard in the vicinity of the famous bay. They sound way out at sea, and never seem to have an explanation, unless it can be the wind playing peculiar tricks with the sound of the heavy seas rolling in from the Atlantic.

*Garrack Hotel, St. Ives, Cornwall*

## SALTWOOD, NEAR HYTHE, KENT

Mysterious lights, and a strange figure, were seen in the densely wooded area around Saltwood a few years ago, and there was much talk of ghosts and black magic in the village.

Four teenagers, walking from Saltwood to Sandling Station [*now disused*], saw a ball of fire on the top of a hill about eighty feet away. Walking down a dip, they lost sight of it, but when they continued up the opposite hill, a figure suddenly appeared on the road ahead, 'like a man in a red cloak carrying a lantern', one of them said.

It shuffled up the hill, and when it reached the railway bridge, disappeared. As they went down to the station, they had to be careful not to slip on the frozen puddles - yet just outside the station, where the figure had vanished, it seemed quite warm.

A young man and his girlfriend were passing the football field at Brockhill School, when they saw a strange light - a kind of glow - coming from behind some trees and lighting up the field. They could see a dark figure standing in the middle of the field. The light seemed brighter as they approached it, and then - abruptly - it disappeared. The girl screamed and fainted.

There are a number of reports of a ghost being seen near Slaybrook Corner, the reputed scene of an ancient battle. The ghost may be that of William Tournay, a wealthy and eccentric landowner who died about sixty years ago, and who is buried on an island in the middle of a nearby lake. According to other reports, the apparition is that of a Roman soldier.

*Hotel Imperial, Hythe, Kent*

## SAMPFORD PEVERELL, NEAR TIVERTON, DEVON

*[The 'haunted house' in 'Higher Town' has since been demolished]*

The scene of a classic ghost story, three years of poltergeist activity, recounted by the Rev. Caleb Colton, in the *Narrative of the Sampford Ghost* (1810).

The house affected was occupied by the servants and family of Mr John Chave. Here the apparition of a woman was seen by an earlier occupant, who had also reported unexplained noises - but these reports were discounted.

A second series of disturbances began in April, 1810. The 'chambers of the house were filled, even in daytime, with thunderous noises, and upon any person's stamping several times on the floors of the upstairs rooms, they would find themselves imitated - only much louder - by the mysterious agency!'

There were a number of women servants, and at night they were frequently beaten the invisible hands - until they were black and blue. Mr Colton stated that he heard upwards of two hundred violent blows in one night delivered upon a bed - the sound resembling that of a strong man striking it with all his might, with clenched fists.

One of the young servant girls - Ann Mills - received a black eye and a swelling as big as a turkey's egg on her cheek. Ann was among those who received blows from an invisible hand while in bed. Mrs Mary Dennis and young Mary Woodbury - two other servants - swore that they were beaten until they were numb, and were sore for many days afterwards.

The disturbances became so bad, that the servants refused to use the room in which they were so severely handled, whereupon Mr and Mrs Chave offered to share their own. Still, there was little peace: candles and candlesticks moved about the room of their own volition.

Once, Mr Chave narrowly missed being hit on the head when a large iron candlestick came hurtling at him in the dark. Colton relates how he 'often heard the curtains of the bed violently agitated, accompanied by a loud and almost indescribably motion of the rings. These curtains, four in number, were - to prevent their motion - often tied up, each in one large knot.

'Every curtain of that bed was agitated, and the knots thrown and whirled about with such rapidity, that it would have been unpleasant to be within the sphere of their action. This lasted about two minutes, and concluded with a noise resembling the tearing of linen - Mr Taylor and Mr Chave, of Mere, being also witnesses. Upon examination, a rent was found across the grain of a strong new cotton curtain.'

Raps, knockings, rattling noises, and a 'sound like that of a man's foot in a slipper coming downstairs and passing through a wall' were repeatedly experienced. Once, says Mr Colton, he was in the act of opening a door, when there was a violent rapping on the opposite side of the same door. He paused, and the rapping continued. Suddenly, he opened the door and peered out, candle in hand. There was nothing to see. Sometimes, the noises were so violent in a room, that he really thought that the walls and ceiling would collapse.

Among the independent witnesses for the Sampford ghost, there is the Governor of the County Gaol - whom came to see the strange happenings, and brought with him a sword, which he placed at the foot of the bed, with a huge folio Bible on top of it.

Both were flung through the air, and dashed against the opposite wall - seven feet away. Mr Taylor, who was in the house at the time, but not with the Gaol Governor, was roused by the shrieks coming from the room, and when he entered, he saw the sword suspended in the air - pointing towards him. Within a moment, it clattered to the floor.

Towards the end of the curious events at Sampford Peverell, there were suggestions that the tenant, Mr John Chave, was faking the disturbances in order to purchase the property cheaply. When this rumour reached the people of the village, and those of Tiverton - five miles away - public sympathy for the occupants of the house quickly melted away, and on more than one occasion, Mr Chave was very severely handled.

The Rev. Caleb Colton rejected this explanation, stating that although the public were given to understand that the disturbances had ceased, in fact, as the immediate neighbourhood well knew, they continued 'with unabating [*not weakening or losing intensity*] influence'.

Mr Chave had no intention of buying the property, said Mr Colton. Indeed, he was making every effort to procure another home - on any terms. As if to confirm all this, the disturbances at length obliged the whole family to leave the house, at a great loss and inconvenience.

Mr Colton was criticized for his participation in the affair. It was not generally known that he offered one-hundred-pounds of the two two-hundred-and-fifty pounds to be paid to anyone who could give such information as might lead to a discovery of the answer to the mysterious events: the money was never claimed.

Years later, it was discovered that the house had double walls, with a passage between, which could have considerably assisted conscious trickery. There was also the possibility that the premises were used by smugglers, who might have produced the weird noises for their own purpose - and of course, many a parson was known to help the smugglers in days gone by.

*Great Western Hotel, Exeter, Devon*

## *SANDFORD ORCAS, NEAR SHERBORNE, DORSET

The fine Tudor manor house here is haunted by the figure of a farmer, who hanged himself from a trap-door - which has since been boarded up.

Colonel Francis Claridge leased the house from the Medicott family. The Claridges became quite certain that strange things happened in the nursery wing of the house when, in 1966, their daughter attempted to spend a night there, but left screaming and returning to her own room in the early hours. Although she had not seen anything, she had heard loud knocks on the door of her room, and also a weird, dragging noise.

Mrs Claridge will tell you that she has several times glimpsed the white-smocked figure of the long-dead farmer 'flitting past the kitchen window, between two-thirty and three-fifty-five p,m.' She has also seen, several times, an old lady in a red dress, mounting a staircase in the house.

Mr and Mrs J. A. Allen, the former footman and housekeeper at the manor, were afraid to go upstairs on their own at night, and thought that the stone carvings of apes above the porch 'laughed in the moonlight', while at the church across the road, 'chains and keys rattled, and footsteps came running down the steps, as though someone was being chased'.

Mrs L. Gates of Taunton spent a night in the chilly little bedroom in the nursery wing and saw the ghost, 'at the foot of my bed, swaying and outlined against the bedroom window. He was in evening dress. His face appeared evil-looking. For what seemed quite a while, he stood there, and then disappeared.'

Other disturbances include mysterious music, which seems to

originate from a harpsichord in an empty room. A curious haze of blue smoke appears in certain rooms. Unexplained voices are heard from the inner courtyard or rear wing, and footsteps pace deserted corridors. A family photograph taken by Mary Claridge in the garden shows a strange unidentified figure, which appears to be wearing a white smock.

The BBC. went to Sandford Orcas, and one of their camera team claimed to see the figure of the man which passed repeatedly the kitchen window. He appeared to be wearing a white milking smock, and an old-fashioned type of farmer's hat. Local people told Colonel Claridge that a good many years ago, the body of the tenant farmer at that time was found hanging in the house: he was wearing a white smock.

*Half Moon Hotel, Sherborne, Dorset*

## *SANDRINGHAM, NORFOLK

The great country house and estate - purchased by King Edward VII when Prince of Wales in 1862 - and ever since a favourite royal retreat, has a ghost that usually gets up to its tricks during the Christmas holidays. There are repeated reports of 'hollow footsteps' being heard in deserted corridors in the servants quarters; of doors that open by themselves - and of lights that switch themselves on and off.

The disturbances usually begin on Christmas Eve, and continue for several weeks. Among the happenings, for which there appear to be no explanation, are:

- Christmas cards which are found moved from one wall to another.

- Bedclothes that are stripped off freshly-made beds.

- And heavy breathing noises that seem to originate from a deserted room off the footmen's corridor on the second floor.

A year or two ago, things were so bad that housemaids refused to enter this room - for cleaning and polishing - unless someone else was also with them. One footman refused to sleep in the room assigned to him, after he claimed to have seen something which he described as 'looking like a large paper sack, breathing in and out like a grotesque lung'.

He also heard heavy and regular breathing apparently emanate from the curious bulging object. King George V died hiere in 1936, and King George VI - in 1952.

*Feathers Hotel, Sandringham, Norfolk*

# SANDWOOD BAY, CAPE WRATH, SUTHERLAND, SCOTLAND

This bleak and isolated beach, on the extreme north-east tip of the mainland of Great Britain, has long been reputed to be haunted. Visitors to this desolate but beautiful district have brought back convincing stories of an apparition and strange happenings at the deserted cottages here.

One autumn afternoon, a crofter and his son strayed into Sandwood Bay as they gathered firewood. The beach was utterly deserted as they collected the timber from long-forgotten wrecks, and they were about to set off home as evening drew on, when suddenly their pony showed signs of fright, and they became aware of a bearded sailor standing close to them.

He was wearing sea-boots, a sailor's cap, and a dark weather-stained tunic with brass buttons. The strange figure that had not been there a moment before, shouted to them that the driftwood was his property, and the crofter and his son promptly dropped the wood they had collected, and fled.

One August afternoon, the same figure was seen by a boy - and the fishing party he was accompanying. The squat figure of a sailor was first noticed close to a sandy knoll, and then walking along the crest of a sand-dune, before disappearing behind a small hill.

Those who saw the figure noticed in particular, the sailor's cap - and the brass buttons on his tunic. Thinking that the man must be a poacher, the boy was sent off to find out what he could. He returned, white-faced and shaken, to report that he could find no one, and there was no trace of any footprints in the sand at the spot where the figure had been seen.

Sandwood Cottage has stood here untenanted for many years - perhaps the most remote and solitary habitation in the whole of Scotland. A few years ago, Angus Morrison - an old fisherman, spent a night at the cottage, and heard footsteps outside, and a tapping at the window on the ground floor. When he looked towards the window, he saw the face of a bearded sailor peering into the cottage.

His visitor wore a peaked sailor's cap, and a tunic with brass buttons. But when Angus opened the door and looked all round the cottage, there was no one there. On another occasion, he was awakened in the cottage by the sensation that he was being suffocated by a thick, black mass, that seemed to be pressing down on him.

A local shepherd, Sandy Gunn, will tell you that he once spent a night at the same cottage, and heard distinct but ghostly footsteps walking about the ground floor. He is quite satisfied that they were not caused by any human being, or by an animal. It is thought that the footsteps may have some connection with a wealthy Australian who came here several times, and seemed to fall completely under the spell of this fascinating spot before he died in Australia some years before the shepherd's experience.

More recently, a couple of English visitors camped at Sandwood Cottage. During the night, they were disturbed by fearful noises, and the whole cottage seemed to vibrate with crashes and bangs that sounded like:

- Doors being flung open and slammed shut.

- Windows being smashed.

- And heavy, tramping footsteps, loud enough to have been made by a horse.

It all seemed to originate from the rooms over their heads. No explanation was ever discovered, and these visitors told the local postmaster that nothing would ever persuade them to spend another night at Sandwood Cottage.

*Garbet Hotel, Kinlochbervie, Sutherland, Scotland*

## *SARRATT, NEAR RICKMANSWORTH, HERTFORDSHIRE

Rose Hall was occupied during my childhood by my maternal grandparents, and was the scene of the first ghost story I ever heard. The account of the brilliantly-coloured ghost which disturbed a visitor by leaning on the bottom of his bed, is recounted by Catherine Crowe in her *Night Side of Nature*.

Falling quickly asleep after a tiring journey, the visitor was first awakened by the barking of dogs, and he heard his host in the adjoining bedroom open his window to quieten them. He went to sleep again, but was soon awakened once more - this time by an extraordinary pressure upon his feet.

By the light in the chimney-corner, he saw the figure of a well-dressed man in the act of stooping and supporting himself on the bedstead. The figure wore a blue coat with bright gilt buttons, but the head was not visible because of the bed-curtains, which looped back so that they just concealed that part of the person.

Since in his haste to get to bed, the visitor had dropped his clothes at the foot of the bed, he thought at first that it must be his host come in to pick them up, which rather surprised him. But as he raised himself upright in bed, and was about to enquire into the reason for the visit, the figure passed on - disappearing.

Realising that he had locked the door, and becoming somewhat puzzled, the house-guest jumped out of bed and carefully searched the room. He found the doors locked on the inside as he had left then, and yet he could discover no trace of his mysterious visitor. He noticed that the time was ten minutes after two, and he returned to bed hoping for some rest, but was unable to sleep again that night. He lay awake till seven - puzzling his brain as to how his visitor could have entered and left the room.

In the morning, when his host and his wife asked how he had slept, he mentioned first that he had been awakened by the barking of the dogs. His host told him that two strange dogs had found their way into the yard, and he had called to his own animals. Then the visitor mentioned his curious experience, fully expecting that this would be explained, or laughed at - but to his surprise, the story received great attention. He was told that there was a tradition of such a spectre haunting that room.

It seemed that many years before, a gentleman so attired had been murdered in the room, under 'frightful circumstances', and his head cut off. From time to time, people occupying the room claimed to see the brightly-coloured figure, but the head was never seen. As proof of the story, the visitor was requested to prolong his visit, to be introduced to the rector of the parish - who would furnish him with such evidence as to leave no doubt in his mind but that the room was haunted. But the thought of another night in the room was too frightening: the traveller took his leave.

A short time afterwards, he was dining with some ladies who came from Hertfordshire, when he chanced to refer to his visit to Sarratt, saying that while he was there, he had met with a very extraordinary adventure which he was totally unable to explain. Thereupon one of the ladies immediately said that she hoped he had not had a visit from the headless gentleman in a blue coat and gilt buttons, who was said to have been seen by many people at that house.

Some years ago, after discovering that in the nineteenth century, the ghost had been so troublesome that a prayer-meeting had been held at Rose Hall, convened for the express purpose of laying the ghost, I took the trouble to get in touch with the Secretary of the Hertfordshire Baptist Association - but he was unable to find any further information on the subject.In 1962, I took a party of Ghost Club members to Sarratt, and three of them had no difficulty in immediately locating the haunted room - although, as far as I know, nothing untoward has happened there for many years now.

The ancient little parish church of Sarratt stands a mile south of the village, on the site of a Roman cemetery. Local tradition explains the considerable distance between the village and the church, by maintaining that it was found impossible to build the church in the vicinity of the village green, some eight hundred years ago. For each morning, after a start had been made, the stones and other materials would be found moved down the long hill a mile away.

At length, it was decided to bow to a possibly 'higher authority', and the church was erected in its present position. The west window is said to be older than Westminster Abbey.

*Victoria Hotel, Rickmansworth, Herts.*

# *SAWSTON, CAMBRIDGESHIRE

*[Sawston Hall is now a Private Residence]*

Sawston Hall, a noble Tudor house, has been the ancestral home of the Huddleston family for over four hundred years. Yet no one - Captain Reginald Eyre-Huddleston told me - can sleep undisturbed in the haunted Tapestry Room.

In the magnificent Great Hall, there is a portrait of Queen Mary Tudor. In 1553, before she became queen, she spent a night in the Tapestry Room. The scheming Duke of Northumberland sent a message asking her to go to London to see her ailing brother - King Edward VI - without telling her that the King was already dead.

Northumberland planned to imprison Mary and to put his daughter-in-law, Lady Jane Grey, on the throne, to retain the power which he exercised over Edward VI. But a message reached Mary when she was at Hoddesdon, warning her that Northumberland's message was a trap. She turned back to Sawston Hall, then the home of John Huddleston - a Papist - where she sought shelter for the night.

At dawn, her rest in the Tapestry Room was disturbed - not by a ghost, but by the arrival of a band of Northumberland's men. Hastily disguised as a milkmaid, Mary escaped in the nick of time with a few friends. At a safe distance from the house, they reined in their horses, and looked back at Sawston Hall.

The house was in flames. Unable to find Mary, Northumberland's men had set the place alight. 'Let it burn, Mary told her companions. 'When I am Queen, I will build Huddleston a finer house' - and she was as good as her word. Stones taken from Cambridge Castle produced the noble mansion that was completed in 1584 - and that still stands today.

The ghost of Queen Mary is said to have been seen in the house and grounds, and MRs Fuller, the Huddlestons' cook, told me that she had seen the ghost 'without the shadow of a doubt'. 'She did not speak, but just drifted out of the room,' said Mrs Fuller, who was born as the clock struck two. She is confident that only those born on the chime of the hour can see ghosts. 'I could never spend a night here by myself,' she added. 'I just couldn't.'

Mrs Huddleston, a grand-daughter of a former Duke of Norfolk, came here when she first married in 1930. In those days, she often heard the sound of a spinet being played when she stood at the bottom of the stairs - although at that time, the only musical instrument in the house was an old harpsichord.

She never had any fear of the ghostly music, although she knew it was of supernormal origin, for it was very lovely, and not in the least frightening. Once too, a friend, staying at the Hall, asked about the same music that she heard, and for which no explanation was ever discovered

Major Anthony Eyre, the Captain's nephew and present owner of Sawston Hall, was the the house, helping to prepare for the opening to the public a few years ago. Suddenly, while he was alone in the hall, waiting for the arrival of the young ladies who were to act as guides, he heard the unmistakable sound of girls' laughter floating down from the upper floor.

An immediate search revealed nobody, and it was not until some time later that the girls actually arrived. Sawston was closed to the public a couple of years ago, when the ceiling of the Great Hall fell in.

Tom Corbett - the clairvoyant - spent a disturbed night in the Tapestry Room, waking each hour on the hour, from four o'clock onwards, to hear someone or something fiddling with the latch of the bedroom door, and footsteps prowling about the room.

Traditionally, the room is haunted by a 'lady in grey' who knocks three times on the door, which then opens to let the grey apparition float across the room. A former maid told her mistress that she had been in the room when the 'grey thing' passed her, and she was so frightened that she ran out of the room and fell down some steps!

Father Martindale, spending a night in a room near to the Tapestry Room (which contains a canopied four-poster believed to be the actual bed in which Queen Mary slept), reported that someone rapped periodically at his bedroom door.

Nothing could convince him that the sound was caused by a human being. An undergraduate spending a night in the Tapestry Room, like Tom Corbett, found himself awakened by the sound of knocking on the door, followed by someone fiddling with the latch - and then silence.

*Blue Boar Hotel, Cambridge*

SCOTNEY CASTLE, SEE LAMBERHURST, KENT

The three-hundred-and-sixty-year-old prison, a notorious Army 'glasshouse' until 1966, is reputed to be haunted by a White Lady who was beheaded here in 1680.

In January 1967, there were reports of:

- Unaccountable bangings.

- The sounds of heavy breathing.

- The feeling that 'someone or something invisible was in one room'.

- A chilling atmosphere that frightened those using the night duty room.

These reports of apparently inexplicable happenings became so numerous, that the prison governor spent a night in the room himself, and then sent a full report to the Home Office, stating: 'I was unable to find any satisfactory explanation for the happenings.'

The governor asked chaplains Prebendary Leonard White and Father Ryan to speak to the worried staff, and afterwards a senior warden said: 'Prebendary White told us to try to forget the incidents, but it isn't easy when you've had this kind of experience. We were all scared stiff, and nobody has yet come up with an explanation.'

Another officer reported an icy feeling on the back of his neck - the sensation that somebody was pushing from the other side when he was trying to lock a door, although in fact nobody was there - and having the unpleasant feeling of being pinned down by the neck.

The paralysed feeling lasted throughout one night. This officer has not entered that particular room since. The attitude of the whole staff was summed up for me by one warden who stated: 'I wouldn't do another night in the duty room for a thousand pounds.' Later, the Home Office told me: 'All is now quiet there.'

*Bowlish House Hotel, Coombe Lane, Shepton Mallet, Som.*

## SHERFIELD, NEAR BASINGSTOKE, HAMPSHIRE

The owner of a fourteenth-century mill used to complain of a 'shadow' that came and stood beside him at night-time when he was hewing stone. He said that the shadow was of a tall man with a long face and beard. He had the distinct impression that the presence was criticizing his methods of doing work. He discovered that a man answering this description used to work at Lailey's Mill many years ago, and that he was an expert in working on stone.

*Red Lion Hotel, Basingstoke, Hants.*

## SHERBORNE, DORSET

Sir Walter Raleigh (1552-1618) lived for many years at the castle here - now a ruin. His ghost is said to walk round the old castle garden on Michaelmas Eve, and to disappear in the arbour - by the tree known as Raleigh's Oak.

*Half Moon Hotel, Sherborne, Dorset*

## *SHERRINGTON MANOR, SELMESTON, SUSSEX

*[Sherrington Manor is now a Private Residence]*

Years ago, tall grey-haired Cecil Chandless - Lord of the Manor - told me about the brown-clad figure that haunted his home, Sherrington Manor.

He saw the ghost several times on the staircase. One summer afternoon, the family were at tea when they were surprised to hear the crunch of horses' hooves and the grind of carriage wheels, which seemed to herald the arrival of a horse-drawn coach. Immediate investigation showed the drive to be deserted, and nothing was ever discovered to account for the noises.

In 1962, I wrote to Mrs Chandless (her husband was then dead), to ask whether I could bring some members of The Ghost Club down to Sherrington, following reports of more unexplained happenings there:

- Doors were said to open and close mysteriously.

- The swish of clothes and the tramp of heavy boots had been heard on the same staircase where Mr Chandless had seen the ghost figure, which he called 'Marmaduke'.

- There were knocks and rattling noises which could not be explained.

We duly went to Sherrington Manor (and went again a few years later). We talked to Mrs Chandless and her daughter Marisa, and other members of the family and household, about the curious experiences that they all have had.

They all fully accept the fact that they have unbidden guests, and indeed would not be without them, for they feel that Sherrington is haunted by happy ghosts, as such a charming house should be.

Theresa, the Austrian maid, once heard the handle of the garden door rattle, and she saw the handle turn. But when she looked over the wall, there was no one on the other side. She was so perturbed, that she gave in her notice, but Mrs Chandless persuaded her to stay, and now Theresa too feels sure that the ghosts are friendly, for they have never harmed or really frightened anyone.

The only unhappy element of the haunting has been outside, in the lovely garden where - very occasionally - one has the overwhelming feeling of being watched by 'someone nasty' - particularly in a neglected corner of the ancient garden. It may be a kind of barrier of misery that dates back to Saxon times.

Within the house, odd things happen from time to time, and occasionally, a ghost is seen - especially when someone in the house is ill. One such a person had a friendly visit from an unknown female, who leaned over her bed and seemed to say, kindly: 'She's asleep.' Once, too, a whole dinner party saw a figure, which certainly had no objective reality, pass through the hall and mount the stairs.

When the family went to the New Forest during the last war, they believe that 'Marmaduke' followed them, and fretted to get back to Sherrington. They heard impatient knocks, and felt something invisible brush against them. They sensed strongly that they were required to return to their Sussex home. 'Now,' Mrs Chandless will tell you, 'none of us feels that we could ever leave here again.'

[*Underwood visited Sherrington Manor and spoke with Mrs Chandless in 1962 during the first annual 'Ghost Club Summer Visit' to haunted houses - an initiative that he inaugurated following his becoming President of the Ghost Club two years earlier*]

*Star Inn Hotel, Alfriston, Sussex*

## SKERRIES, COUNTY DUBLIN, IRELAND

*[It is believed that a local golf club is the site of the 'haunted field']*

A few miles inland, on a large estate, there is a field in the centre of a plantation of trees, which has not been cultivated since time immemorial. In its middle, there is a large depression covering an area of some forty-five square yards.

Legend has it that in the early days of Christianity in Ireland, a holy woman called Saint Mevee and her followers had a settlement here, where many miracles were wrought. Years later, after all traces of the original foundation had long disappeared, the land was bought by a man who laughed at the idea that the land was hallowed, and began to plough it up.

But almost as soon as he had uttered the scornful rhyme: 'Saint Mevee or Saint Mavoe, I'll plough this up before I go', the ground opened, and he was swallowed up together with his horse and the plough, leaving a depression in the field where the ground closed over them.

From that day, the plot of ground has remained untilled, and the depression remains to mock the unbeliever.

*Shelbourne Hotel, Dublin, Ireland*

Upton Court, one of the oldest houses in the county, formerly owned by the Harewood family, has some interesting features, including a priest's hiding-place, and leaded windows with quain Flemish colourings. There is also the ghost of a woman in a bloodstained nightdress.

The story of the apparition is very old, and its origin is now lost, although there have been many people who claimed to have seen the singular figure in the past, usually wandering about the grounds on Friday nights.

*Royal Hotel, Slough, Bucks.*

# *SOUTHFLEET, NEAR GRAVESEND, KENT

*[The Rectory is now a Private Residence]*

The former rectory at Southfleet was long reputed to be haunted by a female figure wearing a brown, nun-like habit. I traced four independent witnesses for this ghost.

A former rector, the Rev. W. M. Falloon, gave me full details of the case when I went to see him on several occasions, evidence that the haunting and the appearance of the ghostly figure dates back nearly a hundred years.

In the Monk's Room, where the apparition most frequently appeared, there is - or was - a stained-glass window commemorating the fact that in 1874, the Bishop of Rochester - the Rev. P. L. Claughton - visited the rectory to exorcize the ghost. During the incumbency of the Rev. J. H. Hazel (from 1891 to 1898), several appearances of the ghost were reported. On one occasion, three visitors apologized at breakfast one morning for coming to stay while there was sickness in the house.

They said they had all been visited by a nurse during the night, whereupon they were told that there was no sickness in the house, and no nurse. Nor had they been visited by any mortal person during the night. Mr Falloon, who saw the ghost in 1942, especially noticed several inches of white material showing at the cuffs of the figure's sleeves.

This would probably account for anyone taking the figure for a nurse. The same figure, I was told, was also seen a number of times by members of the family, and by visitors, during the occupancy of the house by the Alcocks - from 1908 to 1919.

Mrs Walcott Crockett, whose late husband, the Rev. A. W. Crockett, was Rector of Southfleet from 1920 to 1926, tells me that although they loved the old building, there was certainly something strange about parts of it, and she had no doubt that it was haunted.

Her recollection of the origin of the haunting concerned a nurse who came to the rectory many years ago to care for a member of the family then in residence. The person who was ill, died, and there was some dispute about the possession of important family documents in which the nurse was involved. Afterwards, the ghostly figure of a nurse was reputed to haunt the house.

It is interesting to note that as well as being seen, sometimes as a complete ghostly figure, and sometimes only partially visible and indistinct, footsteps of the ghost nurse have been heard at the rectory walking swiftly along a passage. The rustle of papers, and of a starched uniform, have also been heard, and a clicking noise, comparable to that made by locking or unlocking a door - has occasionally been reported.

The Rev. B. S. W. Crockett, Vicar of Mickleover, Derby, and son of the late Rev. A. W. Crockett, recalls a servant seeing and describing the figure of a lady who held rustling papers in her hand, and seemed to be searching for something or someone. He tells me that although the figure has been described as a nurse, he feels almost certain that she is - in fact - a nun. For mediaeval portions of the house were formerly a monastic cell attached to Rochester Priory. Mr Crockett suggests that the unhappy lady may be from a neighbouring convent.

Mrs Gertrude Dancy of Charmouth, Dorset, tells me that while she was in the employment of the Rev. and Mrs Crockett at Southfleet Rectory between 1919 and 1920, she saw the ghost on one occasion. It was about seven-thirty one evening, and Mrs Dancy had to go up to the housekeeper's room to prepare her bed for the night.

This room was situated in the front part of the house. While working on the bed, Mrs Dancy heard a sound like paper being dragged along the passage. She went to the door to see what was happening, but nothing was visible, and the noise ceased as soon as she reached the door. Returning to her task, Mrs Dancy then heard a louder noise, 'like the sound of a rustling skirt', apparently coming from outside the room. Again, she went into the passage, carrying a small lighted lamp with her. Mrs Dancy's report continues:

'I stood at the top of a small stair just outside the room, and to my surprise, saw a nurse dressed in a clean staff uniform, standing at the end of the passage. She looked very human, and had a smile on her face. Feeling a little nervous at seeing her there, I very timidly walked down the three stairs and along the passage towards her.

'As I did so, she began to walk forwards as if to meet me. Then she seemed to go gently backwards, facing me all the time, until she reached the door of a small room at the end of the passage. There, to my surprise, she disappeared backwards through the door.'

Mrs Dancy immediately opened the door through which the 'nurse' had disappeared, and went into the room, but there was no trace of the figure she had seen. Nor, indeed, of anyone. Mrs Dancy tells me that she has never forgotten the experience, and is still absolutely confident that she did see this unexplained figure.

In 1920, Mr Falloon informed me, four friends visited Southfleet Rectory from Bath, and while they were standing together on the landing where Mrs Dancy saw the ghost - waiting for a key to be fetched to unlock a door - they all saw a female figure come out of the Monk's Room, walk forty-two feet along the passage, turn the corner at which they were standing, and go to towards a door at the end of the landing - open it - pass inside, and then closing it again.

When the key for which they had been waiting eventually arrived, they found to their consternation that the door which the apparition had apparently opened and closed, was in fact securely locked.

The Rev. G. A. Bingley, M.A., was Curate at Southfleet from 1923 to 1926, and during that period, he resided at the old rectory. One evening, Mr Bingley tells me, he and his wife (then a fiancee) saw a 'shadowy shape' at the end of a passage about thirty feet away from where they were standing, on the landing above the main staircase.

The form appeared in a passage leading from the Monk's Room. On almost every occasion that this apparition has been seen, it has apparently come out of that place. A solitary exception was mentioned to me by Mr Falloon, concerning the wife of a former rector who once reported seeing the figure in the act of entering the Monk's Room.

Mr Bingley described for me two other seemingly paranormal

happenings. An aunt of the former rector's wife saw a figure, similar to that glimpsed by Mr Bingley and his fiancee, taking shape in the dining room in broad daylight. A nursemaid once reported seeing a figure on the landing above the main staircase one evening. She described the figure she saw as a 'nurse with a flowing veil', and said 'she' crossed the landing with a 'smiling look', and disappeared through a closed door.

At noon on February 7th 1942, the Rev. W. M. Falloon was standing in the hall, when he suddenly saw what he took to be the figure of a nun, between him and the window. He described her to me as being about four feet seven inches in height: dumpy in shape, and wearing a brown serge overall dress - similar to the contemporary nuns' black apparel, with a brown fur scarf reaching to the elbows, and a close-fitting brown woolen cap.

The old rectory occupies the site of a former friary, and tradition asserts that a nun found in the company of a monk inside the friary was bricked up alive in the cellars. Stories of the bricking-up of nuns are not infrequently encountered in nun hauntings, although very sparse evidence exists to suggest that such a barbarous punishment was ever actually meted our in this country. However, on more than one occasion, bones - believed to be female - have been found in suspicious circumstances - for example in the former deanery at Exeter, where such bones discovered between two walls of a bricked-up archway

When I mentioned this fact to Mr Falloon, he told me that about ninety years ago the west door of Southfleet Church was badly blocked with dirt and rubble. After this had been cleared away by churchwardens, they uncovered the stone lid of a sarcophagus in the pathway

This was removed, and can now be seen in the Scadbury pew inside the church. An inscription around the edge states that it marks the burial place of an excommunicated monk. Perhaps, as so often happens, there was a grain of truth in the legend, and a nun and a monk were indeed the chief actors in the Southfleet drama.

*King's Head Hotel, Rochester, Kent*

# *SOUTHAMPTON, HAMPSHIRE

*[Only the Chapel remains]*

The old Indian-style Victoria Military Hospital, Netley - built in 1856 and demolished in 1966 - was long reputed to be haunted by a nurse of the Crimean War, who committed suicide by throwing herself from an upstairs window after discovering that - by mistake - she had administered a fatal overdose of drugs to a patient.

Her ghost was always seen in one particular corridor. Officials and staff at the hospital, as well as clergyman, visitors and patients - have all told of seeing the figure, although stories of the appearances were suppressed for many years, because whenever the ghost was seen, a death took place. A service of exorcism was held here in 1951.

The apparition was reported to be particularly active when the building was being demolished, and one witness stated: 'The figure was dressed in an old-style nurses' uniform of greyish-blue, with a white cap, and was about twenty-five feet away from me when I saw it. She walked slowly away, making no sound, and disappeared down a passage that led to the chapel.'

In 1936, a night orderly saw the 'Grey Lady' pass a ward where a patient died the following morning. A night staff telephone operator, employed at the hospital for twenty seven years, also claimed to have seen the ghost. He said that he heard the rustle of her dress as she passed, and there was a perfumed scent in the air after she had disappeared.

Variations of the legend suggest that the ghost was a nursing sister who fell in love with a patient and, after finding him in the arms of another nurse, poisoned him, and then committed suicide. Another was that the patient died and the nurse jumped from a window because of a broken heart. Or that she is Florence Nightingale, who was mainly responsible for the building of the hospital, and that her frequent appearances in 1966 were an endeavour to prevent its demolition.

*Dolphin Hotel, Southampton, Hampshire*

## SOUTHPORT, LANCASHIRE

In 1969, something of a sensation was caused at the Palace Hotel, when Mr J. Smith and his eleven-man team of demolition workers reported alarming and apparently inexplicable happenings at this thousand-room hotel.

Eerie voices were heard from empty rooms, and corridors, on the second floor. The four-ton lift is said to have moved up and down many times of its own volition. After conducting an investigation, the North Wales Electricity Board asserted that not an amp of power was going into the hotel - electric current having been in fact cut off weeks earlier.

One of the men stated that he entered the foyer in the company of eight others, and they all saw the doors slam shut, and the lift move up - to the second floor.

A Mrs Templeman called at the hotel on the business, and was talking to workmen when she saw the lift suddenly begin to move upwards. She said there was no sound whatsoever. The lift moved about seven feet. Almost to the second floor. And then stopped. Mrs Templeman ran up to the winding room with one of the workmen. They discovered that the lift brake was still firmly at the 'on' position, and there seemed no logical way that the lift could have moved mechanically. The emergency winding handle for cranking the lift had been removed by this time.

At length, it was decided to cut the cables to release the lift, and although this was done, the lift did not budge. Now the main shafts were cut through, and still the lift would not move. It was continually thumped with twenty-eight-pound hammers for twenty-five minutes, before it eventually plunged to the bottom of the lift shaft and buried itself four feet into the cellar.

The workmen all agreed that it was incredible that - although the lift had moved, silently and without apparent effort, by itself on so many occasions - it should have been so difficult to knock down.

During the course of a television broadcast, a dog was shown refusing to pass the second floor landing, although it had no such objection to passing other, apparently identical landings.

*Clifton Hotel, Promenade, Southport, Lancs.*

# *SOUTHWOLD, SUFFOLK

*[The 'Old Vicarage' is now Buckenham Galleries & Coffee House]*

The old vicarage - now divided into club rooms, a bus office, a wool shop, and a paint shop - certainly seems to have been haunted when it was occupied by a family. The daughter of a former rector has told me of the mysterious noises - sometimes all the occupants of the house would hear sounds as though someone had fallen downstairs.

But when they rushed out to offer assistance, no one was there, and nothing could be found to account for the noises that had been heard. One housekeeper left because she heard what she described as the 'clanking of chains' in the unused attic. Sometimes the creak of a chair would be heard, a heavy sigh would follow, and then footsteps would approach the door - followed by silence.

Visitors sleeping in the four-poster bed in the spare room often told of being awakened by 'somebody standing by the bed'.

*Crown Hotel, Southwold, Suffolk*

Thorington Hall, a fine example of a gabled farmhouse, was built in the sixteenth century, and has a dark stairs landing where the ghost of a girl has been seen and heard.

The western wing of the property centres on a magnificent chimney stack, fifty feet high, with octagonal shafts supplying six fireplaces on three floors. In the living room, a sixteenth-century shoe - now in Colchester Museum - was found behind ornamental plaster during repairs in 1937.

A dim passage upstairs is haunted by the ghost of a girl in a brownish dress tied with a cord. Heavy and unexplained footsteps have been heard on many occasions here, and in other parts of the house.

*Red Lion Hotel, Colchester, Essex*

## STOW-ON-THE-WOLD, GLOUCESTERSHIRE

A semi-detached house in Chapel Street - occupied by Mr Stanley Pethrick (fifty-eight), his wife Nancy, and their son David (fourteen), was the scene of remarkable poltergeist activity in 1963 and 1964. Pools of water appeared unaccountably in several rooms, and as soon as the water was mopped up, it reappeared, and then began to seep through the walls.

Three plumbers failed to find fault with the pipes, though all the floorboards in the house were ripped up. Nor could the head of the water board - and a sanitary inspector - find any solution. A sudden gush of water from the kitchen floor steamed up one wall as high was the ceiling. Later, a rhythmic tapping disturbed the occupants.

Search as they would, they could not locate the source. Furniture moved of its own volition. Rasping sounds came from cupboards and drawers. David was tipped out of bed. Sheets were ripped in half. A dressing gown flew from its hook and thrust itself under a mattress. Scratching noises came from David's bed, and when the furniture was moved, it was found that the headboard was gouged and scarred.

Writing appeared mysteriously on the walls, wallpaper was ripped off, and Mrs Pethrick saw a hand appear from the end of her son's bed. At first it was small - like a baby's hand - but it quickly grey to the size of a boy's, and then to that of a large man's hand. Her husband saw it too.

Then a voice spoke, always in the vicinity of David, claiming to be one of the builders of the house, who had died twenty years before - on February 15th. The haunting had commenced on that date. Gradually, the family learned to live with their entity, but when they went on a holiday, it seemed to go with them - and a church they visited 'reverberated with rappings'.

*Wyck Hill House, Stow-on-the-Wold, Glos.*

# STRETTON, RUTLANDSHIRE

*[Stocken Hall Farm is now a Private Residence]*

Stocken Hall Farm was, and perhaps still is, haunted by three ghosts. One is the figure of a woman, dressed in black, with touches of white, who flits away down a corridor as soon as she is seen - or passes with lowered head. At all events, her face is never visible.

During the early 1900s, the occupants and many visitors saw the ghost, who was believed to have been a girl who was strangled in one of the attics. Once, a visitor reported that when she saw the girl - whom she took for a servant - she spoke to her, whereupon the figure vanished.

The second ghost is that of a little white dog, and this phantom, too, was seen by many people for about eighteen months at one period. Often, people opened doors for it, only to find that it had suddenly disappeared. Once, the then occupant of the house and her daughter were going up a narrow staircase, when the creature passed them.

They both felt it touching them as it pressed tightly between them and the jamb of the door on the top of the stairs. But this time the creature was invisible. For hours afterwards, they said, they experience a 'burning chill' where it had touched them. The third apparition was seen by three occupants of the house one December day as they were crossing the park towards Clipsham, at a quarter to three in the afternoon.

The terrier they had with them pricked up his ears and showed signs of fright, when they saw the figure of a man hanging from the bough of an old oak tree. He was dressed in a brown smock, with something white over his face, and the rails of the fence behind him could distinctly be seen through the body.

When they were within about forty yards of the apparition, the figure suddenly disappeared. There is a rumour that a sheep-stealer was hanged hereabouts, and a murder is known to have been committed in the park. The spot was visited on succeeding anniversaries of the date - December 22nd - but nothing further was seen.

*George Hotel, Oakham, Rutland*

## *SUDBURY, SUFFOLK

St Gregory's Church bell-ringers were troubled by mysterious footsteps, and other unexplained noises and curious happenings when I was there a few years ago. In the circumstances related to me, it was quite impossible for the footsteps - in particular - to have had a normal explanation. Preserved in St Gregory's is the head of Archbishop Simon of Sudbury, who built Sudbury Tower, Canterbury, and who was eventually beheaded.

*Four Swans Hotel, Sudbury, Suffolk*

Hylton Castle, three-and-a-half miles to the west of Sunderland, was long said to be haunted by 'the Cauld Lad of Hylton', a naked ghost which was more often heard than seen. Haunting the kitchens and lower parts of the castle, he seems to have been of the 'brownie' order, for he delighted in putting things in order, and only really caused mischief when he became enraged at finding no work to do: then he would smash breakable articles, mix the cooking ingredients, overturn the utensils containing liquids, and generally create havoc.

Understandably, the servants soon learnt to humour him, simply by leaving work for him to do. But there are always those who will not let well alone, and one of the servants heard that the way to ensure seeing such a goblin - and of not being troubled with him again - was to present him with a suit of clothes. Accordingly, a handsome suit of Lincoln green was carefully made, complete with cloak and hood, and left beside the fire - the servants hid in wait for him.

At exactly midnight, the Cauld Lad appeared and stood warming himself by the fire, before he caught sight of the clothes (Queen Mab's own green livery! ['*Queen Mab*' *is a fairy referred to in Shakespeare's play Romeo and Juliet*]), and promptly tried them on.

Finding them a perfect fit, he playfully jumped about the kitchen until it was almost dawn when, drawing his cloak around him, he muttered: 'Here's a cloak, and here's a hood: The Cauld Lad of Hylton will do no more good.' With that he disappeared, and there are only occasional reports of his being seen again.

The precise scene of the Cauld Lad's haunting has long since vanished, which is not surprising, as some say that the Cauld

Lad is the ghost of a young stable-boy, killed by his master in anger some five hundred years ago.

[*The behaviour of the ghost suggests a* **poltergeist** *(German for "noisy ghost" or "noisy spirit"). Other versions of the tale describe the 'Cauld Lad' as an* **elf** *(is a type of human-shaped supernatural being in Germanic mythology and folklore),* **barghest** *(mythical monstrous black dog with large teeth and claws) or* **brownie** *('a personage of small stature, wrinkled visage, covered with short curly brown hair, and wearing a brown mantle and hood') who is under a spell from which he can only be released by being given a gift*].

*The Seaburn Hotel, Sunderland, Co. Durham*

## *SUTTON PLACE, NEAR GUILDFORD, SURREY

This magnificent mansion, with the splendid oak tables once owned by American newspaper magnate William Hearst, as well as the priceless sixteenth-century Brussels tapestries, the gold candelabra, the art treasures - pictures, furniture and rugs - is now the home of Mr Paul Getty [*Jean Paul Getty was born in 1892 and died aged 86 in 1976, five years after the original publication of the* Gazetteer. *The estate is currently owned by Alisher Usmanov, the Russian billionaire*].

With its wonderful gardens, it seems a perfect setting for a haunting, and according to reports, there is more than one ghost at Sutton Place. The ghost of the long gallery for instance - although treated lightly by the present staff - was mentioned by a visitor two hundred years ago. One feels that anything might happen in this history-laden atmosphere, and perhaps the servant who says she saw an unknown figure here was not mistaken.

Then there is the 'lady in white' - another unidentified ghost from the past. Perhaps she is the cause of the curious noises, sounds as though furniture is being smashed, that have been heard from time to time. At all events, multi-millionaire Paul Getty is not worried: 'I am comforted by the advice of a neighbour, who is reputed to have several ghosts,' he will tell you. 'He assures me that they keep their manifestations for visitors and staff, and never appear before the owner of the house.'

*Angel Hotel, Guildford, Surrey*

## SYDERSTONE, NORFOLK

Ill-starred Amy Robsart, the wife of Robert Dudley - afterwards Earl of Leicester - who probably contrived her murder at Cumnor Hall (in conjunction with Queen Elizabeth I) [*see the entry for 'Cumnor Hall'*], lived here at Syderstone Hall before her marriage - and her ghost was said to walk here before the old Hall was demolished.

Then the haunting seems to have been transferred to the nearby rectory, where windows used to open by themselves, after being carefully closed and bolted, and other inexplicable incidents were reported from time to time.

The village green is reputed to be haunted on nights of the full moon by a ghostly highwayman suitably mounted on a ghostly horse. On occasions, words like 'Your money or your life' have been heard as the figure rushes silently past.

*Duke's Head Hotel, King's Lynn, Norfolk*

The Norman Castle has two ghosts: a Black Lady, and a White Lady, who each haunt their own parts of this historic edifice on the banks of the River Trent.

Here, on January 30th 925, Sihtric [*Sigtryggr - an old Norse given name, composed of the elements sig "victory" and trygg "trusty, true"*], the pagan Danish King of Northumbria - was betrothed to Editha, sister of King Athelstan. Although Sihtric accepted baptism, he soon afterwards relapsed into idolatry, and left Editha, who founded a convent and spent the rest of her life in acts of charity and devotion. Tamworth Parish Church is dedicated to her.

After the Norman Conquest, William the Conqueror gave Tamworth Castle to Robert de Marmion for his outstanding bravery at the battle of Hastings. When he took possession, Marmion expelled the nuns, who fled to a nunnery at nearby Polesworth - only to meet a similar fate there, for Marmion had also been granted lands at this second place.

According to legend, one night after Marmion had gone to bed, the ghost of Editha appeared to him, dressed in the habit of a nun or Black Lady, and reproached him for his treatment of her nuns. She is said to have struck him with her crozier [*a stylized staff/long stick*], and prophesied that he would meet a terrible death, unless he allowed the sisters to return to the convent at Polesworth. Bleeding from his wounds, Marmion staggered down the stairway - known to this day as the Haunted Staircase - and promised to make restoration.

The story of a White Lady who haunts the Castle terrace relates how she watched from this point, while her love - Sir Tarquin, an evil Saxon Knight - was slain by Sir Lancelot in

Lady Meadow, below the Castle. Sir Lancelot is then supposed to have rescued forty knights from the Castle.

I am indebted to the Castle Museum Curator, Miss C. F. Tarjan, for the additional information that the Haunted Room - where Marmion is supposed to have met the ghostly Editha, daughter of King Edward the Elder - has long been reputed to be haunted by weird sighs and groans. Some of these have been recorded on tape. A number of people claim to have had very frightening experiences there.

*Castle Hotel, Tamworth, Staffs.*

# *TAVISTOCK - OKEHAMPTON ROAD, DEVON

*[Fitzford Mansion is now occupied by Fitzford Cottages -
but the rebuilt Fitzford Gatehouse remains]*

There is a legend that occasionally - at midnight - the ghost of the Lady Howard leaves the gates of the ruined Fitzford mansion just outside Tavistock, enters her magnificent coach drawn by four jet-black horses, and sets off towards Okehampton, driven by her liveried coachman.

Motorists passing the vicinity late at night have reported seeing her figure or her coach, rolling silently along the road. Some say she is accompanied by a large black dog, while others hear only the sound of horses' hooves and, perhaps, the noise of wheels.

Outside Okehampton churchyard, the coach is said to stop. The huge dog plucks a single blade of grass from the churchyard and return to the coach, where Lady Howard takes it from the foam-flecked dog's mouth, and presses it sadly to her bosom. (Another version says she puts it between the pages of her Bible.) Then the coach turns and heads back to Fitzford, as silently as it came.

*Bedford Hotel, Tavistock, Devon*

TEDWORTH, DRUMMER OF, SEE
TIDWORTH, NORTH WILTSHIRE

## *THAMES DITTON, SURREY

The Home of Compassion has a White Lady that has haunted one room for over ten years.

The present house stands on land owned - and often visited - by Cardinal Wolsey. The original, much larger property, had a long and interesting history. Some of King Henry VIII's officials were at Thames Ditton in the sixteenth century, when a property then known as Stinghaw adjoined Forde's Farm. Horace Walpole, the author of *The Castle of Otranto*, visited it from nearby Strawberry Hill in the eighteenth century.

Later, Forde's Farm became known as Boyle's Farm, although it was never really a farm in the accepted sense of the word. The place was much frequented by the nobility of the day, and the Irish poet, Thomas Moore (1779-1852), attended an elaborate fete here with coloured illuminations and gondolas that carried Italian opera singers. There were character quadrilles danced by the beauties of the season, and Fanny Ayton sang. The event was long remembered as the Dandies' Fete.

A century and a half later, the property stood empty for several years, and the estate was cut up and sold as building plots. The remainder was bought by the Church of England Community of the Compassion of Jesus, and became the Home of Compassion under Mother Mary Margaret. Before long, there was talk of a mysterious figure in white, who used to be glimpsed in one of the rooms.

After Mother Mary Margaret died in 1933, her successor found a charming room locked and unused. She decided to make it into her private room, and had it redecorated. But after one night, she moved out, had the room padlocked, and never used it again. The same thing happened a few years later when a dog bristled, growled, and showed signs of distress on a number of occasions, and its mistress saw a white figure in the room - so it was once again locked, and remained unused for many years.

Mother Eva Mary told me that when she arrived at the Home, she, too, liked the locked-up room, and decided to use it as her bedroom. The first night she spent there, she suddenly found herself awake in the middle of the night and saw, standing quite close to her, at the side of the bed, a female figure in white.

It appeared to be quite solid, and didn't move or speak, but looked sadly at her. Mother Eva Mary felt that it was concerned for her welfare. However, she was not frightened, and became convinced that the White Lady paid her nightly visits, only with love and compassion as her motives. Mother Eva Mary saw the form many, many times, and expected to continue to do so, for she had come to look upon the silent figure as her friend.

In 1962 my friend T. S. Mercer, the historian of Thames Ditton - went to the Home of Compassion to photograph the mural paintings that had been uncovered by workmen stripping the walls. He took five, and when they were developed, four were perfectly ordinary photographs of the murals, but on the fifth he seems to have caught a fleeting apparition.

He submitted the negative to a leading authority, who ruled out all faults due to film, processing or camera, and maintained that some bright object had passed in front of the camera while the shutter was open. Mr Mercer himself saw nothing, and the photograph remains a psychic and photographic puzzle. A few years ago, Holy Communion was held for three days in succession in the haunted room, in an attempt at exorcism, but I am assured on good authority that the room is still haunted.

[*"The Reverend Mother told me when I called there: 'It is true that we have a ghost here, but we never talk about it if we can help [it]….*

*It is the ghost of a nun and it has been seen here for many, many years.... Yes, I have seen the ghost nun myself. It was not a figment of my imagination... but we are not worried about it, it has not harmed anyone.'" - Peter Underwood,* No Common Task *(1983); p.70]*

*Mitre Hotel, Hampton Court, Middlesex*

# TIDWORTH, NORTH; WILTSHIRE

Formerly Tedworth, and the scene of the famous poltergeist case - the 'Drummer of Tedworth', in the early 1600s. Mr John Mompesson - a local magistrate who lived at the Manor House - visited nearby Ludgershall, and heard about a travelling drummer who was demanding money. On examining the fellow's pass and warrant, Mr Mompesson found them to be fraudulent, and ordered the man - one William Drury - to be sent before the Justice of the Peace.

Dury confessed his fraud, but earnestly begged to have his drum back, which Mompesson had taken from him. He was told that if the report from Colonel Ayliff - whose drummer Drury said he was - proved to be favourable, he should have the drum back, but that meanwhile it would be held by the bailiff. Drury was left in the hands of the constable, but the latter, it seems, soon released him.

The following month, as Mompesson was preparing for a visit to London, the bailiff sent the drum to the Manor House. When Mompesson returned from London, his wife told him that while he had been away, they had been very frightened by noises during the night-time. Soon, Mompesson himself heard the noises, which he described as a great knocking at doors and the outside of the house.

He investigated with a brace of pistols, but as soon as he opened a door from which the knocking appeared to be originating, the noise would be heard at another door, which he would then open - but he was always unsuccessful in discovering a cause for the noise.

He went outside the house, and walked around it, but could find nothing - although he still heard the strange and hollow sound, which continued even when he returned to bed. It now seemed to come from the top of the house. Eventually it decreased, and after some time, ceased altogether, seeming to go off into the air.

After this, the thumping and drumming noises were heard very frequently. Usually five nights in a row, and then there was quiet for perhaps three nights. Always the noises sounded on the outside boards of the house. Generally they began as the family prepared for sleep - whether this was early or late.

After several weeks, the noises seemed to come into the house, as if especially attracted to the room where the drum lay. Now, they were heard four or five nights out of seven each week. Just before it commenced, the occupants would hear 'a hurling sound in the air over the house', and when this had gone away, they would hear the beating of a drum 'like that of a breaking up of a guard'.

For two months, the disturbances continued in the same room. Mr Mompesson frequently used the place himself to study the noises. Often the noises were more troublesome during the early hours of the night, and after a couple of hours, they would die away. It was noticed that when the noises were at their height, any dog in the house would stand stock still.

It may be significant that Mrs Mompesson was in the last months of pregnancy, and the night she was away from the house, having the child, all was quiet and continued so for the next three weeks, 'until she had recovered her strength'.

But then the disturbances returned, and in a 'ruder manner' than before. They seemed to follow the young children of the family about the house, annoying them and beating on their bedsteads with great violence.

On holding the shaking children while they were seemingly being hit by something unseen, no blows could be felt, but the children would tremble violently. At this time, the drum would beat for hours on end, sending the 'Roundheads and Cuckolds, the Tattoo [*military drum performance*], and several other points of War, as well as any Drummer'.

Sometimes a scratching noise would be heard under the children's beds - which seemed to lift them up. Later, servants complained of the same inconvenience - their beds being gently lifted up and put down again. At other times, they would feel a great weight on their feet as they lay in bed.

Noticing that a loft in the house had never been troubled, the Mompessons put the children to bed there, hoping for a quiet night. But they had no sooner left the room when they noticed trouble began in the loft - exactly as it had been experienced elsewhere in the house

On November 5th - in daylight - a 'mighty noise' was heard, and a servant in a room full of people observed two floorboards in the children's room begin to move. He asked them to approach him, whereupon the boards, by themselves, moved to within a yard of his feet.

He then asked for one of them to be put into his hand, and his was done. He pushed the board away from him, but it was thrust back against him, and this continued at least twenty times, until Mr Mompesson sent the servant away. Afterwards, a 'sulphurous smell' lingered where the phenomenon had taken place.

During a visit by the local vicar, the drum beat loud and clear - chairs 'walked' around the room - the children's shoes flew over the heads of those present, and practically everything movable in the room moved. Part of the bedstead threw itself at the minister, and hit him on the leg - but so lightly that it might have been 'a lock of wool'. It was noticed that it stopped exactly where it landed on the floor, not rolling or moving at all.

Mr Mompesson now transferred the small children to a neighbour's house, and took the eldest - a girl of ten - to his own bedroom. But as soon as she was in bed, the disturbances began and continued for three weeks - the drumming and other noises seeming to answer or reply to anything that was asked.

The younger children were then brought back and put to bed in the parlour, which had been comparatively free from trouble. But even there they were persecuted by 'something', plucking at their hair and night clothes - although no other disturbances were reported.

Now the drumming sound was less frequent. Instead, a noise - like clinking of money - was heard all over the house. Less violent disturbances followed - clothes being thrown about bedrooms, articles hidden, and bedclothes tugged off beds.

When the house was visited by a son of Sir Thomas Bennet (who had at one time employed the drummer, William Drury), he had no sooner gone to bed than the drumming started, loud and clear. At the same time, Mr Mompesson's servant John heard a rustling sound in his bedchamber, and felt that something dressed in silks approached his bedstead.

He took up his sword, whereupon the presence left him. Shortly afterwards, a singing noise was heard in one of the chimneys, and lights were seen about the house, especially in the children's room. Once the light appeared in Mr Mompesson's room. He described it as blue and glimmering.

After he had seen it, he noticed 'a stiffness in his eyes'. When the light had disappeared, he heard faint footsteps on the stairs as though someone crept upstairs without shoes. The maids asserted that a door opened and closed in their presence, without being touched. When it opened, sounds were heard suggesting that a dozen people had entered the room -

although nothing was visible.

This happened, they claimed, at least ten times. Sounds were also heard inside the room, as though people who had entered were walking about, and among the sounds the maids distinguished was a rustling noise, as of silk. One morning, a little later, Mr Mompesson heard the drum at daybreak outside the chamber he occupied. It then seemed to move to the other end of the house and then 'go off into the air'.

The entity continued to play further tricks, particularly troubling the Mompesson children when they were in bed. It seemed to pass from one bed to another, avoiding the blows that were aimed at it with a sword or other article. Sometimes a panting sound was heard, then a scratching noise, and sometimes knocking and rattling. A voice cried *'a witch, a witch'* at least a hundred times. Once, Mr Mompesson, seeing some wood move in the chimney, discharged a pistol, and afterwards found several drops of blood in the hearth - and on stairs…

After the pistol shot, there was calm in the house for two or three nights. But the disturbances soon returned to worry the children, sometimes carrying away a lighted candle in their room, and disappearing with it up a chimney. Footsteps were heard at midnight, and knocks sounded on Mr Mompesson's chamber door.

When he did not reply, the footsteps moved to another room, where the occupant reported an 'appearance' of 'a great body with two red and glaring eyes' standing at the foot of his bed. After staring steadily at him for a time, the figure disappeared.

It soon returned to trouble the children once again, tugging at their beds with such force that six men could not hold them down. Beds fascinated this poltergeist:

- Chamber pots were emptied into them.

- They were strewn with ashes.

- A long iron pike was put into Mr Mompesson's bed.

- An upright knife was found in Mr Mompesson's mother's bed.

At this time, things would fly about all over the house, and unexplained noises were heard, day and night.

A visiting friend found all the money in his pocket turned black. Mr Mompesson discovered his horse on its back with one of its hind legs in its mouth so tightly that it took several men to lever it out. Sometimes, the house would be visited by seven or eight 'men-like shapes', which would disappear when a gun was discharged.

Meanwhile William Drury - the drummer - was committed to Gloucester Gaol for stealing. There he stated that he had plagued a man in Wiltshire, and would never be quiet 'till he hath made me satisfaction for taking away my drum'.

Thereupon the fellow was tried for a witch at Sarum, acquitted of that charge, but sentenced to transportation - probably as a rogue and vagabond. Somehow (some said by raising storms and frightening the seamen), he contrived to be returned to these shores, whereupon the disturbances at Mr Mompesson's house - which had been quiescent while Drury was aboard ship, recommenced.

The subsequent history of William Drury - and of his drum - is not known, but the Drummer of Tedworth is a classic early account of a poltergeist infestation. It is interesting to recall that John Mompesson - a magistrate - always maintained that the disturbances could not be explained normally.

*White Hart Hotel, Salisbury, Wilts.*

# *TORQUAY, DEVON

*[The Old Spanish Barn is currently Abbey Historic House and Gardens']*

The Old Spanish Barn on the seafront and its immediate vicinity, are haunted occasionally by the ghost of a pretty young Spanish girl. The senorita is said to have disguised herself as a page, and to have arrived with her lover, a Spanish nobleman, aboard the *Nuestra Senora del Rosario*, one of the ships in the ill-fated Spanish Armada.

The young lovers must have been confident of the success of the Spanish invaders, and doubtless thought that in a short time, they would be given some English manor house as part of the conqueror's booty. But the defeat by Drake and the great Tudor navy, their dream was shattered.

Following that great victory in 1588, 397 prisoners - including the young Spanish girl and her lover, were crammed into the tithe barn at Torquay. In the appalling conditions, she was one of the first prisoners to die - although she is said to have received the last rites from a priest of her own religion.

However, this does not seem to have prevented her ghost from reappearing in the park on Torquay seafront, and in the locality of the Spanish Barn - drifting sadly and hopelessly at the scene of her death. Motorists driving along King's Drive, late on moonlit nights, have reported seeing such a figure in recent years.

'Castel a Mere', Middle Warberry Road, was derelict for many years owing to the reputation of being haunted. This is the house referred to in Beverley Nichols' *Twenty-Five*, and Violet Tweedale's *Ghosts I Have Seen*.

The scene of the remarkable experience of Lord St Audries and Beverley Nichols and his brother in the early 1920s. Beverley

Nichols himself related the story at The Ghost Club in 1965, and filled in the detail for me during conversation at his delightful home on Ham Common.

It was a Sunday evening, after prayer-time, that the three young men found themselves outside the fearful-looking and dilapidated empty house, which was said to have long been haunted by strange sounds, screams and footsteps - following a murder there in the long distant past.

Deciding to look over the house, they picked their way through the overgrown garden, and entered through a window on the ground floor. They had a candle, and went from room to room. Each seemed more melancholy that the last.

The plaster had fallen in great lumps from the ceiling. Boxes and planks were scattered all over the place. Wallpaper hung in strips from the rotting walls. They found themselves talking in whispers as they climbed up the narrow twisting staircase to the upper floor.

At this stage, Beverley Nichols went ahead and stood waiting for his companions in the upper hall. He told me that he was not feeling at all 'creepy' - rather disappointed, in fact - that nothing frightening had happened, when he suddenly realized that his mind was working very slowly. His thoughts seemed to be reduced to a frightening slow motion.

Then he became aware that the same thing was happening to his body. He felt as though a black film began to cover the left side of his brain, exactly as the time he had been anaesthetized. Just before everything would - he felt certain - go black, he managed to stagger to the window, half-fall outside, whereby he lost consciousness.

He awakened to find himself sitting on the grass, feeling quite normal, but strangely tired. He wanted no more to do with the house, but his companions - who had experienced nothing strange in the place at all - were determined to return. Having established that Beverley was well again, they clambered back into the dark and silent house.

After some twenty-five minutes spent in avery thorough examination of every corner of the property, including the little room from which Beverley felt the harmful 'influence' had emanated, they returned to him with the conviction that there was nothing whatever to be afraid of - the house was indisputably empty.

After a while, Lord St Audries announced that he was set on exploring the house alone. He felt that Beverley's brother might be a kind of 'anti-influence' keeping the ghosts off - recalling that Beverley's experience had taken place when he had been alone. So, despite the objections of his friends, he went back into the house, after agreeing to take a candle with him, and to whistle every few minutes, in reply to *their* whistle - to show that he was all right.

Beverley Nichols and his brother heard their friend clamber into the house. Heard his footsteps cross the plaster-covered floor of the hall. Heard him climbing the stairs. They heard him walk across the upper hall - and then there was silence. They presumed that he had sat down as he had said he would.

After a moment, they whistled. His whistle came back in reply - or seemed to. For the answering whistle seemed surprisingly faint. They whistled again, and a faint echo came. This went on for some twenty minutes - the answering whistle from the direction of the house seemingly getting stronger. Then both the brothers sensed that something came out of the house and past them - making no sound in the almost unearthly silence.

Nothing was visible - when suddenly, they heard Lord St Audries' voice: a cry, heart-rending and full of anguish. The sort of cry - Beverley Nichols said to me - that a man would make who had been stabbed in the back. He and his brother scrambled to their feet and rushed to the window.

The sounds of a tremendous struggle sounded from upstairs. The wildest thuds and screams - as though a terrific fight were taking place. They didn't know whether to be frightened or relieved when, at length, heavy footsteps staggered down the stairs, and Lord St Audries, a white-faced figure - his hair, clothes and hands covered with plaster and dust - emerged into the garden.

At length, he was able to relate how he had found his attention being brought back time and time again, to the little room Beverley had felt to be malevolent. He had sat with his eyes fixed in that direction. After a while, he noticed a patch of greyish light in the darkness of the corridor. It was the door of the little room. He heard his friends ' whistles, and answered them for twenty minutes.

Then, deciding that he had drawn a blank, he got up, having decided to return to his friends. At this moment, out of the room he had been watching, something came rushing at hims. Something that was black, and seemed roughly the shape of a man, although he could distinguish no face, and the thing made no sound whatsoever.

He found himself knocked flat on his back, and a sickening and overwhelming sense of evil - as though he were struggling with something from hell - pervaded his brain. He fought as he had never fought before, forcing himself to his feet, and then inching himself slowly down the stairs, thinking every second that he could go on no longer.

At last, he reached the bottom of the stairs and blackness, free from his adversary. He staggered outside and met his friends coming to his help. Later, the friends discovered that the murder in the house had been a double one: a semi-insane doctor murdering first his wife, and then a maid. The scene of the murders was the bathroom: the little room at the end of the corridor which had worried Beverley and Lord St Audries so much.

The house stood next to one called 'Asheldon', in Middle Warberry Road, but the site has since been built upon.

*Hotel Hyperion, Cockington Lane, Torquay, Devon*

## *TOTTON, HAMPSHIRE

*[Testwood House was subsequently demolished - the
original gatehouse and driveway still exist]*

Testwood House - formerly a royal hunting lodge, a nobleman's country seat, a well-known gentleman's home a country club - and now the offices of the sherry shippers Williams and Humbert, seems to harbour several ghosts.

Heavy footsteps have been heard walking along passages covered with thick carpeting, footsteps that sounded as though they were walking on boards. They seem to originate in an upstairs corridor, where the dogs refuse to go. One night, the caretaker was making his rounds, after the staff had gone home, when he heard the footsteps.

A year later, unexplained figures were seen outside the house. One autumn night, the caretaker's sixteen-year-old daughter was returning late from a dance, and had almost reached the front door of Testwood House - accompanied by her brother - when they both saw a tall man, apparently trying to open the door. As they approached, he vanished. Neither knew of any ghostly associations of the house.

Shortly afterwards, the same figure was seen by a chef who happened to be working late in the kitchen. He became aware of someone standing silently beside him, watching, only a few feet away. Almost as soon as he became aware of the presence, it vanished. As the chef drove away from the house that night, the headlights of his car picked out the figure of a man on the drive, walking towards the front door.

He noticed that the figure wore a top hat and long overcoat with a short cape, before it suddenly disappeared. A month later, another member of the staff saw a similar figure standing by one of the entrance gates in broad daylight.

A year later, the caretaker and his son were alarmed to hear their dog suddenly start barking late at night. Thinking that there must be intruders in the grounds, they ran across the yard to the main building, where they found that the back door was rattling violently, although there was no sign of anybody.

After they had circled the building, and examined all doors and windows with their torches, the caretaker's son reached the little pantry window, in the oldest part of the house. Here, although the window is unglazed and protected by a metal mesh screen and vertical bars obviating the possibility of reflection, as the torch-light fell on the window, the boy saw the unmistakable face of a young man staring out at him.

The face, long and pale, with grey eyes, looked out unblinking and unmoving as the boy watched, petrified, until his father joined him, whereupon the face faded away. An immediate investigation revealed that the room was heavily padlocked, and no one was inside.

Discussion with former occupants of the house produced other stories of strange happenings here. The owners of the former country club spoke of an unexplained figure of a woman seen in one of the attic bedrooms, and of a coach-and-four dashing up the drive. Local folk told of a murder committed here many years ago, when a manservant killed a cook and dragged her body down the drive, across the main road, and dumped it in a byway still known as Cook's Lane. If there is anything in this story, it could account for:

- The caped figure in the attic - the victim, perhaps?

- The face at the pantry window - the murderer caught?

- The feeling of a presence in the pantry, haunt of the cook...

In 1965, The Ghost Club visited Testwood House, and several members remarked on a curious 'waiting' atmosphere in the upper parts of the interesting old house. We were able to establish that the back door fits tightly, and does not rattle of its own accord.

*Dolphin Hotel, Southampton, Hampshire*

## TUNSTEAD MILTON, NEAR CHAPEL-EN-LE-FRITH, DERBYSHIRE

An old farm in the locality is known as 'Dickie's', on account of 'Dickie's' skull that was kept here for so many years, the preservation of which no one knows the reason for.

There is a suggestion that the skull, incomplete and in pieces, belonged to a Ned Dixon, who was murdered by his cousin in the room where it is kept. Others maintain that, in spite of its name, the skull belonged to a woman.

At all events, it was believed that should the skull be removed from the house, disasters and difficulties would ensue until it was brought back.

Years ago, the skull gained notoriety when the London and North-Western Railway engineers had great difficulty in fixing secure foundations for a bridge as long as they were on the farm land. Eventually, the had to select another site, on land belonging to another farm. The engineers ascribed their difficulties to local sand and bog, but those living in the vicinity maintained that 'Dickie's' skull had been the potent deterrent.

*Alma Lodge Hotel, Buxton Road, Stockport, Cheshire*

## *TWICKENHAM, MIDDLESEX

The waterfront church of St Mary's, an impressive church full of unusual features, is reputed to harbour the ghost of Alexander Pope.

The mortal remains (or most of them) of the man who gave his name to many of the roads in this area lie in the churchyard - and here too is his famous grotto. The deformed and vindictive poet's restless footsteps used to be heard along the main aisle.

Thurston Hopkins - ghost-hunter and collector of ghost-lore, had no doubt about it. He told me: 'The ghost of Alexander Pope used to be seen perambulating the churchyard, muttering to himself. Sometimes raving at the top of his voice. The apparition always faded away - accompanied by a dreadful paroxysm of coughing.'

The haunting seems to date from 1830, when Pope's grave was desecrated, and his skull removed from the coffin. Certainly a skull - stated to be that of Pope - became the showpiece in the private collection of phrenologist Johann Spurzheim.

At one time, the ghost of Pope was said to trouble the parson and sexton of the day, demanding to know what had become of his skull. 'Pope's ghost still walks,' Hopkins told me, 'but his figure is no longer visible - although the sound of his limping footsteps have been plainly heard on many occasions.'

*Richmond Hill Hotel, Richmond Hill, Richmond, Surrey*

## VENTNOR, ISLE OF WIGHT, HAMPSHIRE

*[Craigie Lodge is now a Private Residence]*

Craigie Lodge, near here, was the scene of a mystery that had great publicity some forty years ago [*October 1921*]. The gardener of the tenant at that time was digging in the ground to plant shrubs, when he unearthed the lower jaw of a child, which he took to his mistress - a Mrs Capell. Mrs Hugh Pollock, a psychometrist, happened to be staying with her.

She placed the bone - part of a whole skeleton which was subsequently unearthed here - against her forehead, and stated that another skeleton would be found lying near where the child's bone had been found. A second skeleton was duly discovered - a woman's. It is difficult to suggest a rational explanation for this prediction - and its fulfilment.

*Royal Hotel, Ventnor, Isle of Wight, Hampshire*

WALSALL, STAFFORDSHIRE, SEE
CALDMORE GREEN

## WANTAGE, OXFORDSHIRE

*[Historically part of Berkshire, it has been a part of the district of Oxfordshire since 1974]*

The village of West Hendred seems to possess the ghost of a man who died in a road accident. Margaret Prior (twenty-seven) and Mrs Marcia Colling-Hill (twenty-nine) were driving at night near the spot, when they both saw a man wearing a cap and overcoat, dash in front of their car - yet there was no collision.

Mrs Prior, who was driving, said afterwards: 'I couldn't possibly have avoided hitting him. I braked instantly as I thought I was going to kill him. I prepared myself for the bump, but nothing happened...'

*Bear Hotel, Market Square, Wantage, Berks.*

WARBLETON PRIORY, SEE HEATHFIELD, SUSSEX

## WASHFORD, SOMERSET

*[Bardon House is now a Private Residence]*

Historic Bardon House ['Barton House' in the 1971 edition, which is in Gloucestershire] was occupied for over forty years by artist Edward Collier and his wife. They used to say that ghosts 'pop up all over the place, at any time of the day or night'. Mrs Collier said that although it was sometimes disconcerting when people appeared to walk through walls, the ghosts never troubled them, and in fact, they added to the fun of living at the beautiful old house.

*Luttrell Arms Hotel, Dunster, Somerset*

## WATERFORD, MUNSTER, IRELAND

Legend has it that a beautiful vampire lies buried here, in a little graveyard by the ruined church, near Strongbow's Tower - still ready to kill, in the unearthly fashion of vampires, anyone who lingers here at night-times…

*Acton's Hotel, Kinsale, Ireland*

## WAYLAND WOOD, NORFOLK

This is the wood that is said to have been the original one of the 'Babes in the Wood' story. The babes were Norfolk children and here, where the uncle's ruffian servants left them to die, two little ghostly figures are seen on misty nights, wandering silently among the trees, hand in hand, looking for a way out. Unexplained wailing cries have been heard at night times in this lonely spot.

*Bell Hotel, Norwich, Norfolk*

## WELLINGBOROUGH, NORTHAMPTONSHIRE

*[The Lyric Cinema building was demolished in 1975]*

The Lyric - formerly a cinema, and later a bingo hall - was the scene of a 'ghost hunt' in November 1969, following reports of the spectre of a man said to have been seen on a balcony there. The figure may have had its origin in the mysterious death of a man named Daniel, who was buried in the nineteenth century, on land where the Lyric now stands.

Following several reports of the figure being seen - always on the same balcony, the Rev. Cyril Payne visited the hall, but refused to comment afterwards. The Catholic Bishop of Northampton would not allow a priest to attempt an exorcism. One witness described the figure as 'like a white shadow or statue that had not been unveiled'. Another said: 'It scared me so much that I ran into the street.'

Messages were tapped out, asking for *'Help'*, and such appeals as *'Bring back priest'*. At the time, a number of all-night vigils were kept at the hall by local psychical researchers, who collected evidence suggesting that some paranormal activity had taken place on the foyer balcony.

*Westone Hotel, Fir Tree Walk, Weston Favell, Northampton, Northants.*

The scene of a remarkable haunting in the eighteenth century, when this delightful church was 'infested' by a large black bird for the best part of a hundred years.

People visiting the church and churchyard heard a peculiar knocking sound, which seemed to emanate from the vaults under the church. Once three of them peered through the grating outside, and saw a great black bird perched on one of the coffins inside, pecking away furiously.

They roused the parish clerk, who told them that he had often seen the same bird, or one like it, in the vaults. His wife and daughter declared that they had seen it too, and that it usually appeared on a Friday evening.

Once, when bell-ringers arrived at the church for practice, they were met by a boy who was much agitated by a large black bird, which he had seen flying about the chancel [*the part of a church near the altar*]. Four of the bell-ringers and two of the youths at once armed themselves with sticks and stones, and set out to search for the mysterious bird.

They soon found it fluttering among the rafters - by throwing stones, they eventually drove it from one part of the church to another, hitting it twice with sticks. One of them caught it a hard knock, so that one of its wings drooped, as if the creature were badly crippled. Finally, under a fusillade of blows and hits from stones, it fell wounded, screaming and fluttering, into the eastern end of the church.

Two of the assailants immediately drove it into a corner, and vaulted over the communion rail to seize it as it sank to the floor, apparently exhausted - but, as the men thrust out their hands to seize it - the bird vanished. After that, it was often seen, perched on the communion rails, or fluttering to and from in the vaults.

A resident of West Drayton remarked that local people thought the spectral bird was the restless and miserable spirit of a murderer, who had committed suicide, and had been buried in consecrated ground at the north side of the churchyard, instead of at the crossroads - the traditional place for suicides.

When I took a party of Ghost Club members to West Drayton church in 1962, the rector - the Rev. A. H. Woodhouse - told us about the family coffins in the vault being set upright in readiness for the days of resurrection!

*Skyway Hotel, Bath Road, Hayes, Middlesex*

## WEST GRINSTEAD, SUSSEX

About a mile from West Grinstead, there are the scanty remains of Knepp Castle - one of the six great feudal fortresses of Sussex, where a ghostly white doe is still occasionally seen nibbling the lush green grass.

According to the local legend - in the days of King John - a young girl displeased one of the king's retainers when she refused to submit to his advances. He paid a local hag to bewitch the girl who was turned into a white doe. Next, for some unknown reason, the hag turned herself into a great boarhound, in order to chase the little doe and keep her always on the move.

The hunters of Knapp had strict orders under pain of death never to kill the doe, but one day a youth - anxious to display his skill with the crossbow - sent an arrow through its heart, and a second shaft into the great hound that was chasing it.

So perished the maiden and the witch. But the ghostly doe is still seen feeding on the rich green grass in summer. In winter, usually about Christmas time, when the snow covers the ground, blood-red marks appear on the snow, at the spot where the animals died.

*Ye Olde Kings Head Hotel, Carfax, Horsham, Sussex. [Now an 'Ask' Italian restaurant]*

## WEST HARTLEPOOL, DURHAM

In 1967, the occupants of 18 Dorset Street (Mr and Mrs Harry Parker and their two-year-old daughter) were driven out of their home, and had to spend nights with their next door neighbours, because they were afraid of the house at night-time.

During the course of a sitting, which they had held with friends as a joke, one person saw the outline of a man's hand on the window curtains, and a strip of light suddenly flashed past her. At another seance, 'a figure' was seen standing in front of the fireplace, and was recognized as a deceased relative.

*Grand Hotel, Hartlepool, Co. Durham*

## *WEST WYCOMBE, BUCKINGHAMSHIRE

The fascinating fourteenth-century George and Dragon Inn is reputed to be haunted by a  ghostly girl in white. There is a priest's hole here, too, and a room where Oliver Cromwell used to stay.

The girl, Susan, was a servant at the inn, and her beauty attracted three local young men, but she was intrigued by the visits of an unidentified but prosperous traveller. The local lads became jealous, and sent a note to Susan, purporting to come from her wealthy admirer, asking her to meet him at the nearby raves, so that they could run away and get married.

The three young men thought it a fine joke when Susan kept the tryst, but when their mockery annoyed her, and she began to throw stones at her tormentors, the affair developed into a fight, and Susan fell and fractured her skull.

She was carried back to the inn, but died during the night, in the room which the landlord will show you. Since then, her ghost has haunted the 'George and Dragon', walking along a passage in the early hours of the morning, and causing a supernormal coldness in the bedroom where she breathed her lsat.

*Falcon Hotel, High Street, High Wycombe, Bucks.*

## WETHERAL, CUMBERLANDSHIRE
## (NOW PART OF CUMBRIA)

*[Corby Castle is not currently open to the public]*

Corby Castle, beautifully situated in a forest on the banks of the River Eden, has long been famous for an apparition known as 'the Radiant Boy'. The haunted chamber at Corby is in the old part of the house, and although surrounded by delightful rooms on all sides, the only access to this particular room is through a passage cut into an eight-foot thick wall.

On one wall of the room tapestry was hung for many years, while the rest of the walls were decorated with family portraits and panels of embroidery giving the place an ominous and somehow oppressive feeling.

Many years ago, the apparition so long associated with this ancient seat was seen by a well-known and respected clergyman, who was spending a night in the haunted room. He awoke soon after midnight to find the room in total darkness. And yet, although there was no light, he saw an unmistakable glimmer in the middle of the room which - as he watched - increased to a bright flame.

He thought for a moment that something had caught alight when, to his amazement, he saw - apparently within and part of the radiance - an angelic child clothed in white, 'with bright locks resembling gold', looking steadfastly at him.

After a moment, 'the radiant boy' glided gently and silently towards the chimney, where he vanished. There was no evident place of entry or exit and, indeed, subsequent examination of the wall showed that it was quite sound and unbroken.

In complete darkness once more, the visitor spent a restless night, and arose at dawn, determined never to sleep in that room again. The haunted room was later used as a study, with its dark panelling presenting a sombre appearance on the brightest day, although as far as I know, 'the radiant boy', a rare apparition and a famous one, has not been seen for many years now.

*Crown Hotel, Wetheral, Cumb.*

The famous racing track at Brooklands - now disused and overgrown is, appropriately enough, reputed to be haunted by a ghost in racing cap and goggles. The vast assembly shed, known as The Vatican, juts out onto the former racetrack at the end of the Railway Straight. And it is here that a popular Brooklands figure - Percy Lambert - was thrown to his death when a tyre burst during a record attempt.

It is thought that the mysterious figure in cap and goggles, that night-shift workers claim to have seen over the years, may be his ghost, visiting again his beloved Brooklands.

*Ship Hotel, Monument Green, Weybridge, Surrey*

## WHITBY, YORKSHIRE

Some of the roads hereabouts are said to be haunted by a mischievous ghost named Hob, who seems to have a grudge against travellers, and particular motorists - for he makes them skid into ditches, turns signposts around, and lets down the tyres of cars. At least, that's what late-night motorists to his part of haunted Yorkshire say.

*Metropole Hotel, West Cliff, Whitby, Yorks.*

# *WICKEN, CAMBRIDGESHIRE

*[A farm now stands near this former priory north west of Wicken and a house incorporates masonry from 'Spinney Priory', built in 1775]*

In the heart of the Fen country, and only a mile from Wicken Fen, the stretch of land that has remained unchanged since the days of Hereward the Wake, there stands an isolated collection of buildings grouped round an imposing farmhouse known as Spinney Abbey.

The name was derived from the ancient priory, which formerly occupied the site. Ghostly singing monks, mysterious lights, and strange figures have all been reported here.

The original Spinney Abbey was for the last fourteen years of his life the home of Oliver Cromwell's distinguished son, Henry, who settled here after he had lost his lands with the return of the Stuarts. It was here that the reputed 'stable-fork incident' took place.

King Charles II, returning from Newmarket with his retinue, visited farmer Henry Cromwell, and found him farming contentedly. A member of the King's party thought it a fine jest to take up a pitch-fork and carry it before Cromwell, parodying the fact that the farmer had been mace-bearer when he was Lord Lieutenant of Ireland.

The mortal remains of this well-loved son of the Protector rest in the little village church, where a brass plate tells us that he was the best of Cromwell's sons. Carlyle once said that had *he* been named Protector, English history would have taken a different turn in the seventeenth century.

Now, the occupants are the Fuller family, and I remember that one of the first things Tom Fuller showed me were some fragmentary ruins of the old building, that was built in the twelfth century. Part of it was now a piggery, and I was told that the pigs - although contented enough elsewhere - are often seen to be fighting whenever they occupy that part of their enclosure.

I also recall examining the cellars, remnants of the old building with reputed secret tunnels, and seeing the remains of a grating - and the attachments for primitive handcuffs showing that the cellars were used as dungeons.

One of the most frequent unexplained happenings here was a mysterious twinkling light, which was often seen between the house and Spinney Bank, about a mile away. The lights have been observed within a hundred yards of Spinney Abbey, and once, a local man saw a light move away from him and illuminate a mill almost a mile distant.

Witnesses never seemed to be able to get near the lights, for as soon as they approached, they would drift away. When the observer stops, the lights seem to stop as well. Such lights are often *Ignis Fatuus* (from the Latin: foolish fire), usually seen in the vicinity of marshy places and churchyards, and are sometimes known as 'Will-o'-the-Wisp' and 'Jack-a-Lantern'.

They are generally accepted as being a natural although incompletely understood luminosity, due perhaps to the spontaneous combustion of decomposed vegetable matter. At all events, the Fullers told me that local people will go a long way round to avoid Spinney Bank at night.

Outside the room where I learned of the many strange happenings at Spinney Abbey, Tom Fuller told me of the figure of a monk that he had seen glide slowly along the garden path, before disappearing at an angle of the house.

The hood of the clothing which the figure wore covered its face so that no features were discernible. But Mr Fuller wondered whether the ghostly monk had any connection with the murder of an abbot at the original Spinney Abbey, in 1406. Other people have also seen a ghost friar here, and sometimes ghostly footsteps - slow and measured - sound and resound about this quiet house.

One Sunday morning, unexplained chanting was heard in the west part of the house by six people, including three of the children of old Robert Fuller, who were now telling me about the strange happenings they had encountered over the years.

Music - faint but distinct - accompanied the Latin chanting. The whole thing was over in a few seconds, but all the six people in the room at the time heard and agreed upon the unmistakable sounds. Robert Fuller himself had heard the same sounds some years before, but he heard them in the stack-yard, and they appeared to come from fourteen feet above the ground. 'Clear as a bell.' he said: 'pure and sweet, all in Latin - and just where the old Chapel of the Abbey used to stand.'

Mr Fuller's daughter Unis and her husband told me that they

had heard something they had never been able to explain. It was a curious, uneven, rolling sound - like a coconut being rolled over the floor. After a while it ceased. Then it began again, and it was heard intermittently throughout that one evening, never before and never afterwards.

During the course of a night I spent in the grounds of Spinney Abbey, I placed delicate thermometers, at strategic spots:

- In the piggery [*a farm where pigs are bred or kept: a pigsty*] where the pigs always fought.

- The place where the chanting had been heard.

- Another spot where an unexplained female figure had been seen on one occasion.

- And finally where the monk walked.

Readings were carefully recorded every ten minutes throughout the night. No thermometer showed any abnormality - except one. Each of them steadily declined from around 31 degrees fahrenheit [*of or denoting a scale of temperature on which water freezes at 32° and boils at 212° under standard conditions*] at midnight, to 24 degrees fahrenheit at six a.m. But the thermometer placed where the ghost monk walked showed a sudden and inexplicable drop in temperature of seven degrees!

This occurred at two-ten a.m., and was verified by my two companions - yet the other thermometers showed no similar drop. This one was no more exposed than the others, and in any case, ten minutes later, this thermometer showed the temperature back to normal and in line with the others. I have thought of many possible explanations, but none that I can accept as probably. It is interesting to note that some horses stabled nearby were quiet throughout the night, except at the exact time at which this sudden and unexplained drop in temperature occurred.

At exactly two-ten a.m., the horses suddenly made a terrific noise in their stable, kicking their stalls, whinnying and neighing loudly. Gradually, they quietened down, and by the time the thermometer showed a normal reading at two-twenty a.m., the horses were quiet again. Horses, like cats and dogs, are believed to be super sensitive, so perhaps some shade of a ghost passed near to me that night.

*White Hart Hotel, Newmarket, Suffolk*

# WILLINGTON QUAY, NEAR NORTH SHIELDS, TYNE AND WEAR*

[*'Northumberland' was the previously listed county; it included Newcastle upon Tyne until 1400, and expanded greatly in the Tudor period. Tynemouth and other settlements in North Tyneside (including Willington) were transferred to Tyne and Wear in 1974 under the Local Government Act of 1972]

Some old buildings at this small Tyneside town were formerly a mill house where - well over a century ago - remarkable poltergeist activity was experienced by a staunch Quaker, Joseph Proctor and his family. There is a mass of contemporary evidence for this important case of haunting, which lasted for some twelve years

The first recorded incidents at Willington Mill, for which no normal explanation could be found, were curious noises reported by a young nurse-maid. She described them as sounding like a dull, heavy tread of footfalls. They came from an unoccupied room. It was as though someone were pacing back and forth for ten minutes at a time.

Before long, all the household had heard the same sounds - which continued day after day. Often, the room was examined immediately the noise was heard. Sometimes people sat in the room or occupied it all night, but no cause for the noise was ever discovered.

It seemed impossible for the sounds to have been due to trickery. The affected room had a garret above, and the roof was inaccessible from outside. The house was detached, and most of the time the window was sealed up with laths [a thin flat strip of wood, especially one of a series forming a foundation for the plaster of a wall] and plaster, while the chimney was closed - and so covered with soot that even a mouse must have left traces.

There was no furniture in the room, and at one period, the door was nailed up. No rats or other rodents were seen or heard in the house - although as one witness said, a hundred rats could not have so shaken the floor with their weight as to cause the window to rattle as it did on numerous occasions. The noises were heard at every hour of the day, but more frequently during the evening, and only rarely at night. Other noises included:

- Deadened beats, as of a mallet on a block of wood, near a bedstead in a bedroom.

- Taps on a cradle, causing vibration.

- Footsteps on a gravel path and in a bedroom.

- A sound like the winding-up of a clock.

- The noise of a sack falling.

- A loud chattering and jingling.

- A beating noise and the sound of whistling.

- A voice which seemed to say 'Chuck' twice, and on another occasion, something like 'Never mind', and 'Come and get'.

A neighbour reported seeing a transparent female figure at a window on the second floor of the mill, and the same figure was later seen by two visitors, who described it as 'resembling a priest'. Two of the Proctor children saw - unknown to each other - an apparition. A cook saw 'a distinct shadow', and her bedstead was disturbed. Little Jane Proctor was frightened by the face of an old woman at the foot of her bed, and on the land - while her brother reported seeing a man with grey hair walk into his bedroom.

Once, Mrs Proctor and a nurse felt themselves raised up in their beds, and let down again - three times. One of the boys complained of a similar experience. Another time, Mrs Proctor was awakened by feeling an icy pressure on her face, over one eye - suddenly with much force, and then withdrawn. She often described this experience, and said she found it more distressing than anything she underwent in the house.

The Proctor's diary records these events as happening between 1835 and 1847, when, finding life in the house intolerable, they finally left. Subsequent inhabitants of the property, who divided the mill into separate dwellings, were only occasionally disturbed by unaccountable noises, and reported just once or twice seeing what were thought to be apparitions.

Later, there were rumours of restless nights, and a few exasperating disturbances, but it is probable that with the departure of the Proctor children, the poltergeist could no longer produce the same effects.

*The Sea Hotel, South Shields, Co. Durham*

# WINCHELSEA, SUSSEX

*['Greyfriars' - a country house built in 1819, to which the ruins of the*
*Church of the Greyfriars is attached - is now a Private Residence]*

The picturesque ruins of an old Franciscan monastery, 'Friars', was once the home of two highwaymen brothers, who are said to haunt the roads hereabouts.

George and Joseph Weston lived here under assumed names, and were regarded as country gentlemen, enjoying the highest reputation in Winchelsea. While at night however, they donned their masks. And plied their nefarious trade throughout the surrounding countryside.

They were apprehended in London after robbing the Bristol mail, and executed at Tyburn in 1782. But according to local observers, the brothers are still to be seen from time to time, careering about the district at dead of night. One - believed to be George - has been seen in the shadow of a particular tree, armed but apparently headless, waiting for the opportunity to surprise a phantom coach. Many motorists in the district have been frightened by the sounds of galloping horses' hooves approaching them, which have ceased as mysteriously as they began.

*George Hotel, Rye, Sussex*

## *WINDSOR CASTLE, WINDSOR, BERKSHIRE

A royal palace built by William the Conqueror, where many English sovereigns are buried. It has at least five ghosts: King Henry VIII, Queen Elizabeth I, King Charles I, King George III, and a young guardsman who killed himself in the 1920, while Hector Bolitho has described the ghost with whom he once shared the old Deanery in the castle grounds.

'I used to hear him in the night, walking quickly past my bedroom, until he came to the three steps by the bathroom door', he told me. The odd thing was that the unseen ghost seemed to take *four* steps down before resuming his hurried pace, but later it was discovered that the floor in this part of the old house had been raised from its early level, and in the process one step had been eliminated.

The Cloisters near the Deanery are said to be haunted by the ghost of King Henry VIII. Ghostly groans, and the sound of dragging footsteps - as though made by someone suffering from gout - have been heard in these passages.

Queen Elizabeth I haunts the Royal Library (not open to the public), and witnesses include the Empress Frederick of Germany, and a Lieutenant Glynn of the Grenadier Guards - who heard the 'tap - tap' of high heels sounding on bare boards, when he was in the Library.

The sounds came nearer, and presently the tall stately figure of the Virgin Queen came into view and passed so close to him, that he could have touched her. She entered an inner room, from which there is no other exit, and although Lieutenant Glynn followed her immediately, he found no sign of the figure he had seen in the deserted room.

The Royal Library is also said to harbour the ghost of George

III, the poor old mad king whose ghost has also been seen at Kensington Palace. Canon's house - in the castle precincts - is reputed to be haunted by the ghostly form of King Charles I, recognized by the uncanny likeness to the famous Van Dyck portrait.

A young recruit of the Grenadier Guards was on duty on the Long Walk - where the ghost of Herne the Hunter has occasionally been glimpsed, when he shot himself. A few weeks later, a guardsman was detailed to relieve another on this same duty, and during the bright moonlit night, he saw the ghostly figure of the dead guardsman. When he returned to his quarters, he learned that the guardsman he had relieved had had an identical experience.

*Castle Hotel, Windsor, Berks.*

# *WINDSOR GREAT PARK, WINDSOR, BERKSHIRE

Long reputed to be haunted by the ghost of Herne the Hunter, 'the Foul Fiend of the Forest', as Harrison Ainsworth calls him in his romance *Windsor Castle*. The apparition was usually seen at night-time, wearing horns, and mounted on a fast horse followed by spectral hounds - the whole ghostly band seemingly engaged on a phantom hunting expedition.

The original Herne was a forest keeper in Great Windsor Forest, probably in the reign of Richard II. Falling into disgrace, he hanged himself, or at any rate his body was found hanging from a large oak tree which was only blown down in a storm in 1863.

Queen Victoria had a new oak tree planted in the same sport, for whenever disaster threatened the royal family or the nation, Herne's ghost was said to appear beneath the shadow of the old oak. The figure is said to have been seen in 1931, before the economic crisis, before the abdication of Edward VIII in 1936, and before the Second World War in 1939.

In 1926, there was a remarkable report from Mrs Walter Legge, J.P., a member of the Windsor Board of Guardians, and of the Rural District Council, who lived at Farm House, Windsor. She had just retired one night, when she heard the sound of the baying of hounds coming from the direction of Smith's lawn.

It appeared to increase in volume, and then die away, in the direction of Windsor Castle. A fortnight later, she heard the same sounds, exactly at midnight; and this time, her daughter came into her mother's room, saying she had heard strange sounds, 'almost like Herne the Hunter's hounds'. Mrs Legge and her daughter lived at Windsor for many years afterwards, but never heard the midnight baying again.

The ghost of Herne and his phantom hounds have been reported from various parts of Windsor Great Park. The great shaggy form of Herne usually being glimpsed among ancient trees, and the sound of his baying hounds and a horse's galloping hooves have been heard suddenly, and then the sounds have gradually faded.

Herne's ghost was known in Shakespeare, who refers to it three times in *The Merry Wives of Windsor.* At that time, the enormous oak tree - known as Herne's Oak - seems to have been his special haunt.

*Castle Hotel, Windsor, Berks.*

## *WOBURN ABBEY, WOBURN, BEDFORDSHIRE

The family seat of the Dukes of Bedford is built on the site of a Cistercian abbey. The present structure dates from 1744, and is today one of the most popular stately homes open to the public. But the steady stream of over 25,000 visitors a week during the season has not driven away the ghosts.

In 1963, I had a long talk with His Grace the Duke of Bedford, his wife, and her daughters. They all had curious and unexplained happenings to relate. The thirteenth Duke's introduction to psychic matters came when he was a young man attending a party given by Lord Tredegar, 'a very odd man who was much interested in the supernatural', and at night in one of the enormous rooms of his home in Wales, with an owl flying round the room(!), Lord Tredegar would don cabalistic garb and tell fortunes.

The strange thing was that no sooner had he begun, that the temperature in the room would unmistakably drop. Everyone present agreed on this, and the Duke told me that although he was right in front of a huge fire, he found himself shivering. He never forgot that visit to Wales.

In the private apartments of the Abbey, looking out over the rolling parkland, the Duke told me of an annoyingly persistent manifestation which caused them to move the site of their television room. The phenomenon - which happened times without number - was unexplained door-opening.

Time after time, this door would open, followed by another at the opposite end of the room, just as though someone had walked through and left the doors open. New locks were fitted. The doors were kept locked. But still they opened by themselves, and i the end, the wing of the house was reconstructed. Now there is an open passage where the doors of the television room used to be.

'But now the ghost has turned his attention to other doors!' the Duke went on, and I heard how his son his wife, the servants - and various visitors - had all told him of their bedroom doors opening mysteriously by themselves.

I was shown the beautifully-proportioned bedroom, and the Duke and Duchess told me of curious incidents which they had experienced here - of the continual door-opening, and what seemed like a cold, wet hand passing over one's face. It was not 'really frightening', although the dogs at Woburn didn't like the ghosts.

Often they would stop suddenly in one of the long corridors, crouch down with their tails between their legs, howl piteously, and refuse to move. There does seem to be an indefinable atmosphere in this portion of the house - a kind of restlessness that clairvoyant Tom Corbett told me he sensed immediately on his visit to Woburn. The same feeling is prevalent in the Wood Library, and in a nearby office. The Duke told me that he finds it difficult to concentrate in these rooms - yet he continues to use them.

Sylvie de Cardenal, the administrator of the Stately Antique Market at Woburn, was working late in her office over the courtyard one night, when she noticed that the lights were showing downstairs, although she distinctly recalled switching them off before coming up.

She went down and was astonished to see a tall gentleman, wearing a top hat, walking through the market. The next day, an employee was working late, and when he had finished, he went upstairs and asked about the mysterious gentleman in a top hat, whom he had seen in the Market.

There is an isolated little summer house with an overgrown garden not far from the house, which the Duke feels is haunted by an unhappy ghost. Perhaps it is his grandmother, 'the flying Duchess', to whom the Duke has devoted a fascinating room at the Abbey. She loved the isolation of this summer house - especially towards the end of her increasingly unhappy life, and soon she took off in her Gypsy aeroplane from Woburn - the flight from which she never returned. 'I feel her presence very strongly, every time I come here,' the Duke told me.

*Bedford Arms Hotel, Woburn, Bedfordshire*

## WOODSTOCK, OXFORDSHIRE

*[The 'Bear Inn' is now the 'Macdonald Bear Hotel']*

The twelfth-century Bear Inn seems to have a haunted room where occupants find their possessions moved, hear footsteps, and tell of other evidence of unseen occupants of the bedroom. During the time she stayed there in November 1967 - while making a film in the neighbourhood - actress Maggie Blye found her nights disturbed by footsteps on the creaking floorboards.

Once, at two o'clock in the morning, she awakened to find the dressing-table light switched on. She stated that another member of the film unit moved out of the room after one night there, and the manager, Mr Dennis Fulford-Talbot, is reported to have stated that four people in the preceding two years had told him that unexplained happenings had taken place in Room 16.

*Marlborough Arms Hotel, Woodstock, Oxon.*

# A SELECTION OF THE BEST BOOKS
# ON GHOSTS AND HAUNTINGS

DENNIS BARDENS, *Ghosts and Hauntings,* London 1965

SIR ERNEST BENNETT, *Apparitions and Haunted Houses,* London 1939

JOSEPH BRADDOCK, *Haunted Houses,* London 1956

HEREWARD CARRINGTON AND NANDOR FODOR, *The Story of the Poltergeist Down the Centuries,* London 1953

B. ANDY COLLINS, *The Cheltenham Ghost,* London 1948

J. WENTWORTH DAY, *Here are Ghosts and Witches,* London 1954

J. WENTWORTH DAY, *A Ghost-Hunter's Game Book,* London 1958

NANDOR FODOR, *On the Trail of the Poltergeist,* London 1959

A. GOODRICH-FREER & JOHN, MARQUESS OF BUTE, *The Alleged Haunting of B____ House,* London 1899

DOUGLAS GRANT, *The Cock Lane Ghost,* London 1965

LORD HALIFAX'S *Ghost Book,* London 1936

CHARLES G. HARPER, *Haunted Houses,* London 1907

JOHN HARRIES, *The Ghost Hunter's Road Book,* London 1968

CHRISTINA HOLE, *Haunted England,* London 1940

R. THURSTON HOPKINS, *Ghosts Over England*, London 1953

JOHN H. INGRAM, *The Haunted Homes and Family Traditions of Great Britain,* London 1912

ANDREW LANGE, *The Book of Dreams and Ghosts,* London 1899

SHANE LESLIE'S *Ghost Book*, London 1955

T. C. LETHBRIDGE, *Ghost and Ghoul,* London 1961

ALASDAIR ALPIN MACGREGOR, *The Ghost Book,* London 1955

ALASDAIR ALPIN MACGREGOR, *Phantom Footsteps,* London 1959

ANDREW MACKENZIE, *The Unexplained,* London 1966

ERIC MAPLE, *The Realm of Ghosts,* London 1964

DIANA NORMAN, *The Stately Ghosts of England,* London 1963

ELLIOTT O'DONNELL, *Haunted Churches,* London 1939

ELLIOTT O'DONNELL, Haunted Britain,

HARRY PRICE, *Confessions of a Ghost-Hunter,* London 1936

HARRY PRICE, *'The Most Haunted House in England',* London 1940

HARRY PRICE, *Poltergeist Over England,* London 1945

HARRY PRICE, *The End of Borley Rectory,* London 1947

W. H. SALTER, *Ghosts and Apparitions,* London 1938

PHILIP W. SERGEANT, *Historic British Ghosts,* London N.D.

SACHEVERELL SITWELL, *Poltergeists,* London, 1940

WILLIAM OLIVER STEVENS, *Unbidden Guests,* London 1949

A. M. W. STIRLING, *Ghosts Vivisected,* London 1957

G. N. M. TYRRELL, *Apparitions,* London, 1943

# ABOUT THE AUTHOR

## Peter Underwood

Peter Underwood was President of the Ghost Club (founded 1862) from 1960-1993 and probably heard more first-hand ghost stories than any man alive. He was a long-standing member of The Society of Psychical Research, Vice-President of the Unitarian Society for Psychical Studies, a member of The Folklore Society, The Dracula Society and the Research Committee of the Psychic Research Organisation, he wrote extensively, and was a seasoned lecturer and broadcaster.

He took part in the first official investigation into a haunting; sat with physical and mental mediums and conducted investigations at seances. He was present at exorcisms, experiments at dowsing, precognition, clairvoyance, hypnotism, regression; he conducted world-wide tests in telepathy and extra-sensory perception, and personally investigated scores of haunted houses across the country.

He possessed comprehensive files of alleged hauntings in every county of the British Isles and many foreign countries, and his knowledge and experience resulted in his being consulted on psychic and occult matters by the BBC and ITV. His many books include the first two comprehensive gazetteers of ghosts and hauntings in England, Scotland and Ireland and two books that deal with twenty different occult subjects.

Highlights from his published work include 'Nights in Haunted Houses' (1993), which collects together the results of group investigations, 'The Ghosts of Borley' (1973), his classic account of the history of 'the most haunted house in England', 'Hauntings' (1977), which re-examines ten classic cases of haunting in the light of modern knowledge, 'No Common Task' (1983), which reflects back upon his life as a 'ghost hunter', and 'The Ghost Hunter's Guide' (1986), which gives the reader all the advice necessary to become one. Born at Letchworth Garden City in Hertfordshire, he lived for many years in a small village in Hampshire.

# BOOKS BY THIS AUTHOR

## Hauntings: New Light On The Greatest True Ghost Stories Of The World

In this fascinating account of the best-attested cases of haunting - Hampton Court, the demon drummer of Bedworth, the Wesley ghost, Glamis, Borley Rectory and many others - Britain's foremost ghost-hunter has brought to light a wealth of valuable new evidence. Using the results of many years of research and personal investigation, and providing detailed plans and original photographs, new theories are put forward to change our ideas about these hauntings.

## This Haunted Isle

Peter Underwood has personally visited the historic buildings and sites of Britain, and here presents a wealth of intriguing legends and new stories of ghostly encounters from more than a hundred such throughout the United Kingdom.

From Abbey House in Cambridge to Zennor in Cornwall, this is an A to Z of the haunted houses of Britain. At Bramshill in Hampshire — now a police training college — there have been so many sightings that even sceptical police officers have had to admit that the place is haunted. Beautiful Leeds Castle in Kent has a large, phantom black dog; there is an Elizabethan gentleman (seen by a Canon of the Church of England!) at Croft Castle; a Pink Lady at Coughton Court; a prancing ghost jester at Gawsworth; a spectre in green velvet at Hoghton Tower; six ghosts at East Riddlesden Hall; a headless apparition at Westwood Manor; and then there are some little-known ghosts in Windsor Castle, Hampton Court Palace and the Tower of London, and the strange ghosts of Chingle Hall, perhaps the most haunted house in England.

## Ghosts Of Kent

The first expert exploration of the haunted houses and authentic ghosts of Kent, this volume is filled with fascinating true ghost stories from times past. Read about the curious case of Anne West of Old Bayhall Manor, who 'was always worried that she might be buried while yet alive', or the 'ghostly old gentleman' of Cleve Court in Minster, who, when he turns up, is treated 'more as a guest than a ghost' - because 'the dear old thing means no harm'.

And there is Lympne Castle, where Underwood once took a party of Ghost Club members: 'I had just obtained a description of the room, when one of the Club members rushed into the kitchen begging me to accompany her to one of the towers where "something horrible had once taken place"…'.

## Ghosts Of North West England

The ghostly little monk of Foulridge and the giant apparition from Heaton Norris are just two of the denizens of the North-West you might not care to meet on a dark, stormy evening. But for those intrepid souls whose hearts quicken at the thought of eerie footsteps and muffled groans Peter Underwood has assembled an impressive collection of traditional legends.

## Ghosts Of Hampshire And The Isle Of Wight

Peter Underwood, an acknowledged expert and experienced investigator of haunted houses, presents a selection of hauntings throughout Hampshire and the Isle of Wight. A formidable collection of ghoulies and things that go bump in the night.

This edition includes a foreword by author Alan Williams, as well as an interview Williams conducted with Underwood in 1997.

## The Ghost Hunter's Guide

What are the qualities which make an ideal ghost hunter? You need to be part detective, part investigative reporter, a scientist, with a measure of the psychologist thrown in...

In this book, which is the first real guide to the hunting of ghosts, Peter Underwood manages to cover just about every aspect of this intriguing and mystifying subject.

## Dictionary Of The Supernatural

An A to Z of Hauntings, Possession, Witchcraft, Demonology and Other Occult Phenomena...

The entries cover all known (and some very little known) organisations, individuals, periodicals, terms of reference, and significant cases, events and incidents relevant to the subject. Under each entry there are notes on other appropriate books and further reading.

## Into The Occult

Despite all the answers that conventional science can provide to the earth's mysteries, there remain certain phenomena for which no explanation can yet be found outside the occult. For this reason exploration of the occult and paranormal provides endless fascination.

Here is a survey of all the different aspects of this complex and intriguing subject, including an entire chapter on the relationship between sex and psychic phenomena, a subject on which, until recently, there has been an unwillingness to talk.

## No Common Task: The Autobiography Of A Ghost-Hunter

This is the autobiography of a man who has spent thirty-five years of his life covering scientific psychical research, with detailed investigations into all kinds of manifestation that might be supernatural or paranormal in origin, including spiritualism, ESP, telepathy, hauntings and other occult phenomena. Many of the true experiences from the author's casebook are published here for the first time.

## Deeper Into The Occult

'In an age when voodoo dancers have appeared in London, when Robert Williams, chief psychologist at Kansas State Industrial Reformatory admits to being a practising war-lock; when moon-astronaut Edgar Mitchell conducts extra sensory experiments in space; when the course of a £1,000,000 road is altered to save a 'fairy tree'; when a ghost is officially registered on a census form; when Americans can 'dial-a-horoscope' for a twenty-four hour prophesy; and when the complete skeleton of a cyclops is unearthed by archaeologists — is it surprising that there is a growing interest in the occult, for research in many fields simply proves that things are not what they seem?'

## Nights In Haunted Houses

For over thirty years, in his position as President and Chief Investigator of the Ghost Club of Great Britain, Peter

Underwood was actively involved in undertaking night vigils and carrying out research into ghosts and paranormal activity in controlled, scientific conditions.

## The Ghost Hunter's Guide

What are the qualities which make an ideal ghost hunter? You need to be part detective, part investigative reporter, a scientist, with a measure of the psychologist thrown in…

In this book, which is the first real guide to the hunting of ghosts, Peter Underwood manages to cover just about every aspect of this intriguing and mystifying subject.

## The Ghosts Of Borley: Annals Of The Haunted Rectory

'The Ghosts of Borley' (1973) was the first complete record of the unique Borley Rectory hauntings, detailing all the evidence known about this notorious haunted house from the early days of the Rev. H. D. E. Bull who built Borley Rectory in 1863, through the incumbencies of the Rev. Harry Bull, the Rev. Guy Eric Smith and the Rev. Lionel Foyster, to the investigations by Harry Price and other members of the Society for Psychical Research (SPR).

## The Ghost Hunters: Who They Are And What They Do

A leading psychical researcher takes an in-depth look at ghost hunters, both past and present. Who are these intrepid explorers of the unknown? How do they probe and examine the realms of the seemingly inexplicable? What are their conclusions? In fascinating detail, Peter Underwood profiles the lives and adventures of some of the most famous names in psychical investigation.

## The Vampire's Bedside Companion: The Amazing World Of Vampires In Fact And Fiction

The Vampire's Bedside Companion is a riveting compendium of new facts and fiction on the 'undying' theme of vampirism.

Here is a new theory on the genesis of Dracula (surely literature's most compelling and macabre figure?); thoughts on allusions to vampirism in Wuthering Heights; first-hand experience of Vampires in Hampstead, London; publication for the first time of the story of a fifteenth-century Vampire Protection medallion that Montague Summers presented to the author; an account by a professer of English at Dalhousie University of a visit to 'Castle Dracula' in Transylvania - The Vampire's Bedside Companion contains these and a wealth of other hitherto unpublished material on a subject that is of enduring interest: The Vampire Legend.

## Queen Victoria's Other World

There have been many books about Queen Victoria but there has never been one that has explored her 'other world' - the world of the strange and unusual, the world of death and her fascination for it, and the world of the unseen and the paranormal that she could never resist.

## The Complete Book Of Dowsing And Divining

This comprehensive volume on dowsing and divining - from the twig and the pendulum to motorscopes and bare hands - traces the story of these fascinating and enigmatic phenomena from its origins in the world of fairy tales and mythology to recent theories that the enigma can be explained in terms of present-day psychology.

## Jack The Ripper: One Hundred Years Of Mystery

Jack the Ripper still causes a shudder, synonymous as it is with violent murder and mutilation. But also of mystery and speculation - for the gruesome series of killings in London's East End in that horrific Autumn of 1888 have never been finally solved.

## Exorcism!

Throughout history, the practice of exorcism has been used for the purpose of driving out evil spirits and demons though to possess human beings and the places they inhabit. But there are more startling instances where exorcism has been used: to cure a trawler that seemed to be cursed; to expel demons from Bram Stoker's black 'vampire' dog' even to rid Loch Ness and the Bermuda Triangle of their evil ambience. Peter Underwood explores this frightening ritual in relation to witches, vampires and animals, while his far-flung researches have unearthed dramatic cases in Morocco, Egypt, South Africa and the United States, as well as the British Isles.

## Peter Underwood's Guide To Ghosts & Haunted Places: Cases From The Files Of The World's Leading Paranormal Investigator

Based on 50 years' expert study and investigation, this collection of cases from the files of Peter Underwood - an acknowledged expert and experienced investigator of haunted houses - represents a unique exploration of the world of ghosts, apparitions and psychic phenomena. If you want to satisfy your curiosity about the subject or simply enjoy a riveting read, this guide is for you.

Printed in Great Britain
by Amazon